Swift Recipes

A Problem-Solution Approach

■ ■ ■

T. Michael Rogers

Apress®

Swift Recipes: A Problem-Solution Approach

ISBN-13 (pbk): 978-1-4842-0419-1

ISBN-13 (electronic): 978-1-4842-0418-4

Managing Director: Welmoed Spahr
Lead Editor: Michelle Lowman
Technical Reviewer: Charles Cruz
Development Editor: Anne Marie Walker
Editorial Board: Steve Anglin, Mark Beckner, Gary Cornell, Louise Corrigan, James DeWolf, Jonathan Gennick, Robert Hutchinson, Michelle Lowman, James Markham, Matthew Moodie, Jeffrey Pepper, Douglas Pundick, Ben Renow-Clarke, Gwenan Spearing, Matt Wade, Steve Weiss
Coordinating Editor: Kevin Walter
Copy Editor: Roger LeBlanc
Compositor: SPi Global
Indexer: SPi Global
Artist: SPi Global
Cover Photo: Martijn Vroom

Distributed to the book trade worldwide by Springer Science+Business Media New York, 233 Spring Street, 6th Floor, New York, NY 10013. Phone 1-800-SPRINGER, fax (201) 348-4505, e-mail orders-ny@springer-sbm.com, or visit www.springeronline.com. Apress Media, LLC is a California LLC and the sole member (owner) is Springer Science + Business Media Finance Inc (SSBM Finance Inc). SSBM Finance Inc is a Delaware corporation.

For information on translations, please e-mail rights@apress.com, or visit www.apress.com.

Apress and friends of ED books may be purchased in bulk for academic, corporate, or promotional use. eBook versions and licenses are also available for most titles. For more information, reference our Special Bulk Sales–eBook Licensing web page at www.apress.com/bulk-sales.

Any source code or other supplementary material referenced by the author in this text is available to readers at www.apress.com. For detailed information about how to locate your book's source code, go to www.apress.com/source-code/.

This book is dedicated to my wife, Liz, who single-handedly keeps our family together and functioning, and to my children Catherine, Keira, and Anna. I love you all. I thank them and my other friends and family for their patience and support during all the late nights and long weekends of writing.

Contents at a Glance

Contents at a Glance

Contents

About the Author

T. Michael Rogers fell in love with computers and code when he was 9. Mike has been building software and leading software-development teams for over 18 years. He shares his knowledge and experience by providing training and coaching for software teams and organizations, as an instructor of iOS Boot Camp in NYC and as an author of online courses for developers and managers. Mike can be reached on Twitter @tmichaelrogers and on his blog http://www.brainloaf.com.

About the Technical Reviewer

Charles Cruz is a mobile-application developer for the iOS, Windows Phone, and Android platforms. He graduated from Stanford University with a Bachelor's degree and Master's degree in engineering. He lives in Southern California and runs a photography business with his wife (www.bellalentestudios.com). When not doing technical things, he plays lead guitar in an original metal band (www.taintedsociety.com). Charles can be reached at codingandpicking@gmail.com and @CodingNPicking on Twitter.

Acknowledgments

I would like to thank everyone at Apress who provided support, inspiration, hard work, and long hours in the making of this book. This book is the go-to reference for developers creating Swift-based applications and would not have been possible without the editors and staff who produced it.

Kevin Walter, for his work as the lead editor, who guided me, kept me moving, and coordinated with the entire team to complete this book.

Charles Cruz, for his work as the technical reviewer of the book and for his meticulous verification of every line of code throughout the entire book.

Anne Marie Walker, for her work as Development Editor and ensuring that the organization, flow, and format of the book show the great effort and work that has gone into the book.

Roger LeBlanc, for his work as copy editor on the book and his thoughtful attention to detail, smoothing out the rough edges of my writing.

Michelle Lowman, for her leadership and vision in getting this book to market.

Introduction

Swift is the newest and hottest language in the mobile-development world today. At the 2015 Worldwide Developers Conference (WWDC), Apple announced that it is open sourcing Swift and making it available on other platforms. For developers, this is a huge opportunity to share code inside and outside the Apple ecosystem.

Swift represents an exciting step forward in application development. It brings the power of the latest modern languages, such as functional programming, closures, and extensibility. At the same time, it incorporates tried-and-true concepts, such as type safety and object-oriented structures. This book, *Swift Recipes*, is a reference book on Swift 1.2 for developers who need quick answers to common problems on the iOS and OS X platforms as well as any platform that will support pure Swift in the future.

The book starts out covering core language concepts and provides common problems along with their solutions. Once all the language-specific topics are covered, the book proceeds to offer solutions to common application-development needs and challenges. Each chapter presents recipes in a problem/solution format that can be used individually or in combination with each other. Some recipes build upon each other to form more complex solutions.

In addition to Swift language basics, this book also covers topics such as iOS and OS X application development, multithreading and concurrency, connecting with Web Services and APIs, Core Data, and some advanced iOS 8 topics using Swift.

This book is designed as a reference to help developers get work done. Each chapter includes step-by-step instructions, diagrams, and sample code that explains the concepts behind the solutions, as well as offering the code and patterns required to implement the solutions in your applications.

If you are a developer who develops applications on the iOS or OS X platforms, you will benefit from these solutions. In addition, if you are transitioning from Objective-C to Swift, these recipes will leverage your existing knowledge into creating Swift solutions.

Swift Programming

Welcome to *Swift Recipes*. Swift, announced by Apple at WWDC 2014 and released in September of 2014 is a modern alternative to Objective-C for iOS and OS X developers. In each chapter of this book are recipes or solutions to common situations and challenges you will encounter when developing iOS and OS X applications.

Each chapter follows the same format. A problem is presented, followed by the solution. The solution is discussed in detail in a section named "How It Works." This section explains the implementation of the solution using Swift. Code examples and details about how to apply the code are used to walk you through the solution. Finally, in "The Code and Usage" section, the full listing of the code is provided along with instructions on how to use the full listing.

This chapter will focus on essential recipes you will encounter in Swift. It will provide solutions to common situations you will encounter, such as

- Getting Started with Swift
- Installing Xcode 6
- Working with Playgrounds
- Designing User Interface Elements in a Storyboard
- Dealing with Strings
- Formatting Numbers as Strings
- Getting the Length of a Swift String
- Manipulating Swift Strings
- Manipulating Strings with Native Swift Methods
- Storing Strings on the iOS File System
- Reading a Text File into a String

- Reading and Writing Text Files in Cocoa
- Dealing with Numbers
- Dealing with Dates

Swift is still a young language. In many of the following recipes, you must use Foundation objects such as NSString and NSDate. Many swift classes are "bridged" to Foundation objects and can work together seamlessly. Recipes in this chapter leverage those bridged functions.

1-1. Getting Started with Swift

Problem

You have heard and read good things about Swift since it was released, but you are still wondering about the benefits of working with this new language.

Solution

Swift was created by Apple to provide the development community with a new modern programming language. Swift can be used independently or alongside Objective-C to create Mac OS and iOS applications. Swift does have a large number of modern features that Objective-C does not. Some key features of Swift that are missing in Objective-C are

- **Type Safety.** Type safety helps developers avoid the problems inherent with Objective-C and its use of pointers. All types must have a default value. Variables cannot be nil, unless specified by the developer. An optional type variable may be nil or have a value. The keyword optional is used to define an optional variable.

- **Type Inference.** Swift seeks to make coding more efficient, eliminating some of the artifacts that are present in many languages. The complier can determine the type of most variables using the initial value of the variable. This saves programming time and effort by eliminating the need to explicitly type variables in your code.

- **Enumerations and Structures.** Both can have methods and properties, making them more powerful than ever.

- **Playgrounds.** Playgrounds allow developers to write code in real time and see the results. Developers can code without creating a project, workspace or other typical project requirements. Common playground recipes are found later in this chapter.

1-2. Installing Xcode 6

Problem

You have not yet installed Xcode 6.

Solution

Use the Mac AppStore to install Xcode 6.

How It Works

In order to install Xcode 6, you must have a Mac running OS X Mavericks (10.9) or Yosemite. Launch the Mac App Store, and search for Xcode. Xcode can be downloaded for free from the Mac App Store (Figure 1-1). Once there, click "Get."

Figure 1-1. Click "Install." Xcode will download and install

1-3. Working with Playgrounds

Problem

You want to quickly write some code to explore an idea.

Solution

Xcode 6 and Swift have a new feature called *playgrounds*. Playgrounds let you write code and the playground immediately compiles and executes it. This lets you test an idea without having to create a new project or work within your existing project.

How It Works

Your first step is to launch Xcode. To create a new playground, select File ➤ New ➤ Playground. Provide a name for your playground and for this recipe, choose "iOS" as the platform. Next click continue, and then select a location for your saved playground file (Figure 1-2).

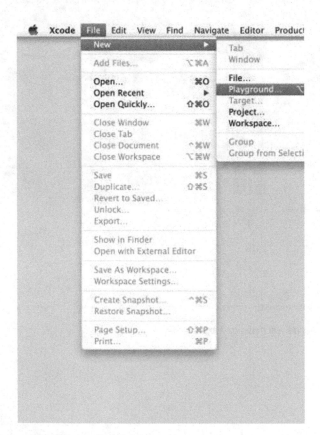

Figure 1-2. Select "New" from the file menu and then select "Playground" in the submenu

Xcode will open a playground window containing sample code. A playground window consists of these areas: the code area on the left, the results sidebar on the right, and the Assistant Editor, which is hidden by default. To see the Assistant Editor, select View ➤ Show Toolbar. Then click the assistant editor icon that looks like a tuxedo. This will open the Assistant Editor to the right of the results sidebar (Figure 1-3).

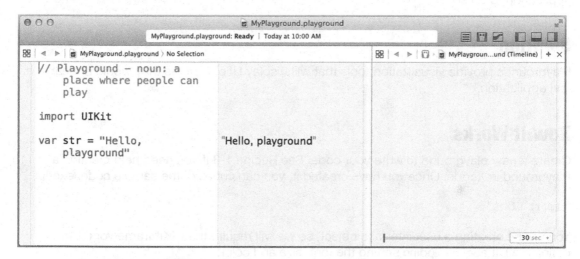

Figure 1-3. The Playground window

The Code and Usage

Working with a playground is designed to be easy. Start writing code in the code editor. Begin with the sample code that Apple has provided:

```
// Playground - noun: a place where people can play

import UIKit

var str = "Hello, playground"
```

The first line is a comment, the second line imports the UIKit framework so that you can access those APIs if you wish, and finally the third line creates a new string variable. If you look, on the same line as the string declaration, in the results sidebar, you will see "Hello, playground". This is the evaluation of the statement var str = "Hello, playground". The result of that expression is the string "Hello, playground".

Add a new variable called "welcome" and assign it a value such as this one:

```
var welcome = "Welcome, playground"
```

The playground will quickly evaluate that statement and display the results on the right column of the window. You will see additional uses for playgrounds in coming recipes.

1-4. Designing User Interface Elements in a Storyboard

Problem

You need to design a user interface element, but you don't want to compile and run an application to do so.

Solution

Playgrounds provide visualization tools that will display UI objects as they would appear in a real application.

How It Works

Create a new playground to write your code. See Recipe 1-3 if you need help creating a Playground in Xcode. Once you have created it, you can cut all of the sample code, except

```
"import UIKit"
```

You will be creating a user interface object, so we will require the UIKit framework. Start by defining a UILabel, including setting the font, size and color:

```
var label = UILabel(frame: CGRect(x: 0,y: 0,width: 300,height: 100))
```

You don't need a class or function. Like the previous recipe, the playground does the work for you. In the results sidebar, mouse over the result and two icons will appear. They are the "Quick Look" and the "Values History" icons (Figure 1-4).

UILabel

Figure 1-4. From left to right, the "Quick Look" and "Values History" icons

Clicking the "Quick Look" icon will display a pop-up that shows the visual results of the statement (Figure 1-5).

Figure 1-5. The pop-up view displaying a visualization of the statement

The "Values History" icon looks like a circle. To view the values of a statement at a particular point in time, click in the circle. The Assistant Editor will appear. Values will appear within boxes for each icon you click on. This allows you to see the incremental effects of your code changes (Figure 1-6).

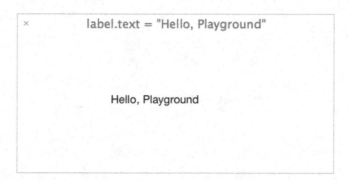

Figure 1-6. *The "Value History" visualization*

The Code and Usage

Enter Listing 1-1 into a new playground. If you need help creating a new playground, see Recipe 1-3.

Listing 1-1. *Create a UILabel*

```
import UIKit

var label = UILabel(frame: CGRect(x:0, y:0, width: 300, height: 100))

label.text = "Hello Playground"

label.font = UIFont(name: "Arial-Black", size: 20)

label.textColor = UIColor.greenColor()
```

Mouse over the statements in the results sidebar, and click the 'Quick Look" and "Values History" icons to see the values. Click each "Values History" button on each line of code. Your values history should look like Figure 1-7.

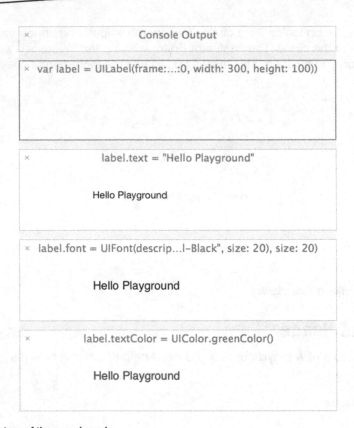

Figure 1-7. Value history of the sample code

1-5. Dealing with Strings

Problem

Frequently you need to convert a string to a number. That number could be an integer, decimal or floating-point number.

Solution

Create a class extension to the `String` class, and use `NSString` to provide the required functions.

How It Works

If you need to convert a String to an integer, then you can use String.toInt.

To convert a String to a decimal or float, you will need to use a different approach. Fortunately, Swift and Objective-C were designed to work well together. You can use classes from the Foundation framework to create a `String` class extension that can provide the conversion methods. The NSNumberFormatter class has the functionality required to convert those strings. The method numberFromString returns an optional NSNumber. If the result is nil, then the string was not a valid int, float or double.

```
var formatter = NSNumberFormatter()

var doubleResult = formatter.numberFromString("40.25")?.doubleValue
```

If it is not nil, you can return the doubleValue or floatValue property to convert the number to the respective type.

The Code and Usage

Copy Listing 1-2 to a new playground. See Recipe 1-3 for details about creating a new playground. Listing 1-2 contains an extension to the String class that will convert the string to an optional number. If the string cannot be parsed, nil will be returned.

Listing 1-2. A String class extension to parse strings to numbers

```
import Foundation

extension String
{
    func toDouble() -> Double?
    {
        var formatter = NSNumberFormatter()

        return formatter.numberFromString(self)?.doubleValue
    }

    func toFloat() -> Float?
    {
        var formatter = NSNumberFormatter()
        return formatter.numberFromString(self)?.floatValue
    }
}
```

Once implemented, these class extensions can be used on any String-type variable. To test the functionality in a *playground*, copy Listing 1-2 into a new playground file. Use the extension methods to convert a string literal to a number using the toDouble and toFloat methods.

```
"100.50394".toDouble()

"0.289".toFloat()
```

Examine the results sidebar in the storyboard window.

1-6. Formatting Numbers as Strings

Problem

You need to convert a number to a string and properly format it.

Solution

Swift `Strings` and `NSStrings` are bridged to allow you access to `NSString` functions, including the string format specifiers. Using format specifiers gives you more control over formatting numbers.

How It Works

In Objective-C, you can format a string such as this:

```
NSLog("The time is %02d:%02d", 10, 4)
```

Swift automatically bridges a `String` to the `NSString` class as well. That means you can access the functions available to you in either class.

The string formatters are exactly the same when using them in Objective-C or in Swift through the `String` class. See Table 1-1.

Table 1-1. *Common Number Format Specifiers*

Specifier	Description
%d	A signed 32-bit integer
%u	An unsigned 32-bit integer
%f	A 64 -bit double
%e	A 64-bit double, printed in scientific notation with a lowercase *e* before the exponent

The Code and Usage

Enter this code into an empty playground file:

```
import Foundation
var time = String(format: "The time is %02d:%02d", 8, 18)
```

Import the Foundation framework. Then you can use the Swift string format initializer. The results sidebar should display the string "The time is 08:18".

1-7. Getting the Length of a Swift String

Problem

You need to find the length of a string, but you can't find a method on the String class. The String class in Swift is bridged with the NSString class. You can call the functions of NSString when using a Swift string. However, there are some exceptions.

Solution

In order to better handle Unicode multibyte characters, Swift has a global method called countElements, which can be used to return the number of characters in a string.

How It Works

The String class handles strings differently than the NSString class. String uses Extended Grapheme Clusters to store Unicode characters as combinations of individual Unicode scalars. Storing strings in this fashion allows for a greater range of characters to be used by developers. For example, you can represent the copyright symbol as a single Unicode scalar

```
let copyrightMark : Character = "\u{00A9}"
```

or decompose it into separate elements

```
let decomposedMark : Character = "c\u{20DD}"
```

This allows two or more characters to be composited together to make a single character. Swift combines these characters in order to display them. However, if you counted the actual characters in the string, for the variable decomposedMark, the value would be 2. Instead, Swift provides the countElements() global that is aware of Extended Grapheme Clusters. Even though the decomposed variable has two physical characters, countElements will return a count of one, representing the single resulting character.

The Code and Usage

Listing 1-3 displays the different behavior between NSString.length and the countElements global. Add this to a new playground. (See Recipe 1-3, "Working with Playgrounds.") NSString.length will return 2, because it counts the Unicode character as two individual characters. The countElements method is able to determine that the Unicode character is an Extended Grapheme and counts it as a single character.

Listing 1-3. Comparing NSString.length with countElements

```
import Foundation

let decomposedMark : String = "c\u{20DD}"

NSString(format:decomposedMark,NSLocale.currentLocale()).length // returns 2

countElements(decomposedMark) // returns 1
```

When you are dealing with strings in Swift, always use countElements to determine the number of composed characters in a string. Using NSString.length on a composed string will give you an incorrect count if the string contains composed characters.

1-8. Manipulating Swift Strings

Problem

Every application at one time or another requires you to perform a manipulation of strings. Swift strings are structured differently than NSString objects. Strings are value types in Swift and behave differently than NSString objects. The method calls are similar between String and NSString, but there are some key differences in names and parameters.

Solution

Swift strings have many built-in features. When a feature is not yet native to Swift, it makes NSString methods available through bridging. Bridging allows you to pass Swift String objects to Foundation classes in place of NSString. In addition, methods available to NSString are made available to Swift String instances, which call the bridged NSString class method.

How It Works

In Swift, mutable strings are created using the var keyword. This allows the string to be updated. If you use the let keyword, the string is immutable and cannot be modified. There is some lack of clarity in the use of the labels "immutable" and "mutable." Swift strings are value types. As a result, when they are passed or assigned, a copy is made. At this time, no NSMutableString functions are available through the String class in Swift. Therefore, most functions return a string rather than operating on the original. The important thing to remember is that if you want to change the contents of a variable, define it with var. If you are not going to change the value, use let. The compiler can optimize those let statements.

To replace a string within a string, you will need to use the NSString function stringByReplacingOccurrencesOfString:withString:

```
"The sky is red.".stringByReplacingOccurrencesOfString("red", withString: "blue")
```

In this function call, the string "red" will be replaced with "blue". Sometimes, you may need to replace a string, but you will want to restrict it to only part of the string.

```
"One, 2, 3.".stringByReplacingOccurrencesOfString("one", withString: "1",
    options: NSStringCompareOptions.CaseInsensitiveSearch,
    range: Range<String.Index>(start: str.startIndex,
        end: advance(str.startIndex, 27 )))
```

The range parameter type is a Swift class called Range, and it is a range composed of String.Index objects, a start and an end. A String.Index object is different from a typical index. Because Swift strings can contain characters that are composed of multiple Unicode characters in an Extended Grapheme Cluster, a `String.Index` must refer to the position of the composed character rather than the physical index. This means that string indexes for different Swift strings cannot be used interchangeably.

To retrieve the starting index of a string, use `String.startIndex`. In order to get the `String.Index` indicating the character five positions in, you use the global function `advance(start: String.Index, n: Int)`. Advance moves the `String.Index` *n* spots to the right. Don't forget to check for index violations. If "n" will advance past the end of the string, your program will crash.

The statement `advance("abc".startIndex,2)` will return a `String.Index` two characters into the string. In this case, it's the position of the letter "b" because there are no decomposed characters.

If you would like to get a substring of a string, there are a number of options, such as `substringFromIndex`, `substringToIndex` and `substringWithRange`. Each requires `String.Index` parameters or a `Range` of `String.Index` objects.

You can append strings using the + operator:

```
var  phrase = "So long" + " and thanks for all the fish."
```

You can also use the += operator to append and reassign the string to itself:

```
var phrase = "So long"
phrase += " and thanks for all the fish."
```

Strings can be inserted into other strings using `stringByReplacingCharactersInRange`, but they use the same index for the `Range` parameter.

```
var r = Range<String.Index>(start: advance(str.startIndex,6),
        end: advance(str.startIndex,6))
"I like pizza.".stringByReplacingCharactersInRange(r, withString: " hot")
```

To delete a range of characters from a string, use `stringByReplacingCharactersInRange` with an empty string.

```
var str = "I like hot pizza."
var r = Range<String.Index>(start: advance(str.startIndex,6), end:
advance(str.startIndex,10))

println(str.stringByReplacingCharactersInRange(r, withString: ""))
```

The Code and Usage

To run the following recipe code, enter it into an empty playground. If you need help creating a playground, see Recipe 1-3. The Swift class `String` is bridged with `NSString` in the Foundation library. This means you can call those methods on any Swift string. Listing 1-4 is an example of some of those methods.

Listing 1-4. Manipulating Swift strings with NSString methods

```
import Foundation

var str = "I would like to replace one with one"

str.stringByReplacingOccurrencesOfString("one", withString: "1")

str.stringByReplacingOccurrencesOfString("one", withString: "1",
    options: NSStringCompareOptions.CaseInsensitiveSearch)

str.stringByReplacingOccurrencesOfString("one", withString: "1",
    options: NSStringCompareOptions.CaseInsensitiveSearch,
    range: Range<String.Index>(start: str.startIndex,
            end: advance(str.startIndex, 27 )))
```

Your results sidebar should look like this:

```
"I would like to replace one with one"
"I would like to replace 1 with 1"
"I would like to replace 1 with 1"
"I would like to replace 1 with one"
```

1-9. Manipulating Strings with Native Swift Methods

Problem

You want to perform string manipulation in pure Swift. You do not want to use the Foundation classes to assist your string processing.

Solution

Strings in Swift can be treated similarly to arrays. This allows you to use powerful functions available in Swift to process both arrays and strings.

How It Works

According to "The Swift Programming Language" published by Apple, strings are a collection of characters in a specific order. Does that sound like an array? It can be treated like one. You can loop through the characters in a string with a for-in loop:

```
for c in "ABCDEFGHIJKLMNOPQRSTUVWXYZ"
{
    println(c)
}
```

Ranges can be used to return a substring from a String value. For example:

```
var str = "ABCDEFGHIJKLMNOPQRSTUVWXYZ"
```

```
str[str.startIndex...advance(str.startIndex, 13)]
```

This can be dangerous, however, because if you exceed the maximum index of the string, you will get a runtime error. You need to check the end index of the string to be sure you do not exceed the bounds. Always check against the range of the string.

You should test the amount you want to index into a string against countElements - 1. This will return the maximum index that can be used. See the substring extension in the following code. Be careful you don't create an off-by-one error.

To test if a string is empty, you can call the global function isEmpty, which returns a Boolean:

```
isEmpty("123")
```

If you need to retrieve a number of characters from the beginning or end of a string, you can use the prefix and suffix functions, respectively. The prefix function will retrieve the first N characters from the String parameter, and N is the second parameter.

```
prefix("ABCDEFGHIJKLMNOPQRSTUVWXYZ",9) // returns "ABCDEFGHI"
```

The suffix method works the same way, except it returns the N characters, starting with the last character and working backwards through the string.

```
suffix("ABCDEFGHIJKLMNOPQRSTUVWXYZ",9) // returns "RSTUVWXYZ"
```

The Code and Usage

Enter the code in Listing 1-5 into a playground window to see the examples in action. This listing shows a number of examples of how you may use global Swift array functions on strings. It also contains a class extension to the String class. This method will use global array functions to return a substring of the original string. Remember strings are value types in Swift, so this method will return a copy of the string.

Listing 1-5. Using array functions with strings

```
var str = "ABCDEFGHIJKLMNOPQRSTUVWXYZ"
// Prints each character of the alphabet in a line by itself
for c in str
{
    print(c)
}

// Get a substring using a range of String.Index
str[str.startIndex...advance(str.startIndex, 13)]

// Return the first 9 characters of a string
prefix(str,9)
```

```
// Return the last 5 characters of a string
suffix(str,3)

// Check to see if a string is empty
isEmpty(str)

// Get the number of characters in a string
countElements(str)

// String extension to add a Swift native substring function
extension String {

    func substring(startix : Int, length : Int) -> String?
    {
        var endPos = 25
        let max = countElements(self) - 1
        if startix + length > max
        {
            return nil
        }

        let start = advance(self.startIndex,startix)
        let end = advance(self.startIndex,startix + length)

        return self[start...end]
    }
}

str.substring(5, length: 5)
```

If you would like to use the string extension substring function in your own code, create a new Swift file named "String-extension.swift" and copy the entire extension into the file. To use the function, add this file to your project.

1-10. Storing Strings on the iOS File System

Problem

Your application needs to store strings in a file on the iOS file system.

Solution

You can write to files located in your application's Documents folder. The Documents folder is part of the application sandbox. Your application can write only to files in your application's sandbox, and other applications have no access to your application's sandbox.

How It Works

In order to write text files in your iOS application, you need to first get a path to the file. To do this in iOS, you use the NSSearchPathForDirectoriesInDomains function:

```
let directories = NSSearchPathForDirectoriesInDomains(
    NSSearchPathDirectory.DocumentDirectory,
    NSSearchPathDomainMask.AllDomainsMask, true) as? [String]
```

This will return an optional array of strings. If the array is not null, the first item in the array is your documents directory. iOS applications have permission to write to the documents folder located within their sandbox. Once you have the directory path, you can append a file name to it:

```
let filename = "SwiftText.txt"
var directory = directories[0];
let path = directory.stringByAppendingPathComponent(filename);
```

> **Note**   You can read from the iOS bundle, but you cannot write back to it. If you want to update a file that you have included in the bundle, copy it to the documents directory and then modify it.

This is the name of the file that contains the content you want to read. Define a variable to store the text, and you can use the function writeToFile to save the contents.

```
let alphabet = "ABCDEFGHIJKLMNOPQRSTUVWXYZ"

alphabet.writeToFile(fullPath, atomically: false,
    encoding: NSUTF8StringEncoding, error: nil)
```

If writeToFile returns true, the file was successfully written. While this is a bridged function of NSString, there are indications that additional functionality will be coming in Swift. An undocumented method writeTo on the string object indicates that a string will be able to be written to objects that implement the Streamable protocol. The current documentation, at the time of publishing, does not have any specifics about the method or Streamable protocol.

The Code and Usage

The code in Listing 1-6 can be executed in a playground or incorporated into an application. To run it now, enter it into a new playground.

Listing 1-6. Writing to a file on iOS

```
import Foundation

let filename = "SwiftText.txt"
// iOS File Path Code
let directories : [String]? = NSSearchPathForDirectoriesInDomains(NSSearchPathDirectory.
DocumentDirectory, NSSearchPathDomainMask.AllDomainsMask, true) as? [String]

var directory : String
var fullPath : String = ""

// Write to file
if let directories = directories {
    directory = directories[0]; //documents directory
    fullPath = directory.stringByAppendingPathComponent(filename)
}
else
{
    println("Error: Could not determine the documents directory path.")
    abort() // Handle this properly in your production code
}

let alphabet = "ABCDEFGHIJKLMNOPQRSTUVWXYZ"

var error : NSError?

alphabet.writeToFile(fullPath, atomically: false,
    encoding: NSUTF8StringEncoding, error: &error)

if let err = error
{
    println("Error reading file: \(err.description)")
}
```

When using an iOS playground, your code is running in a sandbox, just like it would on an iOS device. The file Swifttext.txt will be in a folder for this sandbox on your disk. To view the file the code created, use the "Quick Look" icon in the playground to get the path of the sandbox directory. Click the "Quick Look" icon on this row of code:

```
directory = directories[0]; //documents directory
```

The value of the directory variable will look similar to this:

```
/var/folders/5m/8_xm31b51v91cffgml0s8mkc0000gp/T/com.apple.dt.Xcode.pg/containers/
com.apple.dt.playground.stub.iOS_Simulator.test2-716E9DA4-BBA8-45B9-9AA3-
35C625F6FF8E/Documents
```

Copy the path from the "Quick Look" box by selecting the text with your mouse and using Edit ➤ Copy.

Switch to the finder. Choose Go ➤ Go to Folder. Then paste the path into the text box and click the Go button. A finder window will appear with the location of the file.

1-11. Reading a Text File into a String

Problem

In an iOS application, you would like to read the contents of a file into a string.

Solution

Swift can read from a file using the `stringWithContentsOfFile`. This includes the files from your bundle as well as other files written to the documents directory of the application.

How It Works

You can use the `NSString` class to read text from a file. Swift still relies on Foundation classes in order to read and write text from files. To begin, you need to get a path to the file you wish to read. In order to retrieve the path to the directory in your applications sandbox or bundle, you can use the `NSSearchPathForDirectoriesInDomains` function:

```
NSSearchPathForDirectoriesInDomains(
    NSSearchPathDirectory.DocumentDirectory,
    NSSearchPathDomainMask.AllDomainsMask, true) as? [String]
```

This returns an optional string array. Under normal circumstances, this should always result in the first element of the string array being the path to the sandbox documents directory. Checking for a nil is a good best practice. The function call should not return nil in practice; if it does, it indicates a problem such as a memory issue. The documentation does not specify any potential reasons for this situation. Retrieve the directory path by accessing the first element in the array and append the filename to get the `fullPath` to the file.

```
directory = directories[0] //documents directory
fullPath = directory.stringByAppendingPathComponent(filename)
```

Before we can read a file, it must first exist. Use the code from Recipe 1-10 to create a file. Write the contents of a string to a file. Pass an `NSError` pointer to the `writeToFile` call; it will be populated with an `NSError` object containing information about the problem:

```
var error : NSError?

let alphabet = "ABCDEFGHIJKLMNOPQRSTUVWXYZ"
alphabet.writeToFile(fullPath, atomically: false,
    encoding: NSUTF8StringEncoding, error: &error)
```

Now that the file exists on disk, we can read the file into a string variable. The method `String.contentsOfFile:encoding:error:` will read a file and return the contents of that file as a string.

```
let text = String(contentsOfFile: fullPath, encoding: NSUTF8StringEncoding, error: &error)

if let err = error
{
    println("Error reading file \(fullPath): \(err.description)")
}
```

If an error occurs, it is most likely that the path does not exist. Make sure the file you are attempting to read exists.

The Code and Usage

The code in Listing 1-7 will create a file named "SwiftText.txt" on your disk. Then it will read the contents of that file back into a variable named `text`. Create a new playground in Xcode and pass the contents of Listing 1-7. In the console area, you will see the output indicating the file was written successfully. Otherwise, if an error occurred, you will see an error message.

Listing 1-7. Reading strings from a file on iOS

```
import Foundation

let filename = "SwiftText.txt"
// iOS File Path Code
let directories : [String]? = NSSearchPathForDirectoriesInDomains(
    NSSearchPathDirectory.DocumentDirectory,
    NSSearchPathDomainMask.AllDomainsMask, true) as? [String]

var directory : String
var fullPath : String = ""

if let directories = directories {
    directory = directories[0] //documents directory
    fullPath = directory.stringByAppendingPathComponent(filename);
}
else
{
    println("Err: Could not determine the documents directory path.")
    abort() // Handle this properly in your production code
}

var error : NSError?

// First we need to write to the file
// NOTE: each playground has its own temporary file system
// Files created in one playground will not have the same path
// as those created in another
```

```
let alphabet = "ABCDEFGHIJKLMNOPQRSTUVWXYZ"
alphabet.writeToFile(fullPath, atomically: false,
    encoding: NSUTF8StringEncoding, error: &error)

if let err = error
{
    println("Error writing file \(fullPath): \(err.description)")
}
else
{
    println("Created file at \(fullPath)")
}

let text = String(contentsOfFile: fullPath,
    encoding: NSUTF8StringEncoding, error: &error)

if let err = error
{
    println("Error reading file \(fullPath): \(err.description)")
}
else
{
    println("Successfully read the contents of the file at \(fullPath)")
}
```

In order to access the documents directory, get the path to the file by copying the value of the directory variable. The path will look something like this:

```
"/var/folders/5m/8_xm31b51v91cffgmlOs8mkcOOOOgp/T/com.apple.dt.Xcode.pg/containers/com.
apple.dt.playground.stub.iOS_Simulator.iOS-write-string-to-file-E33AOCB5-906E-4C54-9CE1-
BAC6BCA1AB63/Documents"
```

Switch to the finder. Choose Go ➤ Go to Folder. Then paste the path into the text box and click the Go button. A finder window will appear with the location of the file.

1-12. Reading and Writing Text Files in Cocoa

Problem

You want to read and write text files in your OS X Cocoa-based application.

Solution

OS X applications can read and write files similar to iOS applications.

How It Works

When you build and run your own applications, or download an application from the Internet, not the Mac App Store, a sandbox does not restrict the application.

These applications can access files anywhere on disk. This recipe will read a file in the /tmp path on the hard drive:

```
let filename = "/tmp/SwiftText.txt"
```

In this scenario, you simply need a valid path to the file. Then call the following initializer on String:

```
var text = String(contentsOfFile: fullPath,
    encoding: NSUTF8StringEncoding, error: &error)
```

If there is an error, the variable passed to the error parameter will be populated with the description of the error. You will want to create robust error handling in your code to handle any potential errors, such as being out of disk space, attempting to save to a path without permission, or unknown errors.

The variable "text" is optional in this case, because if there is an error, the string will be nil. So you will want to test the variable before attempting to read it.

To write a file to the Mac OS file system, use the String.writeToFile method:

```
text?.writeToFile(fullPath, atomically: false,
    encoding: NSUTF8StringEncoding, error: &error)
```

Always check the error parameter to see if the write was successful.

The Code and Usage

For the code in Listing 1-8 create a New Project in Xcode. Select "Application" under the OS X section in the left list. Then choose "Command Line Tool." Click next. Give your product a name, such as "ReadWriteText," and select Swift as the language. Choose the location on disk to save the project and click "Create."

The project will have a single .swift file named "main.swift." Open this file, and enter the code. The code will read from a text file you create. Then it will write back to the file to illustrate reading and writing files. The NSString methods are the same as reading from and writing to iOS, but the location of the file is not restricted to the application's sandbox.

Listing 1-8. Reading string from and writing strings to a file on Mac OS

```
import Foundation

let fullPath = "/tmp/SwiftText.txt"

var error : NSError?
var text = String(contentsOfFile: fullPath,
    encoding: NSUTF8StringEncoding, error: &error)

if let err = error
{
    println("Error reading file \(fullPath): \(err.description)")
}
```

```
else
if let contents = text
{
    println("Success: \(contents)")
}

text = "0987654321"

error = nil

text?.writeToFile(fullPath, atomically: false,
    encoding: NSUTF8StringEncoding, error: &error)

if let err = error
{
    println("Error writing file \(fullPath): \(err.description)")
}
```

Next, you need to create a text file to read. You will create a file using the Terminal application.

Switch to the finder. Choose Go ➤ Applications. In the Applications folder is a folder named "Utilities." Double-click that folder to open it. The Terminal application is located in this folder. Double-click the Terminal icon to launch the application.

At the prompt, type **cd /tmp**. This will change the current directory to the /tmp directory. Now you may create the file.

At the terminal prompt, type **cat >SwiftText.txt** and press Enter. Type a few lines of text followed by a carriage return. Then press Control+D. This will end the file.

Run the application. In the output window at the bottom of the Xcode window, you should see "Success:" followed by the contents of the temporary file you created.

Then go back to your terminal window and type **cat SwiftText.txt**. This will display the contents of the file that has been overwritten by the program. You should see the contents of the file as "0987654321."

1-13. Dealing with Numbers

Problem

Typically, before you can display a number on screen or write it to the console, you need to convert it to a string.

Solution

The Swift String class provides you with functionality to convert many different types of numbers to strings.

How It Works

Any type of number can be quickly converted to a string using string interpolation. Swift will substitute the value of the number—whether it is a float, double or integer—into a string. String interpolation is performed by wrapping a variable in parentheses, preceded by the backslash escape character. For example:

```
var n = 110
var s = "This is an integer = \(n)"
This code results in the string "This is an integer = 110".
```

The Code and Usage

When you need to convert a number to a string, create a string literal and use interpolation to display its value.

```
var y = 1701.01

let s = "\(y)"
```

> **Note**   When converting a Float to a string, you may see unpredictable results due to the binary representation of values. If this occurs, use NSString(format: "%.02f", str) to control the precision.

1-14. Dealing with Dates

Problem

Swift does not yet have a Date type, and most of your applications need to deal with dates.

Solution

You have full access to the NSDate class. Using these classes in Swift works similarly to how they are accessed in Objective-C.

How It Works

The NSDate function and other date-related objects in the Foundation framework are available when using Swift. The APIs differ slightly to agree with Swift's simplified syntax. This recipe will provide some helper code to quickly create NSDate objects in a more simplified way.

This function will create a new NSDate using month, day and year parameters:

```
func from(#year:Int, month:Int, day:Int) -> NSDate {
        var c = NSDateComponents()
        c.year = year
        c.month = month
        c.day = day

        var gregorian = NSCalendar(identifier:NSGregorianCalendar)
        var date = gregorian?.dateFromComponents(c)
        return date!
    }
```

As you can see in the preceding code, NSDateComponents encapsulates the different parts of a date. NSDateComponents is used in conjunction with NSCalendar to create and manipulate dates. Be sure to use these classes because they will use important date features such as leap years and daylight savings time when manipulating dates.

Dates can be created from strings as well. The following function will create a date from a formatted date string:

```
func from(string:String, format:String="MM-dd-yyyy") -> NSDate {
        var dateFmt = NSDateFormatter()
        dateFmt.timeZone = NSTimeZone.defaultTimeZone()
        dateFmt.dateFormat = format
        return dateFmt.dateFromString(string)!
    }
```

In this function, NSDateFormatter is used to change the formatted string into a date. The format string you provide to this function can be any valid format that NSDateFormatter can read.

```
var date = Date.from("12/1/2013",format: "MM/dd/yyyy")
```

The Code and Usage

Add Listing 1-9 to a playground or an application. The class extension provides two class methods that facilitate the creation of NSDate instances. The method from(#year:Int, month:Int, day:Int) -> NSDate takes a cardinal year, month and day and returns a corresponding NSDate instance. The method from(string:String, format:String="MM-dd-yyyy") -> NSDate takes a string and an optional format string to create an instance of NSDate. The date format string is an NSDateFormatter format.

Listing 1-9. Date class extension for creating NSDate instances

```
import Foundation

class Date {

    class func from(#year:Int, month:Int, day:Int) -> NSDate {
        var c = NSDateComponents()
        c.year = year
        c.month = month
        c.day = day
```

```
        var gregorian = NSCalendar(identifier:NSGregorianCalendar)
        var date = gregorian?.dateFromComponents(c)
        return date!
    }

    class func from(string:String, format:String="MM-dd-yyyy") -> NSDate {
        var dateFmt = NSDateFormatter()
        dateFmt.timeZone = NSTimeZone.defaultTimeZone()
        dateFmt.dateFormat = format
        return dateFmt.dateFromString(string)!
    }
}

var date = Date.from("12/1/2013",format: "MM/dd/yyyy")
var countdown = Date.from(year: 2015, month: 10, day:21)
```

Chapter 2

Complex Types

Simple types in programming languages are used to store single values. Examples of simple types include Int, Char, and String. These types can have some methods associated with them, which is similar to a complex type. Think of simple types as the building blocks of complex types.

Complex types are made up of other types and have methods and functions that can operate on data. A custom class you create is an example of a complex type. Swift is an object-oriented language, and creating complex types is the heart of the language. In addition to having classes, Swift offers other data structures to create complex types.

This chapter contains recipes to create new complex types, including classes, enumerations, and structures. Swift adds new features and capabilities to these constructs that make it unique from other languages. Topics in this chapter include

- Writing Functions
- Creating Classes
- Adding Class Properties
- Initializing Class Properties
- Adding Class Methods
- Inheriting from Classes
- Implementing Protocols
- Setting Property Observers
- Defining Enumerations
- Creating Structures
- Using Tuples

2-1. Writing Functions

Problem

You need to create a function in order to perform an action on some information, such as a calculation, an update to a user interface, or a manipulation of a block of text.

Solution

In Swift, functions are first class types. They can be passed as parameters, created at runtime, and returned from functions. You can also create functions that are not encapsulated in another class, structure, or enumeration.

How It Works

Functions are defined using the keyword func. Functions can take zero or any number of parameters, and they can return a value to the caller. Function names must start with a non-numeric character. The letters a through z, both uppercase and lowercase can be used as the initial character. Unicode characters can be used as well. After that, you can use the numbers 0 through 9, as well as "_" in addition to the valid characters for the first character. Class names in Swift are upper camel case by convention. Upper camel case is where the first word is capitalized and the rest of the string is camel case, using uppercase letters to define the beginning of a new word. "DessertRecipe" is an example of upper camel case. An example of lower camel case is "getDateAndTime."

By convention, method names are lower camel cased in Swift. Next comes a set of parentheses containing an optional list of parameters, and finally you define the function's body inside curly braces:

```
func foo( a : Int, b: Int)
{ ... }
```

Within the parentheses, you define the parameters for your function. This function takes two parameters, both integers. Parameters are defined by a name and then the type of the parameter. Multiple parameters are added in a comma-separated list. To add more parameters, add a comma and then define the next parameter:

```
func foo ( a : Int, b : Int, c : String )
{ ... }
```

The function foo takes three parameters: two integers and a string. The function then performs some desired actions and completes execution. If you want to return a value, the function is defined similarly. Immediately after the function definition, add -> [Type] to the end of the definition before the opening brace for the body of the function. Put the name of the type your function will return after the "->".

```
func foo ( a : Int, b : Int, c : String ) -> String
```

The Code and Usage

The following function definition takes the two `int` parameters and a string. Then it returns a string containing the string and the two numbers. To run the code, create an empty playground and add this code:

```
func foo ( a : Int, b : Int) -> String
{
    return "\(a) + \(b) = \(a+b)"
}
```

In the results sidebar, you should see the results `coordinates [1,2]`. This is the string that the `foo` function returned.

2-2. Creating Classes

Problem

You want to have your code model real-world objects. For example, an `Order` class could encapsulate data such as the date of the order, the shipping address, and a function to calculate the total cost. This will organize your code for ease of use and maintenance.

Solution

Create classes to organize your code. Classes are an object-oriented structure that allows programmers to encapsulate data and functionality within an object. They allow developers to logically organize parts of a system. This facilitates maintainability and scalability of the code.

How It Works

Swift classes are created using the keyword `class`. Typically classes are written one to a file and the file is named after the class. For example, if you create an `Order` class, save it in a file named `Order.swift`.

Swift classes start with the keyword `class`. Similar to functions, class names must start with a non-numeric character. The uppercase and lowercase letters *a* through *z* can be used as the initial character of a class. However, it is convention to always start a class name with a capital letter. Unicode characters can be used as well. After that, you can use the numbers 0 through 9, as well as "_" in addition to the valid characters for the first character. Class names in Swift are upper camel case by convention. For more information on camel case, see Recipe 2-1. For reference, Table 2-1 contains a chart of acceptable characters for a class name.

Table 2-1. Characters Allowed in Class Names

Part Class Name	Valid Characters
Valid for the first character of a class name	A–Z uppercase and lowercase, Unicode characters
Valid for the remainder of a class name	0–9 and "_", or any character that is valid for the first character

Pumpkin, Apple2, and cherryPie are all valid class names. 3Bears, Apple-Pie, and Banana$ are all invalid names. To instantiate an instance of a class, you first declare a variable or a constant with the var or let keyword. Then you instantiate the class by using the class name followed by parentheses:

```
var pancakes = Recipe()
```

The Code and Usage

Enter this code into a new playground:

```
class Recipe
{
}
```

By itself, this code does not perform any actual work. You will learn about adding properties and methods in coming recipes.

2-3. Adding Class Properties

Problem

You need to store and retrieve data within a class. This will keep all information related to a single object in a single location.

Solution

Add class properties to your class to store and retrieve information.

How It Works

Swift allows developers to create two types of properties: constants and variables. Constants are defined and cannot be changed after that. They are defined using the let keyword:

```
let recipeName = "Apple Pie"
```

This statement creates a constant or "immutable" string. In Swift, you do not have to provide a type when defining a variable or constant as long as you supply an initial value. The compiler can determine the type for you based on that initial value.

By default, properties defined on a class this way are publicly accessible. You can use the `private` keyword to make a property accessible only internally. This means that any classes that reference this class will not have access to this property. You should use private variables in these situations to prevent consumers of the class from using variables that could accidentally change the state of the class and cause bugs.

```
private let internalSum = 5
```

Properties are accessed using *dot notation*. Imagine you have a variable `myRecipe` that is an instance of a class named `Recipe` and that class has a string property name. You would access it using the variable name, dot (.), and the property name:

```
println(myRecipe.name)
```

Private properties can be accessed inside a class just by using the name of the property. They can also be accessed using the `self` keyword, which is a reference to the current instance of the class:

```
println(internalSum)
println(self.internalSum)
```

The result is exactly the same regardless of whether or not you use the `self` keyword.

The Code and Usage

Enter the following code in a new playground file. This code defines two properties: the name, which is of type String, and `minutesToPrepare`, which is of type Int.

```
class Recipe
{
    var name = "Apple Pie"
    var minutesToPrepare = 30
}

var dessert = Recipe()
println("Recipe name: \( dessert.name)")
println("Preparation Time: \( dessert. minutesToPrepare)")
```

Try adding a few additional properties, and make sure you give them an initial value. You can then print them to the console.

2-4. Initializing Class Properties

Problem

Swift is a type-safe language and does not allow variables to be uninitialized unless they are declared as optional types. If you define properties and do not initialize them, your code will not compile. Rather than initializing default values in the property definition, you should initialize the properties to values supplied by the code instantiating the instance.

Solution

Swift allows for non-optional properties to be defined as long as they are initialized with an initializer.

How It Works

Initializers are like class constructors in other languages or the `init` function in Objective-C. If your class uses non-optional properties, the compiler will force you to implement an initializer and initialize those properties. The basic initializer is just `init()`. It is defined by itself with no return type.

Using our example from the previous recipe, our `Recipe` class has two properties, but they are initialized as part of their definition:

```
class Recipe
{
    var name = "Apple Pie"
    var minutesToPrepare = 30
}
```

Initializing class properties inline with their definition is not very extensible, and it can be error prone if some initialization is done inline and additionally in a different method. It is best practice to keep all your initialization code in the same location. In Swift, create initializer methods to handle setting initial values. All initializer methods are declared within the class definition.

The same code using a plain `init()` function would look like this:

```
class Recipe
{
    var name : String
    var minutesToPrepare  : Int

    init()
    {
        self.name = "Apple Pie"
        self.minutesToPrepare  = 30
    }
}
```

This is a little cleaner, but there are still hardcoded defaults. When you might not know an appropriate value before runtime, it is best to create an initializer that takes the initial values as parameters:

```
init( name : String, minutesToPrepare  : Int)
{
    self.name = name
    self.minutesToPrepare  = minutesToPrepare
}
```

Use parameter names that match up exactly with the property names. This makes it very clear for each property which parameter is used to initialize its value. Use the `self` modifier to refer to the instance's variable, and don't use it when accessing the parameters. An initializer defined this way is called a *designated initializer*. It initializes all the properties of the class. If all non-optional properties do not have an initial value at the end of the initializer, the code will not compile.

The Code and Usage

Enter the code in Listing 2-1 into an empty playground. The code defines a class `Recipe` that has a single initializer for the name and `minutesToPrepare` properties. This code instantiates a new recipe and assigns it to the `dessert` variable. Then the properties are printed to the console to illustrate how the properties are accessed.

Listing 2-1. The Recipe class definition, including two properties and a designated initializer

```
class Recipe
{
    var name : String
    var minutesToPrepare  : Int

    init( name : String, minutesToPrepare  : Int)
    {
        self.name = name
        self.minutesToPrepare  = minutesToPrepare
    }
}

var dessert = Recipe("Apple Pie",30)
println("Recipe name: \( dessert.name)")
println("Preparation Time: \( dessert. minutesToPrepare)")
```

You should see the output:

```
Recipe Name: Apple Pie
Preparation Time: 30
```

When appropriate, use this initializer pattern for all the classes you create. It keeps your code understandable and makes it clear how different initializers construct the instance. Note how the properties are initialized in the `init` method. The properties are referred to using the `self` object. This helps the compiler differentiate between properties and parameters with the same name.

2-5. Adding Class Methods

Problem

Your application needs classes that can perform actions to create the desired functionality.

Solution

Swift classes can define methods to accomplish these actions.

How It Works

There are two types of methods that you can add to a class: instance methods and type methods. Instance methods are available only on instances of a class. Type methods can be used without an instance. Methods are formatted like functions, except they are defined within the body of a class. This is an example of an instance method:

```
func add( amount : Double, cupsOf : String  )
```

By default, methods defined on a class are public. If you have a reason to keep a function private to the class, use the `private` keyword before the function definition:

```
private func foo()
```

Swift treats parameter names in a way that is compatible with Objective-C. When a method is called, all parameters except the first are given automatic external parameter names. When a method is called, any external parameter names must be used to identify the parameter. This is done to allow Swift to easily handle the parameter structure of the existing frameworks and their parameter patterns. It also makes function calls more expressive of the method's intent.

For example, calling a function that adds a number of cups of a particular ingredient would look like this:

```
recipe.add(2, cupsOf: "Apples")
```

The intent behind external parameter names is to make the code read almost like a sentence: "With this recipe, add 2 cups of Apples."

If you would like to add a function that is related to your class but does not directly operate on instance data, you should consider creating a type method. Type methods are defined by preceding the function definition with the keyword class. Imagine a conversion function that converts ounces to cups:

```
class func convertOuncesToCups( ounces : Double) -> Double
{
    return ounces / 8
}
```

This type method can be called using the class's name, dot (.), and the function name. For example, if the convertOuncesToCups method was part of the Recipe class, it could be called like this:

```
var cups = Recipe.convertOuncesToCups(16)
```

The Code and Usage

Enter the code in Listing 2-2 into an empty playground. This code defines a class named Recipe. It has three properties: name, minutesToPrepare, and ingredients. It has a designated initializer, a method that will add the name of an ingredient to the ingredients property, and a class method that converts ounces to cups.

Listing 2-2. Class definition for Recipe and example code using the Recipe class

```
class Recipe
{
    var name : String
    var minutesToPrepare  : Int
    var ingredients = [String]()

    init( name : String, minutesToPrepare  : Int) {
        self.name = name
        self.minutesToPrepare  = minutesToPrepare
    }

    func add( amount : Double, cupsOf : String  ) {
        ingredients.append(cupsOf)
    }

    class func convertOuncesToCups( ounces : Double) -> Double {
        return ounces / 8
    }
}

var applePie = Recipe(name:"Apple Pie", minutesToPrepare: 30)
applePie.add(2, cupsOf: "Apples")
Recipe.convertOuncesToCups(16)
```

In the results sidebar, you should see the return value of add and convertOuncesToCups. Next is the value of the newly initialized applePie instance. Then you see the new values of applePie after calling the add method. Finally, you see the results of the Type method convertOuncesToCups:

```
["Apples"]
2.0
{{name "Apple Pie" minutesToPrepare 30 0 elements}}
{{name "Apple Pie" minutesToPrepare 30 ["Apples"]}}
2.0
```

2-6. Inheriting from Classes

Problem

You would like to reuse and extend the features of an existing class. This allows you to organize your code, supports refactoring, and provides a separation of concerns.

Solution

You can inherit from a *superclass* and create subclasses of your classes, Swift language classes, and classes from the other frameworks.

How It Works

To extend an existing class, add a colon and the name of the class you would like to inherit. The subclass will inherit the properties and methods of the parent class.

> **Note**   Swift classes do not inherit from a base class as they do in Objective-C. A new class that does not inherit from a superclass becomes a base class you can extend.

If you want to extend a class, immediately after the name of the class, add a space and a colon (:), followed by another space. Then add the name of the class to extend:

```
class  DessertRecipe : Recipe
```

Consider this Recipe class:

```
class Recipe
{
    var name = ""
    var minutesToPrepare = 0
    var ingredients = [String]()
```

```
var recipeType : String {
    return "Basic"
}

func add( amount : Double, cupsOf : String  )
{
    ingredients.append(cupsOf)
}

class func convertOuncesToCups( ounces : Double) -> Double
{
    return ounces / 8
}
}
```

Although your subclass can reuse methods and properties that are inherited, you might want your subclass to behave differently in certain circumstances. It is possible to override inherited properties and methods. For example, in the Recipe class, there is a recipeType property that currently has the value of "Basic."

When you override properties or methods, the definitions are still placed within the body of the class definition. In the DessertClass, you can override the property to make it specific to the DessertClass. To override a property, use the keyword override. Here's one thing to remember: the type of the overridden property must remain the same.

```
override var recipeType : String {
    return "Dessert"
}
```

If you would like to override a function, you can use the override keyword as well:

```
override func add(amount: Double, cupsOf: String)
```

You then write your own implementation of the method. As is the case with properties, you cannot change the parameters or the return type of the method, but you can redefine the entire method. However, if you need to call the superclass's original implementation in addition to your code, you can use the super property on your instance. This will call the method on the superclass:

```
super.add(amount, cupsOf: cupsOf)
```

> **Note**   Swift classes can inherit only from a single base class.

The Code and Usage

To run the code in Listing 2-3, enter it into a playground. This code defines the class Recipe. Then it defines the subclass DessertRecipe that inherits from the Recipe class. A short code example follows. This creates an instance of Recipe and an instance of DessertRecipe. It then prints out the recipeType property for each. In this example, dinner.recipeType returns "Basic" and dessert.recipeType returns "Dessert."

Listing 2-3. The Recipe class and its subclass DessertRecipe

```
class Recipe
{
    var name : String
    var minutesToPrepare : Int
    var ingredients = [String]()
    var recipeType : String {
        return "Basic"
    }

    init( name : String, minutesToPrepare  : Int) {
        self.name = name
        self.minutesToPrepare  = minutesToPrepare
    }

    func add( amount : Double, cupsOf : String  ) {
        ingredients.append(cupsOf)
    }

    class func convertOuncesToCups( ounces : Double) -> Double {
        return ounces / 8
    }
}

class DessertRecipe : Recipe
{
    override var recipeType : String {
        return "Dessert"
    }

    override func add(amount: Double, cupsOf: String) {
        super.add(amount, cupsOf: cupsOf)
    }
}

var dinner = Recipe(name: "Fish", minutesToPrepare: 15)
var dessert = DessertRecipe(name: "Pie", minutesToPrepare:  30)

println(dinner.recipeType)
println(dessert.recipeType)
```

2-7. Implementing Protocols

Problem

You need to loosely couple functionality between two classes in order to implement a delegate or make your code more maintainable.

Solution

Create a *protocol* that defines a set of functions that a class must implement.

How It Works

Protocols in Swift define a set of methods and properties related to a particular function. A class that implements those methods and properties has "adopted" the protocol. A protocol is similar to an interface in other languages. A protocol allows developers to implement a layer of abstraction between classes. This abstraction allows a class that implements a protocol to be modified or replaced without requiring updates to classes that use an object conforming to a particular protocol.

Protocols can be used to implement the delegate pattern, isolate a set of functions, or allow for dependency injection. Protocols are types in Swift; therefore, you should use upper camel case notation. Protocols can be used the same way any type can. They can be passed as parameters and used to define properties and return types of methods. Protocols are defined with the `protocol` keyword. This is how the definition of the `Sharing` protocol starts:

```
protocol Sharing
```

> **Note**   Swift protocols do not support optional methods or properties like Objective-C protocols.

Properties are declared on the protocol in a similar way to declaring properties on a class. However, you must indicate if the property needs to support `get` and/or `set`. Here are two property definitions, one that supports `get` and `set`, and the second that supports `get`:

```
var username : String { get set }
var error : String { get }
```

In a scenario like this, a username may be used to perform some sort of action and any error message as a result of the action can be retrieved from the `error` property. A method is declared just like it is in a class, except you do not provide any implementation code, just the function name, parameters, and return type:

```
func shareMessage( message : String ) -> Bool
```

This example protocol is designed to abstract sharing a message, via different methods such as email, instant message, or social media. A class using a parameter/property of the protocol type can use an instance of any class implementing this protocol. A class that adopts the protocol indicates so by including it after the class name and a colon, the same way you inherit a superclass. If the class also inherits a superclass, add the protocol to the list after the superclass.

The Code and Usage

In Listing 2-4, the EmailSharing class adopts the Sharing protocol and the Message class is instantiated with an instance of the EmailSharing class. To try the code, add this code to a new playground.

Listing 2-4. Implementing a protocol

```
import Foundation

protocol Sharing
{
    var username : String { get set }
    var error : String? { get }

    func shareMessage( message : String ) -> Bool
}

class EmailSharing : Sharing
{
    private var _error : String?

    var username : String

    var error : String?
    {
        return _error
    }

    init(username : String)
    {
        self.username = username
    }

    func shareMessage(message: String) -> Bool {
        // some code to compose an email
        println("Message from \(username):\n\(message)")
        return true
    } }

class Message
{
    var sharingMethod : Sharing
    var message = "Hello World"
```

```
    init (sharingMethod : Sharing)
    {
        self.sharingMethod = sharingMethod
    }

    func share()
    {
        sharingMethod.shareMessage(self.message)
    }
}

var message = Message(sharingMethod: EmailSharing(username: "Mike"))
message.share()
```

Under the Assistant Editor, the following output should be seen in the Console Output:

```
Message from Mike:
Hello World
```

2-8. Setting Property Observers
Problem

You need to know when a property's value has changed, but you do not want to implement custom getters and setters. You might need to perform an action or update a user interface based on the updated values.

Solution

Swift Property *observers* are triggered when a property's value will change or has changed. Using the willSet: and didSet methods, you can add code to perform the necessary actions when the property has been updated.

How It Works

The willSet: method is called just before the new value is assigned to the property. The willSet method has a single parameter that is passed to it of the same type as the property. It contains the new value. The didSet method is called just after the value has been updated. Both willSet: and didSet are not called during the initialization of the property.

Imagine as part of a class called Recipe that you have a property serves that indicates the number of individuals that a recipe serves:

```
class Recipe
{
    var serves : Int
        {
        willSet( newServes ) {
            println("Will set to value \(newServes)")
        }
        didSet {
            println("Did set")
        }
    }

    init ()
    {
        serves = 0
    }
}
```

In the willSet: method, you can update some status messaging or start an animation in your application. For example, you can have an indicator that data is updating. Property observers can be used to update user-interface elements after some background process has updated a property.

Property observers can be added to existing classes by inheriting the class and overriding the property. This allows you to watch for updates in existing classes and perform your own actions when those values are updated.

The Code and Usage

Paste Listing 2-5 into a new playground. It defines the Recipe class with a single property. Using the willSet: and didSet property observers, the class will print a message to the console when you assign a value to the property.

Listing 2-5. A class with property observers and an example

```
class Recipe
{
    var serves : Int {
        willSet( newServes ) {
            println("Will set to \(newServes)")
        }
        didSet {
            println("Did set")
        }
    }
```

```
    init () {
        serves = 0
    }
}

var g = Recipe()
g.serves = 3
```

If you cannot see the Console Output in the playground editor, click the Values History button on the line g.serves = 3.

2-9. Defining Enumerations

Problem

You need to represent a range of values in a way that is human readable and maintainable. For example, in cooking, there are different types of measuring units. There are cups, teaspoons, and tablespoons. These do not have a character or value that can be represented in code.

Solution

Enumerations are a structure that addresses this issue. Enumerations allow you to define your own sets of values that can be used in code. Swift provides enumerations similar to other languages, but it adds expanded capabilities.

How It Works

Enumerations are structures that define custom values. For example, a recipe takes ingredients of specific amounts to complete. In code, you would like to see values like Cups, Tablespoons, and Ounces. However, it would be inefficient and error prone to contain these values in String type variables or another type that could be hard to update. You could use constants, but constants hold only a single value rather than a range of possible values.

Enumerations are defined with the enum keyword. Values are defined following the case keyword. The following is an example of different measures represented as an enum:

```
enum Measure
{
    case Cup, Tablespoon, Ounce
}
```

Values can be defined on a single comma-separated list after the case keyword, or they can be defined one per line with multiple case statements. The previous and next definitions of the enumeration Measure are functionally the same.

```
enum Measure
{
    case Cup
    case Tablespoon
    case Ounce
}
```

Enumeration values in Swift are different than in other languages. They are types in themselves. In most other languages, enumerations are backed by integers at compile time. They can also be defined by another type, such as a string. Swift enumerations can be of a specific type, but it is not required. To define an enumeration backed by a specific type, define it like you would a variable. Use a colon and then the type. Here is how you define the type of the Measure enum to be Int:

```
enum Measure: Int
{
    case Cup = 1
    case Tablespoon = 2
    case Ounce = 5
}
```

Unique to Swift, enumerations can contain data in what are called *associated values*. Imagine that you have a class that defines the ingredients of a recipe. Each ingredient requires a certain amount to be added to the recipe. Using associated values, you can store that information along with the measurement size. Define the associated values by a list of types contained within parentheses:

```
case Cup (Double)
case Tablespoon (Double)
case Ounce (Double)
```

If you wanted to save two and half cups, you could do so like this:

```
var amount = Cup(2.5)
```

Use the member of an enumeration with an associated value similarly to an initializer. Each variable with the enumerations type can store different associated values. For example, in a recipe, you might need to use a number of items but not a specific measurement, such as *2 eggs*. In this case, you would like to store a whole integer. Add a Quantity item to the enum, and set its associated value to Int.

```
case Quantity (Int)
```

You might want to store more than one piece of data with an enumeration value. In order to do this, you can define multiple associated values. For example, the amount of an ingredient can depend on how it is prepared. You might want to combine that information in another enumeration called `PreparationStyle`. In the definition, you can add multiple types to be captured as associated values:

```
enum PreparationStyle
{
        case Whipped(String, Measure)
        case Boiled(String, Measure)
}
```

Using enumerations in this way can make your code very expressive:

```
var whippedEggs = PreparationStyle.Whipped("Eggs", Measure.Quantity(2))
```

In addition, it allows you to code using the enum values, rather than comparing strings or magic numbers to communicate intent.

Another unique feature of Swift is that enumerations can have methods. Adding a method to an enumeration is the same as adding it to a class. This offers a better way to encapsulate functionality and data because any operations related to the enum can be implemented as part of the definition. In other languages, you would have to create a related class that used the `Measure` enum.

```
enum Measure
{
    case Cup(Double)
    case Tablespoon (Double)
    case Ounce (Double)
    case Quantity (Int)

    func convertToOunces() -> Measure {
        switch (self) {
            case .Cup(let val):
                return Ounce(val * 8)
            case .Tablespoon(let val):
                return Ounce(val * 0.5)
            default:
                return self
        }
    }
}
```

When you need to read values from an enumeration's associated value, use a `switch` statement to extract the values. For each possible enumeration value, add a `case` block. You can use the shortcut dot notation because the compiler can infer the data type of the measure variable. In the statement, use the `Measure` value and, in parentheses, define a variable to hold the extracted value. For example, use this statement: `case .Cup(let val):` If the value of the measure variable is `.Cup`, the associated value is extracted and assigned to the variable `val`.

In this case, `Cup` and `Tablespoon` have just one `Double` value. If the `measure` variable is a `Cup`, it will extract the value from the `Cup` enumeration and return the measure in ounces.

If an enumeration has multiple associated values, provide a variable for each in your case statement. For example, to access the PreparationStyle enumeration, use a case statement, but define two variables for the enumeration values Whipped and Boiled. Both variables are populated with the corresponding associated value.

```
enum PreparationStyle {
    case Whip(String, Measure)
    case Boil(String, Measure)

    func instructions() -> String {
        switch (self) {
            case .Whip(let name, let measure):
                return "Whip \(name)"
            case .Boil(let name, let measure):
                return "Boil \(name)"
        }
    }
}
```

The Code and Usage

Add Listing 2-6 to an empty playground. The Measure enumeration represents the values used to measure the amount of an ingredient. It uses associated values to store the quantity of those measurements. The method convertToOunces in Listing 2-6 shows you how to extract associated values using a switch statement.

The PreparationStyle enumeration shows an example of how to use multiple assigned values using a switch statement. The method instructions returns a string suitable for displaying the instructions for the example ingredient.

Listing 2-6. Enumeration examples

```
enum Measure
{
    case Cup(Double)
    case Tablespoon (Double)
    case Ounce (Double)
    case Quantity (Int)

    func convertToOunces() -> Measure {
        switch (self) {
            case .Cup(let val):
                return Ounce(val * 8)
            case .Tablespoon(let val):
                return Ounce(val * 0.5)
            default:
                return self
        }
    }
}
```

```
var twoCups = Measure.Cup(2)

enum PreparationStyle {
    case Whip(String, Measure)
    case Boil(String, Measure)

    func instructions() -> String {
        switch (self) {
            case .Whip(let name, let measure):
                return "Whip \(name)"
            case .Boil(let name, let measure):
                return "Boil \(name)"
        }
    }
}

var eggs = PreparationStyle.Whip("Eggs", Measure.Quantity(2))
eggs.instructions()
```

2-10. Creating Structures

Problem

You want to create an object that can contain data, but you would prefer that it be treated as a value type rather than a reference type.

Solution

In Swift, structures are value types, and when a structure is passed to functions or properties, a copy is made of the structure.

How It Works

Swift structures, like enumerations, have added features that make them more useful than a traditional structure. Structures in Swift can have properties, methods, initializers, and subscripts, and they can conform to protocols. In Swift, classes and structures are very similar. The key differences are that classes have additional capabilities that structures do not. Structures lack these capabilities:

- Structures cannot inherit other structures.
- Structures cannot be type cast at runtime.
- Structures are value types and do not have references. Any structure that is assigned to a variable will be copied.

Structures are defined in the exact same format as classes, but that is done by using the keyword struct.

```
struct Ingredient
{
    var name : String
    var amount : Measure
    var preparationInstructions : String
}
```

In this example, you have a struct that defines an ingredient. It is indistinguishable from a class at this point.

One feature that structures have and classes do not is *implicit initializers*. In classes, you must define your initializers. Every structure automatically has an initializer with one parameter per property. For a structure with three properties—name, amount, and preparationInstructions—the implicit initializer will have three parameters of the same name and type as the properties:

```
var eggs = Ingredient(name: "Eggs", amount: Measure.Quantity(2), preparationInstructions:
"Beat eggs in a bowl and set aside")
```

Properties and methods of a struct are accessed using dot notation just like you would use for a class. To access the property name, you would use the following:

```
println(eggs.name)
```

> **Note**   Structures can be extended with extensions, have methods, and adopt protocols just like classes.

The Code and Usage

Add Listing 2-7 to a blank playground. This code defines a structure to contain information about an ingredient to be used in a recipe. It creates an instance of Ingredient using the implicit initializer for the structure.

Listing 2-7. Creating and using a struct

```
enum Measure
{
    case Cup(Double)
    case Tablespoon (Double)
    case Ounce (Double)
    case Quantity (Int)
}

struct Ingredient
{
    var name : String
    var amount : Measure
    var preparationInstructions : String
}

var eggs = Ingredient(name: "Eggs", amount: Measure.Quantity(2), preparationInstructions:
"Beat eggs in a bowl and set aside")
```

2-11. Using Tuples

Problem

You need to return multiple values from a function. In other languages, you would typically need to create a class or a struct to hold data.

Solution

Use *tuples* to return an arbitrary number of types from a function or as a parameter.

How It Works

Tuples allow you to pass and return groups of values without creating a new type, using references, or using input parameters. Developers I know hotly debate tuples. No matter what your opinion is on the usage of tuples, if used properly they can add value to your solutions. As with many software design practices in software development, there are passionate opinions on both sides of the argument. There are times when creating a new type would only complicate matters.

A tuple is created by a set of parentheses, with a list of comma-separated values:

```
(10,4,"String")
```

When a tuple is defined as a parameter, or for a return value, you can provide names to each element in the tuple. These names are used to access the values:

```
var x = (average: 1, min: 33, max: 8)
```

The property `x.average`, in the preceding example, would then access the first integer in that tuple.

The Code and Usage

In the example code in Listing 2-8, first we define a tuple by itself. Then `getAverageMinMax` is a function that does multiple operations and returns three results. Enter this code into a blank playground.

Listing 2-8. Tuples

```
func getAverageMinMax( numbers : [Int32] ) ->
    (average: Int32, min: Int32, max: Int32)
{
    var average : Int32 = 0
    var min = Int32.max
    var max = Int32.min

    for i in numbers
    {
        average += i
        if i < min { min = i }
        if i > max { max = i }
    }
    average = average / Int32(numbers.count)

    return (average, min, max)
}

var results = getAverageMinMax([1,2,3,10,110,42])

println(results.average)
println(results.min)
println(results.max)
```

Collections

Collections

Collections are used in almost every application for data storage, retrieval, searching, and sorting. Recipes in this chapter will focus on the most common collection types, Array and Dictionary. Both arrays and dictionaries are generic collections in Swift; however, not all collections are arrays or dictionaries. Swift does provide lower level collection and sequence functions and protocols that perform individual features of the Array and Dictionary generic types.

This chapter focuses on the Array and Dictionary generic types. In Swift, arrays and dictionaries are strongly typed, unless otherwise specified. The recipes presented in this chapter are

- Creating an Array
- Counting the Number of Items in an Array
- Managing Items in an Array
- Searching for Items in an Array
- Sorting an Array
- Replacing a Range of Values in an Array
- Iterating Over an Array
- Saving an Array to the File System
- Populating an Array with the Contents of a plist File
- Using Subscripts
- Creating a Dictionary
- Managing Items in a Dictionary
- Implementing the Hashable Protocol

Chapter 3

- Iterating Through Items in a Dictionary
- Saving a Dictionary to the File System
- Populating a Dictionary with the Contents of a Property List File

3-1. Creating an Array

Problem

Your application needs to store and access data in an ordered list.

Solution

Swift offers arrays to hold collections of objects.

How It Works

Swift is a strongly typed language. Arrays are strongly typed using generic collections. This means that an array can hold only objects of a single type. Generic collections allow reusable classes, such as arrays and dictionaries, to apply to any type, but at compile time, the result is a strongly typed collection. To create an empty array, you use the following syntax. First the Array type is used, and then the specific type for the array is written in between angle brackets "<>".

```
var array = Array<String>()
```

This creates an empty array of strings. Only strings can be stored in this array.

Arrays can also be initialized inline with an array literal, like this:

```
var vehicles = ["Car","Bus","Truck","Plane"]
```

In Swift, arrays are value types. Each time arrays are assigned or passed as parameters, a copy is made. You can use this ability to quickly create a new array:

```
var vehiclesCopy = vehicles
```

The variable vehiclesCopy will contain a copy of the entire array. You can add elements to and remove elements from vehiclesCopy without changing the vehicles array. This does not hold true for the elements of the array. If you create an array containing reference types, the array itself will be copied, but the element will refer to the same reference object in both arrays.

Arrays can be defined as *mutable* or *immutable*. Use the proper definition based on your needs. If you need to store a static list of items and do not need to modify that list, use an immutable array. Arrays defined with the let keyword are immutable. If you will be adding, removing, sorting, or otherwise modifying the elements of an array, create a mutable array. Arrays defined with the var keyword are mutable. Attempting to add elements to or remove elements from an immutable array will result in a compile error.

The Code and Usage

Enter Listing 3-1 into an empty playground. This code creates four array variables: `array`, `vehicles`, `vehicles2`, and `vehicles3`. Each array has different attributes, as indicated by the code comments.

Listing 3-1. Creating arrays

```
// Create a blank array
var array = Array<String>()

//Create an array with an array literal
var vehicles = ["Car","Bus","Truck","Plane"]

//Copy an array to another variable
var vehicles2 = vehicles

//Immutable array
let vehicles3 = vehicles
```

Use these array creation recipes when creating arrays in your applications. In the upcoming recipes, I will discuss how to add, access, and manipulate items in arrays.

3-2. Counting the Number of Items in an Array

Problem

You need to find out how many items are in an array. You might need to know the total size of the array to update a user interface or to create a loop for iteration.

Solution

Arrays have a property named `count`. It will tell you how many items are in the array.

How It Works

The `count` property can be used on any array variable:

```
var vehicles = ["Car","Bus","Truck","Plane"]
```

Accessing the property `vehicles.count` will return 4. In addition, you can access the `count` property on an array literal:

```
["Motorcycle","Bike","Scooter"].count
```

The Code and Usage

Add Listing 3-2 to an empty playground. This code creates an array and then uses the count property to get the number of items in the array. Then it illustrates how you can get the count of an array literal.

Listing 3-2. Counting the number of items in an array

```
var vehicles = ["Car","Bus","Truck","Plane"]
vehicles.count

["Motorcycle","Bike","Scooter"].count
```

In the results side bar, you should see the following:

```
["Car","Bus","Truck","Plane"]
4
3
```

3-3. Managing Items in an Array

Problem

You need to add new items or store new information, or you need to access existing items in your array to retrieve data to process.

Solution

Arrays can be directly indexed by an integer value.

How It Works

Arrays have zero-based indexes in Swift. You can access a particular object in an index using a subscript to indicate the index after the variable name:

```
var vehicles = ["Car","Bus","Truck","Plane"]
var vehicle = vehicles[2]
```

In the preceding code, the variable `vehicle` will contain the string "Truck". You must keep in mind the total number of items in the array when using the subscript. If the index is out of the bounds of the array, a runtime error will occur.

To add a new object to the array, use the append method:

```
vehicles.append("RV")
```

This appends the string "RV" to the array as a new element at the end of the array. If you wish to add the new item somewhere else in the array, you can use the `insert` method:

```
vehicles.insert("RV",atIndex: 1)
```

This method will insert the object at the index provided, and all items in that position through to the end will move 1 index up.

An array can be inserted into another array using the `splice` method. The `splice` method is similar to the `insert` method, but instead it inserts an array rather than just a single item:

```
vehicles.splice(["Quad","Tractor"], atIndex: 3)
```

Two arrays can be concatenated with the + or += operator:

```
vehicles += moreVehicles
```

> **Note**   You can append items only to a mutable array. If you defined the array as a constant with `let`, you will receive a compiler error.

The Code and Usage

Add Listing 3-3 to a new playground. This code creates an array literal and assigns it to a variable `vehicles`. Then it shows an example of indexing into the array, assigning it to the variable vehicle. It then goes on to show a few more examples of inserting, splicing, and concatenating.

Listing 3-3. Managing items in an array

```
var vehicles = ["Car","Bus","Truck","Plane"]
var vehicle = vehicles[2]

// Insert an item at an index
vehicles.insert("RV",atIndex: 1)
// Insert an array at an index
vehicles.splice(["Quad","Tractor"], atIndex: 3)

// Concatenate 2 arrays
var moreVehicles = ["Boat","Train","Helicopter"]
vehicles += moreVehicles
```

Try adding items to the `vehicles` array on your own. Arrays are used frequently for data storage in both iOS and Mac OS applications. These functions will be instrumental to managing data within your applications.

3-4. Searching for Items in an Array

Problem

You need to search for items that match certain criteria, and your application uses arrays for data storage.

Solution

Use the `filter` method of the array. It will return an array of items matching conditions specified by a closure.

How It Works

The `filter` method takes a closure as a parameter. A *closure* is a function that can be declared inline with your code. For more details on closures, see Chapter 4. In a filter, the closure is a function that returns a Boolean result indicating if the item matched. The `filter` method passes a single parameter to the closure. This parameter is the item to be evaluated by your function. If the value matches the comparison made within the closure, it is added to the return array. If you wanted to find a specific string in an array of strings, you could use the `filter` method. For example, to search an array of strings, the closure you could use would look like this:

```
{ c in c=="Car" }
```

It looks very different, but it is just an alternate way of declaring a function. The whole closure is wrapped in a block of braces. The identifiers before the keyword `in` are the parameters of the function. The compiler can infer the type of c from the context. Everything after is in the function body. The `filter` method expects a Boolean result. This function is a single statement that evaluates to a Boolean. In this case, the keyword `return` may be excluded. This is how the closure is used with the `filter` method:

```
var vehicles = ["Car","Bus","Truck","Plane"]
var matches = vehicles.filter({ c in c == "Car" })
```

In the first statement in the preceding code, an array called `vehicles` is created. In the second, the `filter` method is called. For each and every item in the array, the closure will be executed. The `filter` method will pass a single parameter c to the closure. The closure must return a Boolean value indicating if the parameter should be included in the result set. In the example, the closure will look for strings that match the string "Car". The statement `c == "Car"` is evaluated and if it returns `true`, the item is added to the `matches` array. Remember, if your closure has more than one statement, you must use the `return` statement with a Boolean value to indicate if the item matches the criteria in your closure.

Using `filter` with an array of Strings is straightforward. In many circumstances, you might need to filter an array of complex types such as classes or structures. The approach is the same. Here is an array of `Vehicle` structures:

```
var complexArray = [
    Vehicle(name: "Sedan", year: 2008, numberOfWheels: 4),
    Vehicle(name: "Motorcycle", year: 2008, numberOfWheels: 2),
    Vehicle(name: "Tractor", year: 2010, numberOfWheels: 4),
    Vehicle(name: "Trike", year: 2000, numberOfWheels: 3)
]
```

To filter the array for `Vehicle` instances where year property equals 2008, start by creating a closure that takes a single parameter. The array contains the type `Vehicle`, so the parameter will be of the type `Vehicle`. Create a Boolean expression that compares the value of the year property:

```
var results = complexArray.filter({ v in v.year == 2008 })
```

You can make the closure as complex or as simple as you need. However, it is executed once per item in the array. Keep performance and memory usage in mind when filtering large array sets or using complex filtering logic. After the `filter` method completes its work, the array is returned from the `filter` method. Additionally, when the array contains a value type such as a string or structure, remember that the results of the `filter` method will be copies of those objects.

The Code and Usage

Open a new playground, and enter Listing 3-4. This code is the complete listing of the examples in this recipe. First, is an example using `filter` to search an array of `String`. Then there are examples that demonstrate how to filter complex objects like a structure.

The first example searches for a string in an array. Click the Value History circle on line 5, `matches`. You should see the single item "Car" in the array.

The second example searches an array of `Vehicle` objects using a single property. Then a second example is presented using two different properties. In the Playground editor, click the Value History circle on the lines with `matches` and `moreResults`. View the members of the arrays.

Listing 3-4. Using Array.filter

```
// Create an array of vehicle names
var vehicles = ["Car","Bus","Truck","Plane"]
// Filter for items that match the string "Car"
var matches = vehicles.filter({ c in c == "Car" })

struct Vehicle
{
    var name : String
    var year : Int
    var numberOfWheels : Int
}

var complexArray = [
    Vehicle(name: "Sedan", year: 2008, numberOfWheels: 4),
    Vehicle(name: "Motorcycle", year: 2008, numberOfWheels: 2),
    Vehicle(name: "Tractor", year: 2010, numberOfWheels: 4),
    Vehicle(name: "Trike", year: 2000, numberOfWheels: 3)
]
```

```
// filter on one property
var results = complexArray.filter({ v in v.year >= 2008 })
// filter on multiple properties
var moreResults = complexArray.filter(
{ v in v.year >= 2008
    && v.numberOfWheels == 4 })
```

3-5. Sorting an Array

Problem

You need to sort an array of objects before processing them or displaying them onscreen.

Solution

Use the `.sort` method on an array. It will reorder your array using a closure to perform comparisons.

How It Works

The `sort` method takes a closure (for details on closures see Recipe 3-4 and Chapter 4), which is used to sort the items in an array. The `sort` method expects a closure with two parameters. The function must return a Boolean based on the criteria you specify for ordering. Typically, this is accomplished by comparing the two values. The order in which you compare the parameters matters. When comparing, it is best practice to keep the first parameter on the left and the second on the right. This will minimize confusion when using greater than or less than. If you follow this convention, less than will always be ascending order and greater than will always be descending order. The `sort` method reorders the items in the array in place.

Using the list of vehicles from Recipe 3-4, sort the items in the array:

```
var complexArray = [
    Vehicle(name: "Sedan", year: 2008, numberOfWheels: 4),
    Vehicle(name: "Motorcycle", year: 2008, numberOfWheels: 2),
    Vehicle(name: "Tractor", year: 2010, numberOfWheels: 4),
    Vehicle(name: "Trike", year: 2000, numberOfWheels: 3)
]
```

The array contains 4 instances of the `Vehicle` structure. The `Vehicle` class has a number of properties that can be compared to sort the items:

```
complexArray.sort({ p1, p2 in p1.year < p2.year })
```

In the preceding code, the `sort` method is passed a closure that compares the year properties of the two objects. In this case, if the first parameter's year is less than the second parameter's year value, the objects will be ordered in ascending order. If you compared to see if the first parameter is greater than the second, the order would be descending:

```
complexArray.sort({ p1, p2 in p1.year > p2.year })
```

You can use this approach to sort by other properties of the Vehicle structure. However, you might not always want to pass a closure. In this case, you can create functions for each potential sorting method and then provide the function in place of the closure. You can keep your code more organized this way. If you have more than two or three sorting functions, it will be more efficient to create functions and pass a reference to the sorting method rather than repeating the closure.

Implement a sort operation as a function, and pass it to the sort method of the array:

```
func sortYearAscending( v1 : Vehicle, v2 : Vehicle)-> Bool
{
    return v1.year < v2.year
}

complexArray.sort(sortYearAsecending)
```

The Code and Usage

Add the code in Listing 3-5 to a new playground. This is the complete listing of code from this recipe. This listing includes two methods for sorting an array. First it uses an inline closure, and then it uses a method passed as a reference to the sort method. Use the Value History button to see the changes to the array after each sort.

Listing 3-5. Sorting an array

```
struct Vehicle
{
    var name : String
    var year : Int
    var numberOfWheels : Int
}

var complexArray = [
    Vehicle(name: "Sedan", year: 2008, numberOfWheels: 4),
    Vehicle(name: "Motorcycle", year: 2008, numberOfWheels: 2),
    Vehicle(name: "Tractor", year: 2010, numberOfWheels: 4),
    Vehicle(name: "Trike", year: 2000, numberOfWheels: 3)
]

// sort with closure
complexArray.sort({ p1, p2 in p1.year < p2.year }) // Ascending
complexArray.sort({ p1, p2 in p1.year > p2.year }) // Descending

// sort with function
func sortYearAscending( v1 : Vehicle, v2 : Vehicle)-> Bool
{
    return v1.year < v2.year
}
```

```
func sortNameAscending( v1 : Vehicle, v2 : Vehicle)-> Bool
{
    return v1.name < v2.name
}

complexArray.sort(sortYearAscending)
complexArray.sort(sortNameAscending)
```

3-6. Replacing a Range of Values in an Array

Problem

You need to replace a range of values contained in an array in a single function call rather than replacing them item by item.

Solution

Arrays in Swift allow you to get and set ranges of values. This allows you to get or set multiple elements in the array at the same time.

How It Works

You can access a subset of an array using a closed range such as [1...5]:

```
var ingredients = ["Apples","Brown Sugar","Eggs", "Butter"]

ingredients[2...3] = ["Egg Substitute", "Butter Substitute"]
```

In this example, the last two items in the array have been substituted for two new values.

The Code and Usage

Enter Listing 3-6 in a new playground. This code demonstrates how a range of values in an array can be replaced or accessed at once. First an array is defined. Then some elements in the array are replaced. In the final line, only a short range of values is returned. You can see the results of each statement in the results sidebar.

Listing 3-6. Replacing a range of values in an array

```
var ingredients = ["Apples","Brown Sugar","Eggs", "Butter"]

ingredients[2...3] = ["Egg Substitute", "Butter Substitute"]

ingredients[1...2]
```

3-7. Iterating Over an Array

Problem

You need to iterate over the elements in an array to perform an operation with each element.

Solution

There are a number of loop-based solutions to iterate over an array in Swift.

How It Works

The most reliable way to iterate over an array is using a for-in loop. This avoids using numeric indexes and potential "off by one" errors:

```
var ingredients = ["Apples","Brown Sugar","Eggs", "Butter"]

for ingredient in ingredients
{
    println(ingredient)

}
```

In this example, the for loop will loop once for each item contained in that array. The variable ingredient will be set to the next item in the array for each pass through the loop.

The second way to iterate over an array is to use a for loop or a while loop with an index. On each pass through the loop, the index is incremented and the index is used to access an element in the array:

```
for var i=0; i < ingredients.count; i++
{
    println(ingredients[i])
}

var j=0;
while j < ingredients.count
{
    println(ingredients[j])
    j++
}
```

In both of the preceding examples, an integer index is used to access the elements of the array. The first example is a for loop, and the second example uses a while loop. You should use an integer index only if you need to keep track and use the cardinal index of the item in the array. Loops with integer indexes are prime sources for off-by-one errors. With the for-in loop solution, you do not need to worry about numeric indexes.

The Code and Usage

Enter Listing 3-7 into a new playground. It is the complete listing of the code in this recipe. It demonstrates how to use a for-in loop, an index based loop, and a while loop.

Each loop prints each item of the ingredients array. In the Playground editor, click on the Value History button of each println statement to see the output.

Listing 3-7. Iterating over an array

```
var ingredients = ["Apples","Brown Sugar","Eggs", "Butter"]

for ingredient in ingredients
{
    println(ingredient)
}

for var i=0; i < ingredients.count; i++
{
    println(ingredients[i])
}

var j=0;
while j < ingredients.count
{
    println(ingredients[j])
    j++
}
```

3-8. Saving an Array to the File System

Problem

You need to persist the contents of an array to the file system for access at a later time.

Solution

Swift arrays can be saved to disk using the NSArray class from the Foundation library.

How It Works

Arrays in Swift are bridged to the NSArray class. However, Swift arrays are strongly typed and can contain only one type of element, while NSArray can store multiple types of objects. However, it is easy to convert a Swift array to an NSArray by assigning it to a variable of the NSArray type. This will convert the array into an NSArray. When converting from an NSArray to a Swift array, casting can create nil results if the NSArray contains different object types:

```
var nsarray : NSArray = ingredients
```

The NSArray type has a method writeToFile that will save the array data to disk. The writeToFile function takes a string parameter as the path to the file to be written. To get your filepath, you should follow the approach for reading and writing text files depending on your platform: OS X or iOS. See Recipes 1-10, 1-11, and 1-12 for information on the MacOS file system and iOS sandbox. In this example, you will be using a MacOS command-line application so that you can use a fullPath to the file on the hard drive. The /tmp folder is for storing temporary files. Files older than a week are automatically deleted, and all files are removed on a reboot. Use this folder because it is a short path and exists on all OS X machines and allows files to be written.

```
let fullPath = "/tmp/ingredients-array.plist"
nsarray.writeToFile(fullPath, atomically: true)
```

The method writeToFile creates a plist file. The first parameter is the full path to the file to be written.

> **Note**   An existing file with the same file path will be overwritten. In your code, you might need to check to see if the file exists before writing to the file. See Chapter 7 for recipes dealing with the file system.

The second parameter for writeToFile is a Boolean. If this parameter is set to true, the contents of your file are written to a temporary file until the process is complete. Then it is renamed and will replace the existing file (if there is one). This ensures that a partial file is not written or an existing file is not corrupted if the application crashes or fails to complete writing.

writeToFile returns true or false, indicating if the file has been successfully written.

The Code and Usage

In Xcode, create a new project and select OS X Application. Then select "Command Line Tool." Give your project a name, and select "Swift" as the Language. Add Listing 3-8 to the "main.swift" file. Run the program.

Listing 3-8. Saving an array to the file system

```
import Foundation

var ingredients = ["Apples","Brown Sugar","Eggs", "Butter"]

var nsarray : NSArray = ingredients

let fullPath = "/tmp/ingredients-array.plist"

if !nsarray.writeToFile(fullPath, atomically: true)
{
    println("Error writing array file \(fullPath)")
}
else
{
    println("Successfully wrote to file")
}
```

When you run the program, view the output console in Xcode. You should see the text "Successfully wrote to file." To view the plist file, open a Terminal window and then type **cat /tmp/ingredients-array.plist**. This will display the contents of the file in the Terminal window.

Note   This code will work only if the array contains simple types. I discuss archiving data with complex types in Chapter 7, Recipes 7-7 and 7-8.

3-9. Populating an Array with the Contents of a plist File

Problem

You need to load the values of a plist file into an array.

Solution

Use the NSArray class to load an array from a plist file.

How It Works

The method NSArray.initWithContentsOfFile creates and populates an array with the contents of a plist file and returns the new array. Before calling the function, you need to have a full path to the plist you wish to read:

```
let fullPath = "/tmp/ingredients-array.plist"
```

In Swift, the syntax of the initializer for NSArray works as shown in the following code line. The parameter contentsOfFile is the file path to be read to create the array. Use the as keyword to cast the NSArray to a Swift array. If the conversion fails or the file cannot be loaded, the ingredients variable will be "nil":

```
var ingredients = NSArray(contentsOfFile: fullPath) as [String]?
```

If the array is returned, it was successfully loaded and cast to a Swift String array. If you do not cast the array, you will have an instance of an NSArray.

If the ingredients array is not nil, it was successfully loaded.

The Code and Usage

Listing 3-9 is the code of a command-line application that loads a plist file and prints the contents to the console. Listing 3-2 is the contents of a sample plist file you can use to run the code. First, create the plist file. Select File ➤ New ➤ File and choose Resources under iOS. Select Property List, and click Next. In the file dialog, place your cursor in the Save As text box. Type **/tmp**. The Go To Folder dialog will open. Click Go. Now save the file as **ingredients-array.plist**.

The file will open in the Property List editor. Change the Root item's type to Array. Then add four string items. Update the Values of each to be Apples, Brown Sugar, Eggs, and Butter. Save the file. The editor should look like Figure 3-1.

Key	Type	Value
▼ Root	Array	(4 items)
Item 0	String	Apples
Item 1	String	Brown Sugar
Item 2	String	Eggs
Item 3	String	Butter

Figure 3-1. Content of ingredients-array.plist

Next, create a new project in Xcode. Select "OS X", "Applications," and then "Command Line Tool." Give your project a name such as "ArrayFromFile." Add the code from Listing 3-9 to the main.swift file. Then run the application.

Listing 3-9. Load an array from the plist file

```
import Foundation

let fullPath = "/tmp/ingredients-array.plist"

var ingredients = NSArray(contentsOfFile: fullPath) as [String]?

if let ingredientsArray = ingredients
{
    for ingredient in ingredientsArray
    {
        println(ingredient)
    }
}
else
{
    println("Could not load plist")
}
```

In the output window, you should see the names of the ingredients in the file. It should look like this:

```
Apples
Brown Sugar
Eggs
Butter
Program ended with exit code: 0
```

3-10. Using Subscripts

Problem

You are writing a custom class and want to make it easier for users of that class to get and set items contained within an internal array.

Solution

You can define a subscript on any class, structure, or enumeration in Swift. The subscript allows a consumer of an instance to use square brackets "[...]" and a value to be used by the class to return a value.

How It Works

A subscript looks like a combination of a function and a property. It is defined with the keyword subscript. You provide parameters and a return type for the subscript. The following code shows a subscript that takes an Int as the subscript and returns a String:

```
subscript(index : Int) -> String
```

Subscripts can even have multiple parameters. In the following example, the subscript has two parameters:

```
subscript (var i : Int, var b: Bool) -> String
```

You would use the subscript in the following manner:

```
foo[2,true]
```

In your code, use the values passed as parameters to determine the response and return a specific value.

The Code and Usage

Listing 3-10 defines a `Recipe` class. That class has a property, `ingredients`, which is an array of Strings. You can access the individual ingredients using the subscript.

> **Note**   Implement your subscripts defensively. This is a simple example to illustrate the usage of subscripts. Always validate the input to the subscript. For example, check for out-of-bounds indexes.

Enter Listing 3-10 into a new playground. In this example, the value of `recipe[2]` is "Flour".

Listing 3-10. Using subscripts in a class

```
class Recipe
{
    var name : String
    var ingredients : [String]
    var prepTimeInMinutes : Int

    init(name :String, ingredients : [String], prepTimeInMinutes : Int) {
        self.name = name
        self.ingredients = ingredients
        self.prepTimeInMinutes = prepTimeInMinutes
    }

    subscript (var i : Int) -> String {
        return ingredients[i]
    }
}

var recipe = Recipe(name:  "Recipe x",
    ingredients:["Sugar","Apples","Flour"],
    prepTimeInMinutes: 3)

recipe[2]
```

3-11. Creating a Dictionary

Problem

You need to store a collection of key/value pairs and retrieve values by a unique key.

Solution

The Dictionary type can store and retrieve key/value pairs.

How It Works

The Dictionary type is a generic class and strongly typed. It can contain only values of a single type, and the key is only of a single type. This is different than the NSDictionary and NSMutableDictionary in Objective-C.

Any type can be used as a key value as long as it conforms to the Hashable protocol. To define a dictionary, use the type "Dictionary" followed by two comma-separated types contained in angle brackets "<>". Dictionaries can be mutable or immutable. If you use the keyword let, the Dictionary will be immutable, and items cannot be added or removed. Immutable dictionaries are useful if you have a frequently accessed dataset and want to keep it in memory. To create a mutable dictionary, use the keyword var:

```
var d = Dictionary<Int, String>()
```

This will create a dictionary with an integer key and string values. A dictionary can be initialized with a comma-separated list of key/value pairs. As its name indicates, a key/value pair is made up of the key used to retrieve the value from the dictionary. The type of the key can be any Swift type that implements the Hashable protocol. The Hashable protocol is discussed in Recipe 3-13. This recipe uses an Int for the key. The value can be any Swift type.

```
var e = [ 1:"One", 2:"Two", 3:"Three"]
```

The variable e is a Dictionary<Int, String>(). As with other variable definitions, the compiler automatically types the dictionary for you.

The Code and Usage

Create a new playground, and add Listing 3-11. It creates a dictionary with an Int as the key and String as the contents of the dictionary.

Listing 3-11. Creating a Dictionary

```
var d = Dictionary<Int, String>()

d[1]="First"
d[2]="Second"
d[3]="Third"

var e = [ 1:"One", 2:"Two", 3:"Three"]
```

Inspect the contents of the dictionary variable d. Click the "Value History" icon on line 7 to see the values contained in the variable e.

3-12. Managing Items in a Dictionary

Problem

In order to support your application's required functionality, you need to be able to add, remove, and update items in the dictionary.

Solution

The Dictionary class provides the methods required to manage the contents of a dictionary.

How It Works

First, you must create a new dictionary. Create a mutable Dictionary using the var keyword:

```
var d = Dictionary<Int, String>()
```

To add a value to the dictionary, use subscript notation to assign a new value to an existing key:

```
d[1]="First"
```

The type of the key used must match the type provided to define the dictionary. The same is true for the value. For example, if you initialized the dictionary with var d = Dictionary<Int,String>(), you must provide an Int as the key and String as the value.

> **Note**   If you provide a key that does not exist in the dictionary, nil is returned. All values returned from the dictionary are optional. For example, in our example dictionary, the return type is an optional String.

Items added to the dictionary can be referenced by their key. To remove an item from a dictionary, use the removeValueForKey method. The item with the matching key will be removed from the dictionary:

```
d.removeValueForKey(2)
```

The Code and Usage

Enter Listing 3-12 into a new playground. This code creates a new Dictionary and then removes the item for key value 2.

Listing 3-12. Managing items in a Dictionary

```
var d = Dictionary<Int, String>()

d[1]="First"
d[2]="Second"
d[3]="Third"

d.removeValueForKey(2)
```

Click the Values History button to examine the contents of the variable d after the item has been removed. You should see that the dictionary now contains two values: "First" and "Third".

3-13. Implementing the Hashable Protocol
Problem

You have a custom object that you want to use as a key in a Dictionary.

Solution

A Dictionary key can be any object that implements the Hashable protocol.

How It Works

The Hashable protocol requires the hashValue property to be implemented. There are many hashing algorithms that you can implement. The purpose of the hash is to create a unique value based on the content of the key. For this recipe, create a simple hash by concatenating all properties into a String and use String.hashValue:

```
"\(self.name) \(self.year) \(self.numberOfWheels)".hashValue
```

The Hashable protocol is an extension of the Equatable protocol. Any object implementing the Hashable protocol must also implement the Equatable protocol. The only requirement for the Equatable protocol is to implement the "==" operator for that type.

The "==" operator is defined in the global scope, not within your object. It takes two parameters, named left and right. To implement the operator, compare the hashValue properties of the two parameters:

```
func == (left: Vehicle, right: Vehicle) -> Bool
{
    return left.hashValue == right.hashValue
}
```

> **Note**   Hash values are not required to be consistent across different invocations of your application. It is advisable to store the value for future comparisons.

The Code and Usage

Add Listing 3-13 to a new playground. The code implements a struct Vehicle that conforms to the Hashable and Equitable protocols. The example at the end of the listing creates an instance of Vehicle. Examine v.hashValue to see the result of the hashing function.

Listing 3-13. Implementing the Hashable protocol

```
struct Vehicle : Hashable
{
    var name : String
    var year : Int
    var numberOfWheels : Int

    var hashValue : Int
    {
        get
        {
            return "\(self.name) \(self.year) \(self.numberOfWheels)".hashValue
        }
    }
}

func == (left: Vehicle, right: Vehicle) -> Bool
{
    return left.hashValue == right.hashValue
}

var v = Vehicle(name: "Sedan", year: 2008, numberOfWheels: 4)
v.hashValue
```

3-14. Iterating Through Items in a Dictionary

Problem

You need to iterate through the values in a `Dictionary`.

Solution

The `Dictionary` class provides two properties: keys and values. These return a collection of the keys stored in a dictionary and the values stored in the dictionary.

How It Works

When you have a dictionary, it is possible to get a list of all keys and values:

```
var d = [1:"One",2:"Two",3:"Three"]
```

In the preceding example, the variable d is initialized to a `Dictionary<Int,String>` with three initial values. The properties `d.keys` and `d.values` return a collection of items. The type of the keys or values collection is not an Array but a lower level collection. Therefore, if you need to access methods and properties related to an array, you must convert it to the type `Array`.

```
var keyArray = Array(d.keys)
```

The most efficient way to access the items in the keys or values collection is to use a for-in loop:

```
for k in d.keys
{
    println("The value for key \(k) is \(d[k]!)")
}
```

The dictionary literal in the preceding code defines a dictionary as a comma-separated list of key/value pairs separated by a colon.

> **Note**   The order in which items are returned from the dictionary is not guaranteed. If you require an ordered list, use an Array.

To retrieve the values in the dictionary, you can use the key to retrieve the value:

```
var value = d[k]!
```

If you need only the collection of values and do not require the keys, you can loop through the collection:

```
for v in d.values
{
    println(v)
}
```

The variable v will be populated with the values contained in the array. If you need to get the number of items in the dictionary, use the count property:

```
d.count
```

The Code and Usage

Create a new playground, and copy Listing 3-14. This code creates an array and then illustrates how to loop through the collection of keys and values. It will loop through the keys and print out the value for each key. Then it will loop through the values and print the values.

Listing 3-14. Iterate through items in a dictionary

```
var d = [1:"One",2:"Two",3:"Three"]

var keyArray = Array(d.keys)

println("Loop and print keys")
for k in d.keys {
    println("The value for key \(k) is \(d[k]!)")
    var value = d[k]!
}

println("Loop and print values")
for v in d.values {
    println("The value is \(v)")
}
```

Click on the value history icons for both `println` statements. You should see the following in the "Console Output":

```
Loop and print keys
The value for key 2 is Two
The value for key 3 is Three
The value for key 1 is One
Loop and print values
The value is Two
The value is Three
The value is One.
```

3-15. Saving a Dictionary to the File System

Problem

You need to persist the contents of a dictionary to the file system for access at a later time.

Solution

Save a Swift dictionary to disk using the NSDictionary class from the Foundation library.

How It Works

The Swift Dictionary type does not have the ability to save its contents to a file. However, it is easy to convert a Swift dictionary to an NSDictionary. Assign the dictionary to a variable that is defined as an NSDictionary:

```
var nsarray : NSArray = ingredients
```

The NSDictionary type has a method writeToFile that will allow you to save your data to disk.

The writeToFile function takes a string with the path to the file to be written. Create the file path by following the approach for reading and writing text files for your platform: OS X or iOS. See Chapter 7, Recipe 7-7 and 7-8. In this recipe, you will be using an OS X command-line application.

```
let fullPath = "/tmp/ingredients-dictionary.plist"
```

The NSDictionary method writeToFile creates a plist file. The first parameter is a string containing the full path to the file to be written.

> **Note** If a file exists at the path passed to writeToFile, that file will be overwritten. You will need to check to see if the file exists if you want to handle this situation. Recipes for the file system are available in Chapter 7.

The second parameter of writeToFile is a Boolean. If set to true, the contents of your file are written to a temporary file until the process is complete. When it has finished writing, it is renamed and will replace the existing file (if there is one). This prevents a partial file from being written or corrupting an existing file, if the application crashes and fails to complete writing.

```
nsarray.writeToFile(fullPath, atomically: true)
```

The method writeToFile returns true or false to indicate whether the file has been successfully written.

> **Note**   If an NSDictionary contains objects other than valid property-list objects (instances of NSData, NSDate, NSNumber, NSString, NSArray, or NSDictionary), it will return `false` and fail to write the file to disk. Saving custom classes is covered in Chapter 7.

The Code and Usage

Listing 3-15 contains a command-line application that will save a dictionary to the file path /tmp/numbers-strings.plist. In Xcode, create a new project and select OS X Application. Then select "Command Line Tool." Name your project **DictionaryToFile**, and select "Swift" as the Language. Add the contents of Listing 3-15 to the main.swift file. Run the program and view the output console in Xcode. If the file was written successfully, you should see the following text:

```
Successfully wrote to file
```

Listing 3-15. Saving a Dictionary to the file system

```
import Foundation

var dictionary = [ "1":"One", "2":"Two", "3":"Three"]

var nsDictionary : NSDictionary = dictionary

let fullPath = "/tmp/numbers-strings.plist"

if !nsDictionary.writeToFile(fullPath, atomically: true)
{
    println("Error writing dictionary file \(fullPath)")
}
else
{
    println("Successfully wrote to file")
}
```

To view the plist file, open a Terminal window, and then type **cat /tmp/numbers-strings. plist**. This will display the contents of the file in the Terminal window. The contents should look like Listing 3-16.

Listing 3-16. Contents of numbers-strings.plist

```
<?xml version="1.0" encoding="UTF-8"?>
<!DOCTYPE plist PUBLIC "-//Apple//DTD PLIST 1.0//EN" "http://www.apple.com/DTDs/
PropertyList-1.0.dtd">
<plist version="1.0">
<dict>
    <key>1</key>
    <string>One</string>
    <key>2</key>
```

```
    <string>Two</string>
    <key>3</key>
    <string>Three</string>
</dict>
</plist>
```

3-16. Populating a Dictionary with the Contents of a Property List File

Problem

Your application needs to load and access values from a property-list file into a `Dictionary`.

Solution

Use the `NSDictionary` class to load the contents of a `plist` file and then cast it to a dictionary.

How It Works

This recipe builds on Recipe 3-15. This recipe creates a file that you can read in this recipe. Complete Recipe 3-15 before proceeding.

`NSDictionary`'s method `initWithContentsOfFile` will instantiate a new dictionary and load the contents of a property-list file. First, you need to have a full path to the plist you wish to read. For recipes related to getting the proper paths to files based on platform, see Chapter 7, Recipes 7-7 and 7-8.

```
let fullPath = "/tmp/numbers-strings.plist"
```

The dictionary is created using the `NSDictionary` initializer. `NSDictionary` does not know the types of the keys and values it is loading. In order to get a Swift `Dictionary`, the `NSDictionary` can be typecast using the as keyword:

```
var dictionary =
    NSDictionary(contentsOfFile: fullPath) as Dictionary<String,String>?
```

An optional `Dictionary<String,String>` is returned. If dictionary is `nil`, the file could not be loaded. Even if the `plist` file can be loaded, the cast might still fail if your types do not match. If the types stored in the `plist` do not match, the invalid cast will throw an exception.

The Code and Usage

Before continuing, complete Recipe 3-15 and run that application. It will create a file >/tmp/numbers-strings.plist. Listing 3-17 is a command-line application that will load the contents of a property-list file.

Create a new OS X Command Line Application, selecting Swift as the language, and copy the contents of Listing 3-17 to main.swift. Run the application.

Listing 3-17. Main.swift

```swift
import Foundation

let fullPath = "/tmp/numbers-strings.plist"

var dictionary = NSDictionary(contentsOfFile: fullPath) as Dictionary<String,String>?

if let numbersDictionary = dictionary
{
    for k in numbersDictionary.keys
    {
        println("The value for key \(k) is \(numbersDictionary[k]!).")
    }
}
else
{
    println("Could not load dictionary from plist: \(fullPath)")
}
```

It will load the file that the application in Recipe 3-15 created and print the information to the console. It should look like this:

```
The value for key 2 is Two.
The value for key 1 is One.
The value for key 3 is Three.
Program ended with exit code: 0
```

Chapter 4

Advanced Swift Programming

This chapter will cover more advanced recipes that you can use when creating applications using Swift. Recipes in this chapter will cover the following topics:

- Writing Closures
- Writing Trailing Closures
- Overloading the Equality Operator
- Checking for Reference Equality
- Implementing Generic Functions
- Implementing Generic Classes
- Working with Local Dates and Times
- Creating a Unit Test Project
- Writing a Unit Test
- Performance Testing with XCTest
- Creating Mock Objects for Testing
- Testing Asynchronous Code

4-1. Writing Closures

Problem

Your application needs to pass a function as a parameter to another function. For example, a method requires a callback function that is executed upon completion.

Solution

In Swift, you can define a closure and supply it as the parameter for one-time use code. This can make the code more readable by keeping function calls and callback methods in proximity to each other.

How It Works

Closures are self-contained functions that capture the variables of the surrounding scope. Closures are defined using the following syntax:

```
{ (optional parameter list) -> optional return type in
    statements
}
```

Define the parameter list following the same rules as a traditional function. Providing the return type is optional. Following the parameter list and return type, indicate the start of the closure's code using the in keyword. A closure can even be assigned to a variable because functions are a first-class type in Swift. An example of a function that returns an Int follows. It takes no parameters:

```
var foo = { ()-> Int in
    var a = 1

    var b = 3

    return a + b
}
```

If you are writing a function and want the consumer to provide a closure, declare the closure as a parameter of the function being called:

```
doSomething("ABCDE", { () in println("Finished") })
```

The Code and Usage

Put Listing 4-1 into a new Playground. The doSomething method takes a String parameter and a closure. When you add the code to a Playground, click the Values History button on line 17, which reads println("I did it!"). You will see the text "I did it" followed by the text "Finished" in the console output.

Listing 4-1. Writing closures

```
// Closure with no parameters
var foo = { ()-> Int in
    var a = 1

    var b = 3

    return a + b
}
```

```
// Closure with parameters
var add = { (a: Int,b: Int) -> Int in return a + b }

add(2,2)

// The second parameter is a closure without a return value
func doSomething( str: String, finished: ()->Void) {
    println("I did it!")

    finished()
}

doSomething("ABCDE", { () in println("Finished") })
```

4-2. Writing Trailing Closures
Problem

You want your closure code to be readable. Writing larger closures with multiple lines of code can begin to get confusing if they are contained within a function call's parameter list.

Solution

Use *trailing closures* to place your code after the parameter list.

How It Works

A trailing closure is a great code-organization tool; however, it can be used only in certain circumstances. If a method call's final parameter type is a function, you can use a trailing closure. To create a trailing closure, complete all the parameters except the final one and close the parenthesis. Take the following method call for instance:

```
doSomething("ABCDE", { () in println("Finished") })
```

It takes two parameters: a string and a function. This works when the closure provided is a single line of code, but it can get confusing if there are multiple lines of code in the closure:

```
doSomething("ABCDE", { () in
    println("Finished")
    for i in 1...10
    {
        println(i)
    }
})
```

Instead, complete the function call:

```
doSomething("ABCDE")
```

Then define the closure immediately after the call:

```
// Trailing Closure
doSomething("ABCDE")
{
    () in
    println("Finished")
    for i in 1...10
    {
        println(i)
    }
}
```

The Code and Usage

Create a new Playground, and enter Listing 4-2. Closures are frequently used for asynchronous callbacks and event handlers. Trailing closures allow you to better format and organize your code by removing it from the tangle of the parameter list. The code in Listing 4-2 defines a function.

Listing 4-2. Trailing closure examples

```
// The second parameter is a closure without a return value
func doSomething( str: String, finished: ()->Void) {
    println("I did it!")

    finished()
}
// Trailing Closure
doSomething("ABCDE") { () in

    println("Finished")
    for i in 1...10 {
        println(i)
    }
}
```

4-3. Overloading the Equality Operator

Problem

You created a custom class and frequently need to test two instances for equality.

Solution

Overload the "==" operator to create a custom method that will compare two instances of your custom type.

How It Works

Usually operator overloads are defined in the body of a class. The equality operator is an exception. It is defined as a global function. The global function definition is specific to your class, so you might want to keep the definition in the same file as the class.

To override the operator, define a method using the operator as the name:

```
func == (left: Contact, right: Contact) -> Bool
```

The first parameter passed to the function is the object on the left side of the operator, and the second is the object on the right side of the operator. The equality operator returns a Boolean. Write the logic of function to check for the equality of all necessary properties:

```
return left.name == right.name
    && left.phoneNumber == right.phoneNumber
    && left.email == right.email
```

In this example, there are three properties, and each is a string. Return the results of a Boolean expression that tests the value of each property.

The Code and Usage

Enter Listing 4-3 into a new Playground file. This listing creates a Contact class, which is the class that will be tested for equality. It creates a few sample Contact instances. Then it defines the global function that overrides the == operator. In the example comparisons, c1 and c3 are different instances of the Contact class. The expression c1==c3 is true since the values of the properties match.

Listing 4-3. Overloading the equality operator

```
class Contact
{
    var name : String
    var phoneNumber : String
    var email : String

    init( name: String, phoneNumber: String, email: String)
    {
        self.name = name
        self.phoneNumber = phoneNumber
        self.email = email
    }
}

var c1 = Contact(name: "Ben Franklin", phoneNumber: "555-1212",
    email: "benfranklin@continentalcongress.gov")
```

```
var c2 = Contact(name: "John Adams", phoneNumber: "555-2498",
    email: "jadams@xpresidents.com")

var c3 = Contact(name: "Ben Franklin", phoneNumber: "555-1212",
    email: "benfranklin@continentalcongress.gov")

func == (left: Contact, right: Contact) -> Bool
{
    return left.name == right.name
    && left.phoneNumber == right.phoneNumber
    && left.email == right.email
}

c1 == c2

c1 == c3
```

4-4. Checking for Reference Equality

Problem

You need to determine if two variables reference the same object in memory.

Solution

Use the triple equals operator (===) to test for reference equality.

How It Works

If you have two references and you attempt to test for equality with the double equals operator (==), you will receive an error. This is because the compiler searches for an overload of the (==) operator for the custom type you are comparing. In order to test object references, use the === operator:

```
left === right
```

The Code and Usage

Create an empty Playground, and add the contents of Listing 4-4. The code creates three sample instances of the Contact class. Note the results of the comparisons in the results sidebar. Note that the result of c1 === c2 is false. The result of c1 === c3 is true because it references the same object.

Listing 4-4. Checking for reference equality

```
class Contact
{
    var name : String
    var phoneNumber : String
    var email : String

    init( name: String, phoneNumber: String, email: String)
    {
        self.name = name
        self.phoneNumber = phoneNumber
        self.email = email
    }
}

var c1 = Contact(name: "Ben Franklin", phoneNumber: "555-1212",
    email: "benfranklin@ continentalcongress.gov")

var c2 = Contact(name: "Ben Franklin", phoneNumber: "555-1212",
    email: "benfranklin@continentalcongress.gov")

var c3 = c1

c1 === c2
c1 === c3
```

4-5. Implementing Generic Functions

Problem

You want to refactor a function that performs a common function, does not need to know the type of object being processed, and maintains type checking at compile time.

Solution

In Swift, you can optimize your code for re-use by creating generic functions.

How It Works

Generic functions allow you to reuse code that could apply to many different types of input. Generic functions allow you to create a placeholder for a type in a function's definition. Frequently, this is illustrated by the capital letter "T." However, you can name the placeholder however you prefer. In the following function, areEqual, the function takes two parameters of the same type as indicated by the use of the placeholder T. The method returns true or false based on their equality:

```
func areEqual<T : Equatable> (a : T, b : T) -> Bool
```

The first step in defining a genericized function is to use angle brackets "<>" and define your placeholder. In the example, the placeholder is T: Equatable. The placeholder is "T" and then following the placeholder is an optional list of types or protocols. If the optional types are provided, only types that conform to or inherit from the list of types can be used. In this example, the type must conform to the Equatable protocol.

Since the parameters are a type that conforms to the Equatable protocol, use the == operator to make the comparison and return the result:

```
return a == b
```

To call the function, pass two parameters of the same type to the function and the Swift compiler will infer the type for you.

The Code and Usage

Create a blank Playground, and enter Listing 4-5. The listing contains a definition for a generic function that tests for equality. In this case, the function will work with any type that implements the Equatable protocol. In order for your code to compile, any operations you apply to the generic parameters must conform to a protocol, inherit from a superclass, or use operations that can be applied to any type that can potentially be passed to the generic function.

The two example function calls will return false and true, respectively.

Listing 4-5. Implementing generic functions

```
func areEqual<T : Equatable> (a : T, b : T) -> Bool
{
    return a == b
}

areEqual(22, 99)
areEqual("Apple", "Apple")
```

4-6. Implementing Generic Classes

Problem

You have code that is used in multiple places in your application, but you might not be able to refactor it into a superclass or a class extension. You still want to create a reusable class that can be used with multiple types.

Solution

Create a generic class to encapsulate the functionality that is type agnostic. This will allow for code reuse and maintain type safety.

How It Works

Generic classes allow developers to create class "templates" that are applied at compile time. You may have common functions that can be used with any number of types in your code. The most common examples of generic classes are arrays and dictionaries. Since collection classes can hold any number of items and need to be flexible, they use generic classes to provide that functionality, but they maintain strict typing.

When defining a generic class, supply a list of type placeholders within angle brackets "<>" after the definition of the class name.

This list of placeholders will be used throughout the class to represent the types that are provided when a concrete instance of the class is created. In the following example, the class LIFOStack requires one placeholder. This placeholder is the type of object that can be stored within your stack. LIFOStack implements a Last In, First Out stack:

```
class LIFOStack<T>
```

A generic class is implemented the same as any other class. However, when defining variables and parameters, use the placeholder to indicate the generic type. At compile time, the compiler will merge the generic class and your type to create a concrete type. For example, the following line initializes an internal variable to be used for storage:

```
items = [T]()
```

This works because the Array class is a generic class. The placeholder T holds the place of the generic type. When the code is compiled, the T is replaced with the type you specify.

Next, create two functions push and pop, to add and remove items on the stack. Both have a parameter of type T. T is the type placeholder declared in the class definition. In the push definition, T is used to denote the type of the parameter. In the pop definition, the placeholder is used to indicate the return type:

```
func push(item : T)
func pop() -> T?
```

The Code and Usage

Create a new Playground, and add Listing 4-6. Listing 4-6 implements a generic class for managing LIFOStack. The code creates a stack with the type String. As strings are pushed onto the stack, you can see the strings are added to the items array. As the strings are popped from the stack, they are printed to the console. If you attempt to pop more items that have been pushed onto the stack, pop will return nil.

Listing 4-6. Implementing a generic class

```
class LIFOStack<T>
{
    var items : [T]

    init()
    {
        items = [T]()
    }

    func push(item : T)
    {
        items.insert(item, atIndex: 0)
    }

    func pop() -> T?
    {
        if items.count == 0
        {
            return nil
        }
        var item = items[0]
        items.removeAtIndex(0)
        return item
    }
}

var lifo = LIFOStack<String>()

lifo.push("Apple")
lifo.push("Pear")
lifo.push("Peach")

println(lifo.pop())
println(lifo.pop())
println(lifo.pop())
println(lifo.pop())
```

The results sidebar should look something like this:

```
{["Apple"]}
{["Pear","Apple"]}
{["Peach","Pear","Apple"]}

Optional("Peach")
Optional("Pear")
Optional("Apple")
nil
```

4-7. Working with Local Dates and Times

Problem

You need to handle the display and input of dates to cover all possible geographies around the world.

Solution

Use the NSDate localization functions in Swift to properly localize date usage in your applications.

How It Works

As of the publishing of this book, Swift does not have native classes for dates and date localization. You can use the Foundation class NSDate to perform date functions and NSDateFormatting to manipulate dates.

The best way to store dates and transmit them between devices is by using UTC (Coordinated Universal Time). UTC is not a time zone, and no country officially uses UTC as a local time. UTC is a standard that supports time and time zones around the world. GMT (Greenwich Mean Time) is a time zone and is used by some European and African countries. The value of UTC and GMT is always the same. These facts are important because NSDate will never return a date value in UTC time. It will always return it as GMT.

Fortunately, NSDate stores the date and time as UTC. However, when you inspect the variable in Xcode or display it in any way (such as printing it to the console or debugger), the string representation is not displayed in UTC time. NSDate displays the date in the current local time zone of the device.

Use NSDateFormatter to display the date, and you need to specify a time zone other than the default of the local device. NSDateFormatter requires three pieces of information: the date format, time format, and time zone. Dates and times are formatted using the NSDateFormatterStyle enumeration. See Table 4-1 for the enumeration options and example strings for both the date and time formats.

Table 4-1. NSDateFormatterStyle Definitions

Enum Value	Date Example (en_US)	Time Example (en_US)
FullStyle	Wednesday, November 26, 2014	5:54:49 PM GMT
LongStyle	November 26, 2014	5:58:41 PM GMT
MediumStyle	Nov 26, 2014	5:59:06 PM
ShortStyle	11/26/14	5:59 PM
NoStyle	[Blank]	[Blank]

The examples in the table are shown as en_US format dates and times. What NSDate is running on a device in a different region or the time zone is set to a different region. Set the date style using the dateStyle property of NSDateFormatter:

```
formatter.dateStyle = NSDateFormatterStyle.FullStyle
```

The format used to display the time is set using the timeStyle property of NSDateFormatter:

```
formatter.timeStyle = NSDateFormatterStyle.FullStyle
```

If you want to hide the date or the time from the string output, use NoStyle for the date style or the time style.

To specify the time zone to be used, set the timeZone property of NSDateFormatter with an instance of NSTimeZone. To create an NSTimeZone, use the time zone ID for the time zone. A complete list of time zone IDs can be found using the method NSTimeZone. knownTimeZoneNames. For example, this is how you set the time zone to New York:

```
formatter.timeZone = NSTimeZone(name:"America/New_York")
```

If you do not set the time zone explicitly, the application uses the current time zone of the device. For special time zones like UTC and GMT, use NSTimeZone(abbreviation:"UTC") or NSTimeZone(abbreviation:"GMT"). Apple does not recommend using abbreviations to initialize NSTimeZone because the abbreviations are not standardized or unique.

The Code and Usage

Listing 4-7 contains example statements that cover the date and time localization approaches discussed previously. Comments in the code indicate the usage of the statements.

Listing 4-7. Working with local dates and times

```
import Foundation

// Create date with current date and time
var d = NSDate()

// Create NSDateFormatter instance used to set
// the style of date and time and provides methods to format NSDate objects
var formatter = NSDateFormatter()
formatter.dateStyle = NSDateFormatterStyle.LongStyle
formatter.timeStyle = NSDateFormatterStyle.LongStyle

// No timezone specified
formatter.stringFromDate(d)

// New York time zone
formatter.timeZone = NSTimeZone(name:"America/New_York")
formatter.stringFromDate(d)

// Los Angeles time zone
formatter.timeZone = NSTimeZone(name:"America/Los_Angeles")
formatter.stringFromDate(d)

// UTC, NOTE: UTC is not a time zone, but value is the same as GMT
formatter.timeZone = NSTimeZone(abbreviation:"UTC")
formatter.stringFromDate(d)

// GMT time
formatter.timeZone = NSTimeZone(abbreviation:"GMT")
formatter.stringFromDate(d)

// Get a list of time zone abbreviations and full strings
var timeZoneStrings = NSTimeZone.abbreviationDictionary()
var locales = NSLocale.availableLocaleIdentifiers()

// Format for Istanbul Time
formatter.timeZone = NSTimeZone(name:"Europe/Istanbul")
// Set the locale to get the proper format date
formatter.locale = NSLocale(localeIdentifier: "tr_TR")
formatter.stringFromDate(d)
```

4-8. Creating a Unit Test Project

Problem

You need to add a unit-testing project to your application in order to create unit tests.

Solution

Xcode 6 comes with XCTest, a unit-testing framework. It can be used to create unit tests for both iOS and Mac OS applications, and it works with Swift or Objective-C.

How It Works

Test-driven development, *unit testing*, and *test automation* are best practices that many developers are embracing. Unit tests are added to the project as a new target for the build. You create a "Cocoa Touch Testing Bundle" for iOS applications and a "Cocoa Testing Bundle" for Mac OS applications. To add a new target, open the project in Xcode. Next, select File ➤ New ➤ Target. Both the iOS and OS X sections in the list on the left have a choice for "Other." Depending on your application type (iOS or OS X), select "Other" in the list on the left. For iOS applications, you will see a choice for "Cocoa Touch Testing Bundle." For OS X, you will see a choice for "Cocoa Testing Bundle." Select the bundle you want, and click "Next." Fill in the project information, and click "Finish." Don't forget to choose "Swift" as the language.

The Code and Usage

A new target is added to your solution as well as a template Swift file. The project will contain a templated test-case file similar to Listing 4-8.

Open an existing project for an application, or create a new console application. Then follow the previous instructions to add a new target for the test bundle. In order to run the tests, you must make sure the Tests target is selected. As shown in Figure 4-1, select the Tests target and then choose a device where the tests will be run.

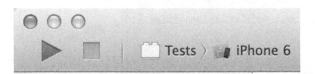

Figure 4-1. Select the Tests target

Run the tests by selecting Product ➤ Test in the menu or pressing Command-U. You will see a success message indicating the tests passed. In the output panel, you will see the status as the test runner executes each test. It will report which tests pass and which fail. After all tests are run, you will see a status update like the following example:

```
Executed 4 tests, with 0 failures (0 unexpected) in 0.722 (0.727) seconds
```

Listing 4-8. XCTestCase Swift template

```swift
import UIKit
import XCTest

class Sample: XCTestCase {

    override func setUp() {
        super.setUp()
        // Put setup code here. This method is called before
        // the invocation of each test method in the class.
    }

    override func tearDown() {
        // Put teardown code here. This method is called after
        // the invocation of each test method in the class.
        super.tearDown()
    }

    func testExample() {
        // This is an example of a functional test case.
        XCTAssert(true, "Pass")
    }

    func testPerformanceExample() {
        // This is an example of a performance test case.
        self.measureBlock() {
            // Put the code you want to measure the time of here.
        }
    }
}
```

4-9. Writing a Unit Test

Problem

You need to add a unit test that validates the execution of a component's code.

Solution

Unit tests are written in a class that extends the XCTestCase class. Xcode will run these tests using the XCTest framework.

How It Works

Unit tests are written by first extending the XCTestCase class. This class provides the basic tools and resources required for automated unit testing. One of the first rules of unit testing is, "Keep your tests mutually exclusive." Tests should not depend upon data created by another, nor should they require tests to be run in a certain order. XCTestCase has two methods to aid developers in following this rule: setupUp and tearDown.

You override setupUp to create objects that need to be initialized, create data, and set up preconditions. This method is called before each and every test case is run. The method tearDown is used to remove and reset any data or preconditions that tests might have created. You do not want data or state information to remain between test runs. For example, if your class under test is a sorting algorithm, the setUp method would contain code to create the data to be sorted. The tearDown method would remove all the data.

The setUp and tearDown methods should be used to create and reset data and state that apply to all tests because they run before every test. For individual tests or small subsets of tests that share common needs, create other helper functions to create data. XCTest can identify methods that are test methods and will ignore any other methods you create.

For this recipe, follow the three As of unit testing (Arrange, Act, Assert). First, arrange the preconditions for the test, then perform the action you are testing, and then assert that the results are correct to verify the post-conditions. Here is an example of a test for a method that will add two numbers and store the results in a property:

```
func testAdd() {
// Arrange
        var calc = Calculator()
        // Act
        calc.add(4, b: 2)
        // Assert
        XCTAssertEqual(6, calc.sum, "Sum does return a + b")
    }
```

In the preceding example, the preconditions are set up by creating an instance of Calculator. Next, it calls the method add, which is the method under test. Finally, you assert that the instance's property sum has the correct sum for the two parameters passed to the add method.

XCTAssertEqual is an assertion function provided by XCTest. The first parameter is the expected value. The second is the actual value. In this test, if the "sum" property does not contain the correct sum of 6, the assertion will fail and the test runner will display a failure. If the sum does match the expected outcome, the assertion passes and the test runner will indicate the test passed.

Many assertions are available in XCTest. Table 4-2 contains some of the most common assertions to be used in your tests.

Table 4-2. XCTest Assertions

Assertion	Description
XCTAssertEqualObjects	Assertion passes when the two objects are the same object.
XCTAssertNotEqualObjects	Assertion passes when the two objects are not the same object.
XCTAssertEqual	Assertion passes when the value of the parameters passed are equal.
XCTAssertNotEqual	Assertion passes when the value of the parameters passed are not equal.
XCTAssertGreaterThan	Assertion passes when the first parameter is greater than the second.
XCTAssertGreaterThanOrEqual	Assertion passes when the first parameter is greater than or equal to the second.
XCTAssertLessThan	Assertion passes when the first parameter is less than the second.
XCTAssertLessThanOrEqual	Assertion passes when the first parameter is less than or equal to the second.
XCTAssertNil	Assertion passes when the parameter passed is equal to nil.
XCTAssertNotNil	Assertion passes when the parameter is not equal to nil.
XCTAssertTrue	Assertion passes when the parameter is equal to true.
XCTAssertThrows	Assertion passes when the expression passed throws an exception.
XCTAssertThrowsSpecific	Assertion passes when the expression passed throws a specific expression passed as the second parameter.
XCTAssertNoThrow	Assertion passes when the expression passed does not throw an exception.

The Code and Usage

Create a new Command Line Tool project called "UnitTesting." Add a new target for "Cocoa Testing Bundle" or "Cocoa Touch Testing Bundle." See Recipe 4-8 for help adding the new target. Name the target "Tests." Add two new Swift files to the project: `Calculator.swift` and `CalculatorTests.swift`. Add the contents of Listing 4-9 to the file `Calculator.swift`, and add Listing 4-10 to the file `CalculatorTests.swift`.

Listing 4-9. Calculator.swift listing

```swift
class Calculator {
    var sum : Int = 0

    func add( a : Int, b : Int) {
        sum = a + b
    }
}
```

Listing 4-10. CalculatorTests.swift

```swift
import XCTest
class CalculatorTests : XCTestCase {
    func testAdd() {
        // Arrange
        var calc = Calculator()
        // Act
        calc.add(4, b: 2)
        // Assert
        XCTAssertEqual(6, calc.sum, "Sum does return a + b")
    }
}
```

The testing bundle is a separate target from the main application. In order to test a class, you must add it to the testing target so that it will be compiled along with the test. To add a Swift file to an additional target, select the file in the Project Navigator on the left. Refer to Figure 4-2. In the File Inspector on the right, you will see a section labeled "Target Membership." Check the box next to the Tests target located in the "Target Membership" section of the far right column.

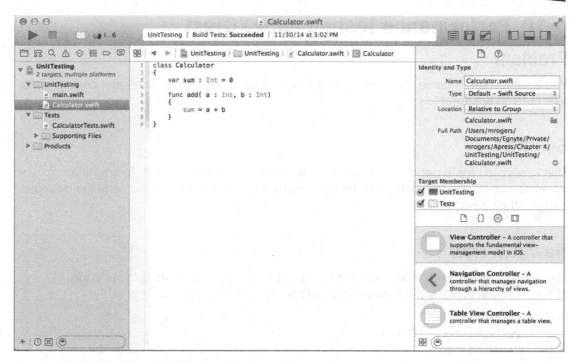

Figure 4-2. Select Target Membership

Now compile and run the tests by pressing the key combination Command-U. First, make sure your project builds. Next, in the Xcode toolbar, you will need to make sure that your unit test target is selected. It should be already, but it may not always be the active target. Choose "Tests" from the "Product Menu." See Figure 4-3.

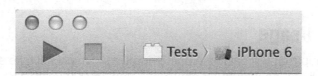

Figure 4-3. Select the unit test target

After running the tests, you should see similar output to the following in the Xcode console:

```
Test Suite 'All tests' started at 2014-11-30 19:26:11 +0000
Test Suite 'Tests.xctest' started at 2014-11-30 19:26:11 +0000
Test Suite 'CalculatorTests' started at 2014-11-30 19:26:11 +0000
Test Case '-[Tests.CalculatorTests testAdd]' started.
Test Case '-[Tests.CalculatorTests testAdd]' passed (0.001 seconds).
Test Suite 'CalculatorTests' passed at 2014-11-30 19:26:11 +0000.
     Executed 1 test, with 0 failures (0 unexpected) in 0.001 (0.001) seconds
Test Suite 'Tests.xctest' passed at 2014-11-30 19:26:11 +0000.
     Executed 1 test, with 0 failures (0 unexpected) in 0.001 (0.002) seconds
Test Suite 'All tests' passed at 2014-11-30 19:26:11 +0000.
     Executed 1 test, with 0 failures (0 unexpected) in 0.001 (0.003) seconds
```

4-10. Performance Testing with XCTest

Problem

You want to performance test critical code in your application and be notified if performance falls outside acceptable ranges.

Solution

Use XCTest to create performance testings. XCTest provides functionality to create a baseline of performance data, and then generates a failure if a test run exceeds the baseline performance parameters.

How It Works

Measuring performance in XCTest uses closures to test particular parts of your code. XCTest.measureBlock is the method you call and then provide a closure:

```
self.measureBlock() {
        performance.countPrimes()
}
```

Any code within that closure will be profiled. XCTest runs the code 10 times to establish a baseline. The first time you run your performance test, it will fail because it has not yet established a baseline. On subsequent runs, the code will be run 10 times again and compared to the baseline. If there is a large divergence, the test fails. Baseline information is stored on per device/simulator basis. If you switch machines or devices, XCTest will establish a new baseline the next time you run the tests.

The Code and Usage

Listing 4-11 has a loop that will calculate prime numbers, which will take some processing time. The method will test each number between 1 and 15,000 using a loop. It is not a practical solution, but it is used to illustrate how you can run performance tests.

To use the code, see Recipes 4-8 and 4-9 to create a new project with unit tests. Create a new class that will hold your performance tests. Add a new Swift file Performance.swift. Press Command-N. The new file dialog will appear. Choose Source under iOS, and then select the Swift file template. Save the file as Performance.swift. Copy the contents of Listing 4-11 into the new Performance.swift. Create a second Swift file, Tests.swift, which will contain the unit tests. Add the contents of Listing 4-12, to the Tests.swift file. Press Command-R to run the tests.

Listing 4-11. Performance.swift

```swift
class Performance
{
    func countPrimes()
    {
        for num in 1...15000 {
            var i = 2
            while i <= num {
                if num % i == 0 {
                    break
                }
                i++
            }
        }
    }
}
```

Listing 4-12. Tests.swift

```swift
import XCTest

class Tests : XCTestCase {

    func testPerformanceExample() {
        var performance = Performance()

        self.measureBlock() {
            performance.countPrimes()
        }
    }
}
```

In the output section of Xcode, you will see the output from the tests. Remember, the first time you run the tests they will fail. Run it again and the tests will pass.

4-11. Creating Mock Objects for Testing

Problem

You are writing unit tests for a class, and the functionality of the class under test depends on values from another class. You need to return a known value from this class to validate your class.

Solution

Define a local class, and override the methods you need to return a consistent result. This local class will be used only for testing.

How It Works

Swift is a statically typed language, and this creates some difficulties when implementing the traditional "mock object" pattern in unit testing. In order to mock something like a database connection, inherit the class and override the function you need to modify. In Swift, you can declare a class within a class. This subclass will be available only within that test class, isolating it to prevent accidental usage in production code. In this example, the Mock DB class extends Database as a Mock to simulate a database connection:

```
class MockTesting: XCTestCase {
    class MockDb : Database {
        override func getRecords() -> [Record] {
```

The class Database has a method getRecords that returns all the records in the database. Normally, this function would query the database and return an array of Record instances. Instead, it is overriden and returns an array of known data. This removes the dependency of a database.

The Code and Usage

Create a new Command Line Application in Xcode, and add a Unit Testing target. See Recipes 4-8 and 4-9 for details. In this new project, create a file name MockTesting.swift. Press Command-N, select Source under iOS, and choose the Swift file. Save the file and then copy the contents of Listing 4-13 into it. Then create a file named Database.swift using the contents of Listing 4-14. Finally, create a TestMe.swift file with the contents of Listing 4-15.

Select each file, and use the identity inspector for each file to make sure the testing target is selected in the "Target Membership" section. Run the tests by pressing Command-U, or select Product ➤ Test from the menu

Listing 4-13. MockTesting.swift, the MockTesting class

```
import Cocoa
import XCTest

class MockTesting: XCTestCase {
    class MockDb : Database {
        override func getRecords() -> [Record] {
            var records = [Record]()
            records.append( Record(id: 2,data: "Test2"))
            records.append( Record(id: 3,data: "Test3"))
            records.append( Record(id: 1,data: "Test1"))
```

```
        return records
    }
}

func testExample() {
    // Arrange
    var mockDb = MockDb()
    var testTarget = TestMe(db : mockDb)

    // Act
    var results = testTarget.getSortedRecords()

    // Assert
    XCTAssertEqual(3, results.count)

    // Check that items are in ascending order
    XCTAssertEqual(1, results[0].id)
    XCTAssertEqual(2, results[1].id)
    XCTAssertEqual(3, results[2].id)
    }
}
```

Listing 4-14. Database.Swift with the Database and Record classes

```
class Record {
    let id : Int
    var data : String

    init(id : Int, data : String)
    {
        self.id = id
        self.data = data
    }
}

class Database {

    func getRecords() -> [Record] {
        // Pretend this connects to a database and returns records
        return [Record]()
    }
}
```

Listing 4-15. TestMe.swift, the class to be tested

```swift
// This is the class to be tested
public class TestMe {
    let db : Database

    init( db : Database) {
        self.db = db
    }

    func getSortedRecords() -> [Record] {
        var results = db.getRecords()

        results.sort({ r1, r2 in r1.data < r2.data })

        return results
    }

}
```

The tests should succeed. In the output console, you should see output similar to the following:

```
Test Suite 'All tests' started at 2014-12-15 18:35:11 +0000
Test Suite 'MockTesting.xctest' started at 2014-12-15 18:35:11 +0000
Test Suite 'MockTesting' started at 2014-12-15 18:35:11 +0000
Test Case '-[MockTesting.MockTesting testExample]' started.
Test Case '-[MockTesting.MockTesting testExample]' passed (0.011 seconds).
Test Suite 'MockTesting' passed at 2014-12-15 18:35:11 +0000.
    Executed 1 test, with 0 failures (0 unexpected) in 0.011 (0.012) seconds
Test Suite 'MockTesting.xctest' passed at 2014-12-15 18:35:11 +0000.
    Executed 1 test, with 0 failures (0 unexpected) in 0.011 (0.012) seconds
Test Suite 'All tests' passed at 2014-12-15 18:35:11 +0000.
    Executed 1 test, with 0 failures (0 unexpected) in 0.011 (0.013) seconds
```

4-12. Testing Asynchronous Code

Problem

You need to test code that executes asynchronously.

Solution

Use the class XCTestExpectation from XCTest framework. This is used to test asynchronous code by allowing the test execution to pause and wait for the asynchronous code to run.

How It Works

Swift makes use of functions for asynchronous calls. Asynchronous system functions rely on a callback function to notify its caller of completion. You cannot use the traditional means of testing because the callback function might not have executed by the time the test runner reaches your assertions. In order to deal with asynchronous methods, the class XCTestExpectation is used to wait for the desired expectation.

The method XCTestCase.waitForExpectationsWithTimeout will wait for a specified timeout. If the expectations are fulfilled before it times out, the test passes. If the timeout is reached, the test will fail.

An instance of XCTestExpectation is created using the expectationWithDescription method of XCTestCase:

```
let expectation = expectationWithDescription("NSURLSession.dataTaskWithURL")
```

Imagine you wanted to test NSURLSession.dataTaskWithURL. Normally, you wouldn't test a function from an existing framework, but this is an example for the purposes of this recipe. The dataTaskWithURL method takes two parameters: an NSURL and a closure. The task can be used to download a URL from the Internet.

Make a call to expectation.fulfill() inside the callback closure. This will complete the expectation, and it verifies that the asynchronous task has completed. If fulfill is not called within the timeout parameter passed to waitForExpectationsWithTimeout:, the test will fail. Additionally, you will need to add additional assertions to validate the state of the class under test after the asynchronous task has completed. In this example, you could test to see if the parameter data in the callback is not null and that the error parameter is null. This should be the state if a URL was successfully downloaded. In the following code, a call to NSURLSession.dataTaskWithURL will retrieve the data from a URL and then execute the callback. In the callback, expectation.fulfill is called:

```
let dataTask = session.dataTaskWithURL(url!) {
        (data: NSData!, response:NSURLResponse!,
        error: NSError!) -> Void in
            expectation.fulfill()
            XCTAssertNotNil(data, "data should not be null")
            XCTAssertNil(error, "error should be null")
    }
```

Use waitForExpectationsWithTimeout:handler: to wait the number of seconds indicated and, optionally, trigger a callback. The second parameter is an optional callback. A callback is used if the timeout period has expired before the expectation was fulfilled. In this example, nil is passed since the callback is unused. You would use it to perform tasks such as cleaning up objects that have been created or maybe temporary files that have been written to the file system.

```
waitForExpectationsWithTimeout(30, handler: nil)
```

The Code and Usage

Create a new OS X Command Line application named "AsyncTesting." Add a Cocoa Test target. See Recipes 4-8 and 4-9 for help adding the target. Next, add a new Swift file called AsyncTests.swift and add the contents of Listing 4-16 to the new file.

Make sure that your unit test target is selected. It should be already, but it might not always be the active target. Choose "Tests" from the "Product Menu." Run the tests by pressing Command-U, or select Product ➤ Test from the menu.

Note   The NSUrlSession calls will attempt to download the Google home page. You must be connected to the Internet or the test will fail.

Listing 4-16. Testing asynchronous code

```
import Cocoa
import XCTest

class AsyncTests: XCTestCase {

    func testFoo() {

        let expectation =
            expectationWithDescription("NSURLSession.dataTaskWithURL")

        let url = NSURL(string: "http://www.google.com")
        let session = NSURLSession.sharedSession()

        let dataTask = session.dataTaskWithURL(url!) {
            (data: NSData!, response:NSURLResponse!,
            error: NSError!) -> Void in
                expectation.fulfill()
        }
        dataTask.resume()

        waitForExpectationsWithTimeout(100, handler: nil)
    }
}
```

If the test is successful, the output console should contain details similar to the following:

```
Test Suite 'All tests' started at 2014-12-15 22:04:29 +0000
Test Suite 'AsyncTests.xctest' started at 2014-12-15 22:04:29 +0000
Test Suite 'AsyncTests' started at 2014-12-15 22:04:29 +0000
Test Case '-[AsyncTests.AsyncTests testFoo]' started.
Test Case '-[AsyncTests.AsyncTests testFoo]' passed (0.234 seconds).
Test Suite 'AsyncTests' passed at 2014-12-15 22:04:29 +0000.
    Executed 1 test, with 0 failures (0 unexpected) in 0.234 (0.235) seconds
Test Suite 'AsyncTests.xctest' passed at 2014-12-15 22:04:29 +0000.
    Executed 1 test, with 0 failures (0 unexpected) in 0.234 (0.236) seconds
Test Suite 'All tests' passed at 2014-12-15 22:04:29 +0000.
    Executed 1 test, with 0 failures (0 unexpected) in 0.234 (0.237) seconds
```

To see what an expectation failure would look like, remove the line dataTask.resume from the test code, the expectation will fail because the callback will not be executed and, as a result, expectation.fulfill() is not called. In this case, the output will look similar to the following:

```
Test Suite 'All tests' started at 2014-12-15 22:17:00 +0000
Test Suite 'AsyncTests.xctest' started at 2014-12-15 22:17:00 +0000
Test Suite 'AsyncTests' started at 2014-12-15 22:17:00 +0000
Test Case '-[AsyncTests.AsyncTests testFoo]' started.
/Users/mrogers/Documents/Egnyte/Private/mrogers/Apress/Chapter 4/AsyncTesting/AsyncTests/
AsyncTests.swift:28: error: -[AsyncTests.AsyncTests testFoo] : Asynchronous wait failed:
Exceeded timeout of 30 seconds, with unfulfilled expectations:
"NSURLSession.dataTaskWithURL".
Test Case '-[AsyncTests.AsyncTests testFoo]' failed (30.053 seconds).
Test Suite 'AsyncTests' failed at 2014-12-15 22:17:30 +0000.
    Executed 1 test, with 1 failure (0 unexpected) in 30.053 (30.054) seconds
Test Suite 'AsyncTests.xctest' failed at 2014-12-15 22:17:30 +0000.
    Executed 1 test, with 1 failure (0 unexpected) in 30.053 (30.054) seconds
Test Suite 'All tests' failed at 2014-12-15 22:17:30 +0000.
    Executed 1 test, with 1 failure (0 unexpected) in 30.053 (30.056) seconds
```

iOS Applications

This chapter contains recipes for the creation of iOS applications, adding user-interface controls, and working with a `UITableView`. Many of the user-interface topics in this chapter can be accomplished using *storyboards*. The recipes in this chapter focus on using Swift to add, position, and interact with user-interface controls. The full list of topics includes

- Creating a New iOS Application
- Adding a `UILabel` to a View
- Adding a `UIButton` to a View
- Adding a `UITextField` to a View
- Positioning `UIViews` in Auto Layout Using `NSConstraints`
- Repositioning a View to Accommodate the Keyboard
- Displaying an Alert with `UIAlertController`
- Using `UIAlertController` to Collect User Input
- Creating a `UITableView`
- Swiping to Delete an Item from a `UITableView`

5-1. Creating a New iOS Application

Problem

You want to create a new iOS application.

Solution

Xcode offers a number of application templates to get you started. Choose Single View Application to start your application.

How It Works

Launch Xcode and then select File ➤ New ➤ Project from the menu. (See Figure 5-1.)

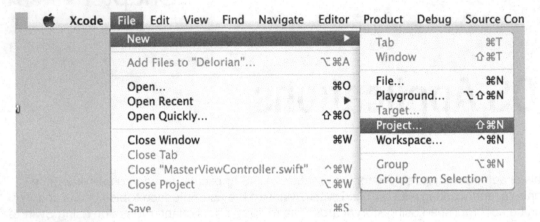

Figure 5-1. Creating a new project

Xcode displays a list of templates. (See Figure 5-2.) Select "Single View Application."
The Single View Application template contains the least amount of bells and whistles.
That makes it a good starting point for small projects. Click the "Next" button.

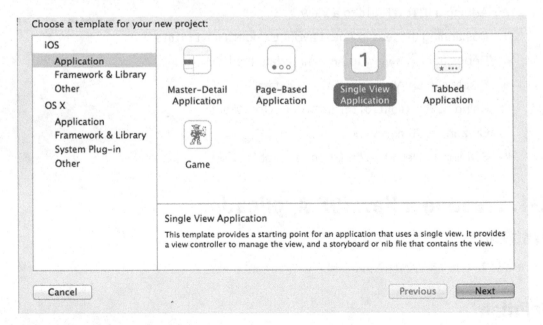

Figure 5-2. Select "Single View Application"

Give the application a name, such as "NewApplication." Select "Swift" as the language and
"Universal" for the "Devices" option. (See Figure 5-3.)

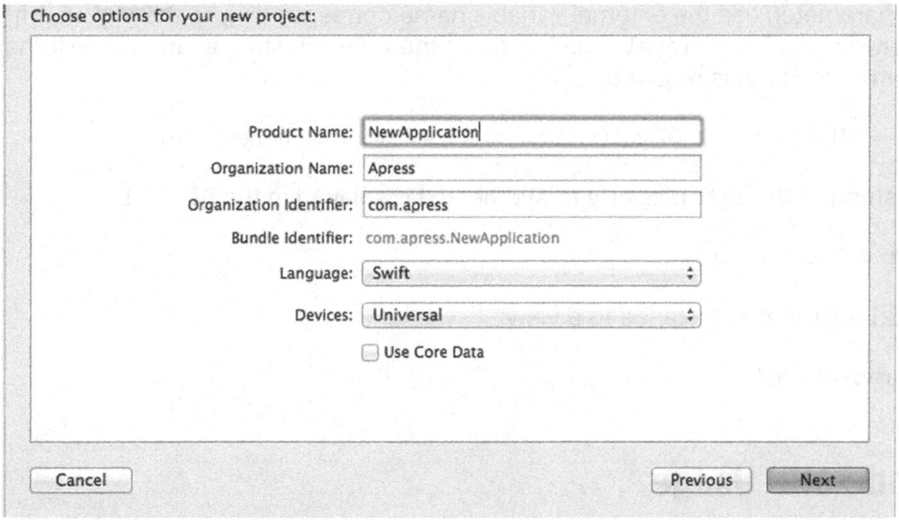

Figure 5-3. Choose options for your new project

Then click "Next." Choose a location for the project on your disk, and click "Create." Your new application has been created and is opened in Xcode.

5-2. Adding a UILabel to a View

Problem

You would like to add static text to a UIView. You would also like to set the font and color of the text.

Solution

Use the UILabel class to display static text.

How It Works

You can see the UILabel in most applications. UILabel is useful for displaying static text that a user cannot interact with. Text can be updated by your application, but the user cannot select the text or edit it in any way. UILabel has a property named text that is used to get and set the text displayed by the label.

To use a label, create an instance of UILabel, set the desired properties, and add it to a view. The UILabel initializer requires a CGRect to define its frame. The frame dictates the label's position and size. Use the text property to get and set the displayed text.

In Swift, the CGRect initializer looks like the following:

```
CGRect(x: 10, y: 50, width: 200, height: 20)
```

For each parameter, use the external variable name corresponding to the x, y, width, and height parameters. The UILabel initializer takes the CGRect instance, and the external parameter name frame is required:

```
var label = UILabel(frame: CGRect(x: 10, y: 50, width: 200, height: 20))
```

Assign a string to the text property to set the text displayed in the UILabel:

```
label.text = "Swift Recipes"
```

Finally, add the UILabel instance to a view:

```
view.addSubview(label)
```

The Code and Usage

Create a new single-view application as described in Recipe 5-1. Open the file ViewController.swift, and add Listing 5-1 to the contents of the viewDidLoad: method. The viewDidLoad: method was added by the project template when the project was created. Run the application.

Listing 5-1. ViewController with a UILabel added

```
import UIKit

class ViewController: UIViewController {

    override func viewDidLoad() {
        super.viewDidLoad()

        var label = UILabel(frame: CGRect(x: 10, y: 50, width: 200, height: 20))
        label.text = "Swift Recipes"
        view.addSubview(label)
    }
}
```

In the simulator, the application will display the label as shown in Figure 5-4.

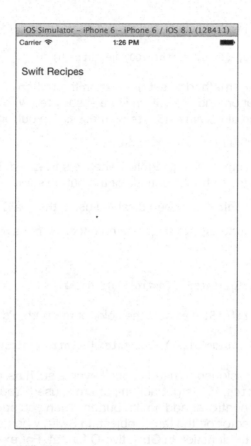

Figure 5-4. UILabel in the running application

5-3. Adding a UIButton to a View

Problem

You want to add a button to your application and handle users' touch events.

Solution

Add a UIButton to the view.

How It Works

Buttons are everywhere in iOS. They are one of the most used elements in applications. Create buttons with a CGRect to determine a button's position and height. UIButton has a class method named buttonWithType that returns a new instance of UIButton. The return value is of type AnyObject. Cast it to UIButton:

```
var button = UIButton.buttonWithType(UIButtonType.System) as? UIButton
```

Set the frame of the button with a `CGRect` to indicate its position and size:

```
button.frame = CGRect(x: 10, y: 50, width: 200, height: 20)
```

Use the `setTitle:forState:` method to set the text on the button. Two parameters are required: the text of the button and the button state associated with the text. The `forState` parameter is a combination of `UIControlState` bit masks. The button states are

- `Normal` – The default state of the button.

- `Highlighted` – A button is highlighted when it is touched. It changes on touch up or the touch tracks outside of the button's frame.

- `Disabled` – The control has been disabled using the `enabled` property.

- `Selected` – For buttons, this state has no effect on behavior.

Call the `setTitle` method:

```
button.setTitle("Tap Me!", forState: UIControlState.Normal)
```

The method `setTitleColor:forState:` sets the color of the button's text:

```
button.setTitleColor(UIColor.blueColor(), forState: UIControlState.Normal)
```

Different methods can be assigned to handle touch events such as `TouchDown` and `TouchUpInside`. With `UIButton`, the target/action pattern is used. You give the control a target delegate, usually the view controller adding the button. Then you specify a Selector so that the button can call the Selector on the target object. In Swift, when a parameter requires a Selector, use the name of the function in Objective-C format. For example, for a function with a single parameter, use the string `functionName:`. Make sure you add the colon to indicate that it takes a parameter. Use the `addTarget` method to create a new target/action combination:

```
button.addTarget(self, action: Selector("tapped:"), forControlEvents:
UIControlEvents.TouchUpInside)
```

A list of common touch events is provided in Table 5-1 for your reference. One of the most commonly used touch events is `TouchUpInside`. This event is used to indicate a user tapping on a button. When the `UIButton` is tapped, the target/action associated with the button will attempt to call the Selector indicated in the `action` parameter. In the preceding code example, when `button` is tapped, iOS will call a function named `tapped:`. on the `ViewController`.

Table 5-1. Common Touch Events from UIControlEvents

TouchEvent	Description
TouchDown	The user has touched the button on screen.
TouchDownRepeat	Occurs when multiple touches are made within the same control.
TouchUpInside	When a user touches down on a control, does not move their finger outside of the control, and releases their finger without leaving the bounds of the control, this event is triggered.

Finally, add the button to the view:

```
view.addSubview(button)
```

The Code and Usage

Create a new iOS single-view project as described in Recipe 5-1. Open the file ViewController.swift. Replace the contents with the code from Listing 5-2. The function tapped: is called when a button is tapped. Run the application, and tap the button. In the Xcode output console, you will see the text "tapped."

Listing 5-2. ViewController with a UIButton added

```swift
import UIKit

class ViewController: UIViewController {

    override func viewDidLoad() {
        super.viewDidLoad()

        var button = UIButton.buttonWithType(UIButtonType.System) as! UIButton
        button.frame = CGRect(x: 10, y: 50, width: 200, height: 20)
        button.setTitle("Tap Me!", forState: UIControlState.Normal)
        button.setTitleColor(UIColor.blueColor(), forState: UIControlState.Normal)

        button.addTarget(self, action: Selector("tapped:"), forControlEvents:
        UIControlEvents.TouchUpInside)
        view.addSubview(button)
    }

    func tapped(sender : UIButton!) {
        NSLog("tapped")
    }
}
```

5-4. Adding a UITextField to a View

Problem

You want a user to enter a short amount of text.

Solution

UITextField is a simple text-entry field for iOS.

How It Works

UITextField is a UIControl subclass that accepts text input from a user. Optionally, when the user clicks the return button, it will send an action to a target object. UITextField should be used when you want to collect small amounts of text. It is designed for a single line of text.

The UITextField is initialized with a CGRect defining its frame:

```
var textField = UITextField(frame: CGRect(x: 10, y: 50, width: 300, height: 30))
```

The placeholder property is a string displayed in the field to communicate information to a user. It is not required to provide placeholder text, but using one sometimes helps you avoid needing to use a label to indicate the field's use. The placeholder text is hidden when the field is focused (i.e., becomes the first responder). The placeholder has a lighter color text to indicate that it is not a value entered in the text field, but placeholder copy:

```
textField.placeholder = "Enter your name"
```

The typeface and size of the field's font is controlled by the font property. You can change the font using the UIFont class. There are a number of default fonts available on iOS that you can use. You will need to know the postscript name of the font to supply to the UIFont initializer. The font size in points is provided as well. For this recipe, you will use a specific font. By default, all user-interface components use the "system" font. System is not a font itself, but it tells iOS to use the default system font for the version of iOS. The system also defines the font size based on the version of operating-system device. If possible, use the system font to maintain a consistent look and feel between your application and the iOS design. The default font size for body text is 17. For legibility, Apple recommends that you do not use text smaller than 11 points.

> **Tip**   The web site iOS Fonts (http://iosfonts.com) is a great resource to determine the list of included fonts for every version of iOS since 4.0.

```
textField.font = UIFont(name: "Arial-BoldMT", size: 22)
```

The style of a text field's border is set using the borderStyle property. Table 5-2 describes the possible styles you can specify for the borderStyle property.

Table 5-2. UITextBorderStyle Options and Examples

Border Style	Example from iOS 8.0.1
UITextBorderStyle.None (Default)	Enter your name
UITextBorderStyle.Line	Enter your name
UITextBorderStyle.Bezel	Enter your name
UITextBorderStyle.RoundedRect	Enter your name

Send the border of textField to UITextBorderStyle.RoundedRect:

textField.borderStyle = UITextBorderStyle.Line

Finally, add the text field to the view:

view.addSubview(textField)

The Code and Usage

Follow Recipe 5-1 to create a new single-view iOS application. Open the file ViewController.swift. Copy the code from Listing 5-3, and replace the contents of ViewController.swift. Run the application.

Listing 5-3. Adding a UITextField within a view controller

```
import UIKit

class ViewController: UIViewController {

    override func viewDidLoad() {
        super.viewDidLoad()

        var textField = UITextField(frame: CGRect(x: 10, y: 50, width: 300, height: 30))

        textField.placeholder = "Enter your name"
        textField.font = UIFont(name: "Arial-BoldMT", size: 22)
        textField.borderStyle = UITextBorderStyle.Line

        view.addSubview(textField)
    }
}
```

In the simulator, you should a screen like the one in Figure 5-5.

Figure 5-5. UITextField application running in simulator

5-5. Positioning UIViews in Auto Layout Using NSConstraints

Problem

You want your application's user interface to automatically adjust to different screen sizes and orientations.

Solution

Use Auto Layout to manage the position, size, and alignment.

How It Works

Auto Layout is a system used to define the positions and size of user-interface elements in relation to each other. Apple created this model to provide developers with a method for writing adaptive interfaces that can conform to multiple screen sizes and resolutions.

Constraints are applied to user-interface controls on your view. The constraints give Auto Layout a set of rules to follow when views are drawn on screen. For example, you can set a constraint to keep the height of a control set to 30, and constrain the top, right and left sides of the control to be 10 points in distance from the top, right and left of the superview's frame. These rules allow the control to grow in width. The control will grow in width if the superview grows in width but the other values remain set.

When using constraints, take care to avoid conflicting rules. For example, if you set the height of a view to 30 but then create another constraint that may need the height to change, you will get a runtime error. Depending on the severity of the error, your view may not appear. Xcode tries to fix inconsistent constraints by choosing one to break. This can affect the look and operation of your interface. The following is the output of a constraints conflict:

```
2015-02-05 11:17:30.336 AutoLayout[96434:2259116] Unable to simultaneously satisfy
constraints.


[REMOVED FOR BREVITY]

(
    "<_UILayoutSupportConstraint:0x7f8b18483410 V:[_UILayoutGuide:0x7f8b18481c20(20)]>",
    "<_UILayoutSupportConstraint:0x7f8b18482ce0 V:|-(0)-[_UILayoutGuide:0x7f8b18481c20]
        (Names: '|':UIView:0x7f8b18481910 )>",
    "<NSLayoutConstraint:0x7f8b18493a30 V:[UITextField:0x7f8b18480f70(30)]>",
    "<NSLayoutConstraint:0x7f8b184941b0
        V:[_UILayoutGuide:0x7f8b18481c20]-(10)-[UITextField:0x7f8b18480f70]>",
    "<NSLayoutConstraint:0x7f8b18494200
V:[UITextField:0x7f8b18480f70]-(NSSpace(8))-[UIButton:0x7f8b1848e540'Tap Me!']>",

[REMOVED FOR BREVITY]

Will attempt to recover by breaking constraint
<NSLayoutConstraint:0x7f8b184941b0 V:[_UILayoutGuide:0x7f8b18481c20]-(10)-
[UITextField:0x7f8b18480f70]>
```

Make a symbolic breakpoint for `UIViewAlertForUnsatisfiableConstraints` to catch this in the debugger.

The methods in the `UIConstraintBasedLayoutDebugging` category on `UIView` listed in `<UIKit/UIView.h>` may also be helpful.

Note the output towards the end, "Will attempt to recover by breaking constraint." This is Auto Layout attempting to fix the issue on its own. When you see errors like this, it is important to resolve them; otherwise, your user-interface layout may be unpredictable.

Let's look at an example of positioning a `UITextField` using constraints. First you define the `UITextField` variable, but you do not use a `CGRect` to initialize:

```
var textField = UITextField()
textField.placeholder = "Enter your name"
```

To set the top position of the `UITextField`, you need to add a constraint that will move the `UITextField` to the desired point on the y-axis. In most applications, you will need to account for the status bar at the top of the screen. There is a property named `topLayoutGuide` on the `ViewController` class. This property takes user-interface elements, such as the status bar and navigation bars. You should use `topLayoutGuide` for any positioning based on the top of the screen. Create a variable that references the `topLayoutGuide`. This will be used later:

```
var topGuide = self.topLayoutGuide
```

The method `NSLayoutConstraint.constraintsWithVisualFormat:` will create a constraint and return it. In order to use it, you need some prerequisites. First, you need a dictionary containing the controls to be constrained. Each control has a string key associated with it. The key may be anything, but it is recommended that you name it the same as the variable:

```
let views = ["textField":textField]
```

Each control is given a key. This key is used again later. Now the constraint is created using `constraintsWithVisualFormat`. The method takes a number of parameters: a visual format string, options, metrics, and a dictionary of views.

```
let verticalPositions:NSArray =
    NSLayoutConstraint.constraintsWithVisualFormat("V:|-10-[textField]-[button(34)]",
    options: NSLayoutFormatOptions(0), metrics: nil, views: views)
```

In this example, the `options` parameter is set to `NSLayoutFormatOptions(0)`. This is the equivalent of `nil` for the `options` parameter. The `metrics` parameter is unused as well. The `views` parameter is assigned the dictionary of views involved in creating the constraints.

The first parameter to the method is a visual format string. This is how you can describe constraints within Swift code. Let's break down the format string.

The first character is V. This means you are creating vertical constraints. When dealing with horizontal constraints use H instead. A colon follows the orientation:

```
V:|-10-[textField]-[button(34)]
```

Next, a list of views is provided, indicating the spacing between the views, as well as other constraints, such as height. In the example "`[topGuide]-10-[textField]-[button(34)]`", the `topGuide` represents the bottom of the status bar and navigation bar if they exist.

Next, the `-10-` means ten points of separation between the views. `textField` is put in brackets, indicating it is the key associated with a view that was added to the views dictionary. Any view or control referenced in the visual format string must be included in the dictionary. The value between the [ ] indicates the key of the view in the dictionary. Next is a just one dash "-". This indicates the default spacing of 8 points. Then a UIButton is added to the dictionary under the key button. The parentheses after button indicate additional constraints. Since you are creating vertical constraints, this sets the height to 34. If the string indicated horizontal constraints, the number would be the width. See Figure 5-6 to see how the visual format relates to the user interface.

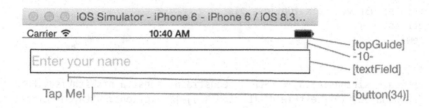

Figure 5-6. *How a visual format string relates to the resulting user interface*

The Code and Usage

The following code illustrates how to use Auto Layout to position user-interface elements in a view. To use this code, create a single-view iOS application. Then replace the contents of ViewController.swift with the contents of Listing 5-4. Run the application.

Listing 5-4. Positioning views with constraints and Auto Layout

```
import UIKit

class ViewController: UIViewController {

    override func viewDidLoad() {
        super.viewDidLoad()

        var textField = UITextField()

        textField.placeholder = "Enter your name"
        textField.borderStyle = UITextBorderStyle.Line
        textField.setTranslatesAutoresizingMaskIntoConstraints(false)
        view.addSubview(textField)

        var button = UIButton.buttonWithType(UIButtonType.System) as! UIButton
        button.setTranslatesAutoresizingMaskIntoConstraints(false)
        button.setTitle("Tap Me!", forState: UIControlState.Normal)

        button.addTarget(self, action: "tapped:", forControlEvents:
        UIControlEvents.TouchUpInside)
        view.addSubview(button)
```

```
        var topGuide = self.topLayoutGuide

        let views = ["textField":textField,"button":button,"topGuide":topGuide] as [NSObject
        : AnyObject]

        // height constraint
        let textFieldHeight:Array = NSLayoutConstraint.constraintsWithVisualFormat(
            "V:[textField(30)]",
            options: NSLayoutFormatOptions(0),
            metrics: nil,
            views: views)

        // vertical position
        let verticalPositions:Array = NSLayoutConstraint.constraintsWithVisualFormat(
            "V:[topGuide]-10-[textField]-[button(34)]-|", options: NSLayoutFormatOptions(0),
            metrics: nil,
            views: views)

        // right and left side constraints
        let textFieldHorizontal:Array = NSLayoutConstraint.constraintsWithVisualFormat(
            "H:|-10-[textField]-10-|",
            options: NSLayoutFormatOptions(0),
            metrics: nil,
            views: views)

        // right and left side constraints
        let buttonHorizontal:Array = NSLayoutConstraint.constraintsWithVisualFormat(
            "H:|-[button(75)]",
            options: NSLayoutFormatOptions(0),
            metrics: nil,
            views: views)

        view.addConstraints(textFieldHeight
            + verticalPositions
            + textFieldHorizontal
            + buttonHorizontal)      }

    func tapped( sender : UIButton )
    {
        NSLog("Tapped")
    }
}
```

The application will appear with a UITextField and a button positioned at the top of the
screen.

5-6. Repositioning a View to Accommodate the Keyboard

Problem

You need to reposition the screen when the keyboard covers user-interface elements.

Solution

Use a `UIScrollView` to reposition the screen elements so that they can be seen above the keyboard.

How It Works

The onscreen keyboard can use quite a bit of screen real estate, even on newer devices. Developers need to be aware when a keyboard could appear and adjust the user interface to accommodate it. You can use a `UIScrollView` to reposition elements of a view when the keyboard appears.

To begin, assume you are working on iOS 8 and running the application in the simulator for the iPhone 6. This recipe can be used on any device running iOS 7 or iOS 8, but for this recipe you will use this exact configuration.

In order to use the `UIScroll` view to reposition controls, you need a property to reference the `UIScrollView`. In addition, you need a property for a `UITextField`, `UIButton`, and `Bool`. All `UIView` properties should be implicitly unwrapped optionals, since they are initialized later in `viewDidLoad:`. The Boolean can be initialized inline:

```
var scrollView : UIScrollView!
var button : UIButton!
var textField : UITextField!
var isKeyboardUp : Bool = false
```

In the `viewDidLoad:` method, initialize the `scrollView` variable and add the new `UIScrollView` to the view controller. Make the `UIScrollView` the same size as the existing view:

```
scrollView = UIScrollView(frame: self.view.frame)
self.view.addSubview(scrollView!)
```

In this recipe, the size of the `UIScrollView`, `UITextArea`, and `UIButton` will be set to an exact frame. This is done to keep the code focused on handling keyboard events. In reality, you should leverage Auto Layout to position and size `UIViews` and subviews on the screen. This will make your code flexible, and it prepares your app to run on multiple devices and resolutions.

Next, initialize the textField property and the button. The UIButton will call a method named tapped:. Initialize the button, and add it to scrollView:

```
textField = UITextField(frame: CGRect(x: 10, y: 400, width: 200, height: 30))
textField.placeholder = "Enter your name"
textField.borderStyle = UITextBorderStyle.Line

button = UIButton.buttonWithType(UIButtonType.System) as UIButton
button.frame = CGRect(x: 10, y: 440, width: 200, height: 30)
button.setTitle("Tap Me!", forState: UIControlState.Normal)
button.addTarget(self, action: "tapped:", forControlEvents:
UIControlEvents.TouchUpInside)
scrollView.addSubview(button)
```

Create a stub method named tapped: with a UIButton for its only parameter. This method will be implemented later:

```
func tapped( sender : UIButton ) {
}
```

Next you need to listen for a notification that the keyboard will be shown on screen or will be hidden. The keyboard sends notifications using NSNotificationCenter. Add an observer for each of the two notifications the application needs to know about: UIKeyboardWillShowNotification and UIKeyboardWillHideNotification. You will want to be a good citizen and add observers only when required and remove them when they are no longer needed, even if the view controller is not currently active. Use the viewWillAppear: delegate method to add your observers. Later you will remove them in the viewWillDisappear: method. This sets up the view controller so that when it is active and on screen, the observers are present and when the application transitions away or the view controller is superseded by another controller, the observers are removed.

The addObserver method takes a reference to the target to be notified; in this case, it is self. It also requires a Selector for the method that will be called by NSNotificationCenter. In Swift, a selector is created using the object Selector and passing it the method signature as a string. For example, Selector("keyboardWillShow:") will create a selector for a method named keyboardWillShow with a single parameter. Note that the colon must be used to indicate that the method takes a parameter. The third parameter to addObserver is the name of the notification you will be listening for. Finally, the fourth parameter, object, can be nil:

```
override func viewWillAppear(animated: Bool) {
    NSNotificationCenter.defaultCenter().addObserver(self,
        selector: Selector("keyboardWillShow:"),
        name: UIKeyboardWillShowNotification, object: nil)

    NSNotificationCenter.defaultCenter().addObserver(self,
        selector: Selector("keyboardWillHide:"),
        name: UIKeyboardWillHideNotification, object: nil)
}
```

When keyboard posts a notification, the Notification Center will call the Selector on the target object. The Selector is not verified at compile time. If you make a typo in the name of the method, you will receive a runtime error:

```
AdjustViewForKeyboard[96718:2265471] *** Terminating app due to uncaught exception
'NSInvalidArgumentException', reason:
'-[AdjustViewForKeyboard.ViewController tapped:]:
unrecognized selector sent to instance 0x7fca151082b0'
```

Create two methods, keyboardWillShow: and keyboardWillHide:. The functions called within these methods do not exist yet, but you will add them soon. The Notification Center passes an NSNotification instance to these methods. The information about the keyboard's size is contained within this notification. Both methods work similarly. When the keyboard is going to appear, you want to get the height of the keyboard and then reposition scrollView to ensure your text field and button are visible. When the keyboard is hidden, you need to restore everything back to its original position:

```
func keyboardWillShow( notification : NSNotification) {
    if !isKeyboardUp {
        scrollView( getKeyboardHeight(notification) , scrollingUp: true)
    }
}

func keyboardWillHide( notification : NSNotification ) {
    if isKeyboardUp {
        scrollView( getKeyboardHeight(notification) , scrollingUp: false )
    }
}
```

To get the height of the keyboard, you need to retrieve that information from the notification. Create a new function getKeyboardHeight:. It will have one parameter, notification. The keyboard height is stored in the property notification.userInfo. The userInfo property is an optional dictionary of values. The position and size of the keyboard are accessed with the key UIKeybordFrameBeginUserInfoKey. Cast the result to an NSValue, and then convert the result to a CGRect. Return the height property of the converted value. This is the height of the keyboard:

```
func getKeyboardHeight( notification : NSNotification ) -> CGFloat {
    return (notification.userInfo?[UIKeyboardFrameBeginUserInfoKey] as NSValue).
CGRectValue().height
}
```

Now you have a function to return the height of the keyboard. This will help calculate how far you need to scroll to move the text field and button to be visible above the keyboard. Create a method named scrollView:scrollingUp:. The first parameter, points, is the number of points the UIScrollView needs to be scrolled. The value for this will be calculated by the getKeyboardHeight method. The parameter scrollingUp indicates if you are moving position of scrollView up (true) or down (false). For example, if the keyboard is 216 points high, you will need to move elements that could be hidden behind the keyboard up at least 216 points toward the top of the screen.

> **Caution** Never use a fixed value for the size of the keyboard. It is constantly changing based on rotation, the operating system, and the type of keyboard. Always use the notification events to determine the current size.

When scrolling up, the method to move the contents of the scrollView consists of two steps. First, you expand the height of scrollView by the height of the on-screen keyboard. This is done to add vertical space to the scroll view. This will allow the scroll view to scroll. Before you extend the height, the scroll view is the same size as the superview and will not scroll. Then set the contentOffset property of scrollView to bring the elements into view above the keyboard. You are adding the equivalent blank space to scrollView and then scrolling the view up. The keyboard hides the blank space, and textField and button are moved above the keyboard.

Use the y coordinate of the button's origin to calculate how far you must scroll. This will ensure that the field you desire to be visible will be positioned closely to the keyboard. In this example, you want the textField and button to be visible. Then set isKeyboardUp=true to prevent the view from being moved up more than once.

To reset the view when the keyboard disappears, you perform the opposite actions: remove the excess height from scrollView, and reposition the scrollView back to its original position. In this case, you are using 0. However, if you have a longer scrollView with many controls, you will need to keep track of the original offset so that you can restore it when the keyboard disappears:

```
func scrollView ( points : CGFloat, scrollingUp: Bool ) {
    var newRect = scrollView!.frame

    if scrollingUp && !isKeyboardUp {
        newRect.size.height += points
        scrollView.frame = newRect
        scrollView.setContentOffset(CGPoint(x: 0.0,y: button!.frame.origin.y - points),
        animated: true)
        isKeyboardUp = true
    } else
    if !scrollingUp && isKeyboardUp {
        newRect.size.height -= points
        scrollView.frame = newRect

        scrollView.setContentOffset(CGPoint(x: 0.0,y: 0), animated: true)
        isKeyboardUp = false
    }
}
```

In order to dismiss the keyboard, resign `firstResponder` from `textField`. This will cause the keyboard to dismiss itself. Add this code to the `tapped` method:

```
func tapped( sender : UIButton ) {
    textField.resignFirstResponder()
}
```

Observers were created to listen for the notification in the `viewWillAppear:` method. They should be removed when they are no longer needed. In the `viewWillDisappear:` method, call `removeObserver:`. This will remove all observers associated with the object provided as the parameter:

```
override func viewWillDisappear(animated: Bool) {
    NSNotificationCenter.defaultCenter().removeObserver(self)
}
```

The Code and Usage

Create an iOS single-view application in Xcode, and name it "AdjustViewForKeyboard." See Recipe 5-1 for details on creating a new project. Open the `ViewController.swift` file. Copy the code from Listing 5-5, and replace the contents of `ViewController.swift`. Run the application.

Listing 5-5. Adjusting a screen with UIScrollView to accommodate the keyboard

```
import UIKit

class ViewController: UIViewController {

    var isKeyboardUp : Bool = false
    var scrollView : UIScrollView!
    var button : UIButton!
    var textField : UITextField!

    override func viewDidLoad() {
        super.viewDidLoad()

        // Setup user interface elements.

        scrollView = UIScrollView(frame: self.view.frame)

        self.view.addSubview(scrollView!)

        textField = UITextField(frame: CGRect(x: 10, y: 400, width: 200, height: 30))
        textField.placeholder = "Enter your name"
        textField.borderStyle = UITextBorderStyle.Line
        scrollView.addSubview(textField)

        button = UIButton.buttonWithType(UIButtonType.System) as! UIButton
        button.frame = CGRect(x: 10, y: 440, width: 200, height: 30)
        button.setTitle("Tap Me!", forState: UIControlState.Normal)
```

```
        button.addTarget(self, action: "tapped:", forControlEvents: UIControlEvents.
        TouchUpInside)
        scrollView.addSubview(button)
    }

    override func viewWillAppear(animated: Bool) {
        NSNotificationCenter.defaultCenter().addObserver(self,
            selector: Selector("keyboardWillShow:"),
            name: UIKeyboardWillShowNotification, object: nil)
        // Keyboard Down
        NSNotificationCenter.defaultCenter().addObserver(self,
            selector: Selector("keyboardWillHide:"),
            name: UIKeyboardWillHideNotification, object: nil)
    }

    func getKeyboardHeight( notification : NSNotification ) -> CGFloat {
        return (notification.userInfo?[UIKeyboardFrameBeginUserInfoKey] as!
        NSValue).CGRectValue().height
    }

    func keyboardWillShow( notification : NSNotification) {
        if !isKeyboardUp {
            scrollView( getKeyboardHeight(notification) , scrollingUp: true)
        }
    }

    func keyboardWillHide( notification : NSNotification ) {
        if isKeyboardUp {
            scrollView( getKeyboardHeight(notification) , scrollingUp: false )
        }
    }

    func scrollView ( points : CGFloat, scrollingUp: Bool ) {
        var newRect = scrollView!.frame

        if scrollingUp && !isKeyboardUp {
            newRect.size.height += points
            scrollView.frame = newRect
            scrollView.setContentOffset(CGPoint(x: 0.0,y: button!.frame.origin.y - points),
            animated: true)
            isKeyboardUp = true
        } else
        if !scrollingUp && isKeyboardUp {
            newRect.size.height -= points
            scrollView.frame = newRect

            scrollView.setContentOffset(CGPoint(x: 0.0,y: 0), animated: true)
            isKeyboardUp = false
        }
    }
```

```
override func viewWillDisappear(animated: Bool) {
    NSNotificationCenter.defaultCenter().removeObserver(self)
}

func tapped( sender : UIButton ) {
    textField.resignFirstResponder()
}
}
```

When you tap and put the focus in the text field, the keyboard will appear. The UIScrollView will be scrolled to move the view upward. Then tap the button "Tap Me." The keyboard will be dismissed, and the scroll view will be reset.

5-7. Displaying an Alert with UIAlertController

Problem

You need to display an alert dialog in iOS 8 and later.

Solution

Use UIAlertController to display an alert. UIAlertController replaces UIAlertView, which is deprecated in iOS 8.

How It Works

In iOS 8, UIAlertView and UIActionSheet have been deprecated and, in its place, developers are advised to use UIAlertController instead. UIAlertController provides a more generalized and rich interface. It replaces both UIAlertView and UIActionSheet. To instantiate a UIAlertController, specify the title, message, and alert style. The alert style can be either Alert or ActionSheet. The Alert style is a dialog that appears in the center of the screen. The ActionSheet style is a control that slides up from the bottom with a series of buttons. The following code is a simple alert:

```
let baconAlert = UIAlertController(title: "More Bacon?",
    message: "Would you like some more bacon?", preferredStyle: .Alert)
```

This alert looks like Figure 5-7.

Figure 5-7. Example Alert style dialog created with UIAlertController

An Alert and an Action Sheet have very common elements, which is why Apple refactored them into UIAlertController. UIAlertController has a collection of actions that you add to the controller to respond to different actions. To add a "Cancel" action and "OK" action to the baconAlert controller, use UIAlertAction and UIAlertController.addAction:. For each UIAlertAction the controller adds a button with a title, a style, and a callback. There are three styles to choose from:

- Default – Use this style to confirm an action, gather input, or answer a question.

- Cancel – Use this style to indicate that an action will cancel the operation and no data will be updated.

- Destructive – Use this style to indicate that the action may change or delete data.

To ask the question "Do you want more bacon?" add two actions: one cancel style and one default style. Supply a trailing closure as the second parameter. The closure is called when the user taps the corresponding button:

```
let cancelAction = UIAlertAction(title: "No", style: .Cancel) { (action) in
    self.dismissViewControllerAnimated(true, completion: nil)
}
baconAlert.addAction(cancelAction)

let OKAction = UIAlertAction(title: "Yes", style: .Default) { (action) in
    self.dismissViewControllerAnimated(true, completion: nil)
}
baconAlert.addAction(OKAction)
```

A destructive action only changes the style of the button. Your callback method must handle all actual changes that should happen.

```
let NoMoreBacon = UIAlertAction(title: "Don't ask again", style: .Destructive) { (action) in
    self.dismissViewControllerAnimated(true, completion: nil)
}
baconAlert.addAction(NoMoreBacon)
```

The Code and Usage

To use the code from Listing 5-6, create a new single-view iOS application. See Recipe 5-1 for guidance on creating a project. Open the file ViewController.swift, and replace the contents with Listing 5-6. Run the application.

Listing 5-6. UIAlertController in action

```
import UIKit

class ViewController: UIViewController {

    override func viewDidAppear(animated: Bool) {
        let baconAlert = UIAlertController(title: "More Bacon?",
            message: "Would you like some more bacon?", preferredStyle: .Alert)

        let cancelAction = UIAlertAction(title: "No", style: .Cancel) { (action) in
            self.dismissViewControllerAnimated(true, completion: nil)
        }
        baconAlert.addAction(cancelAction)

        let OKAction = UIAlertAction(title: "Yes", style: .Default) { (action) in
            self.dismissViewControllerAnimated(true, completion: nil)
        }
        baconAlert.addAction(OKAction)
```

```
        let NoMoreBacon = UIAlertAction(title: "Don't ask again", style: .Destructive) {
        (action) in
            self.dismissViewControllerAnimated(true, completion: nil)
        }
        baconAlert.addAction(NoMoreBacon)

        self.presentViewController(baconAlert, animated: true, completion: nil)
    }
}
```

When the application launches, the alert will be displayed immediately. Tapping one of the action buttons will trigger the closure associated with that action and the alert will be dismissed.

5-8. Using UIAlertController to Collect User Input

Problem

You need to prompt the user for short text-based input.

Solution

Use UIAlertController with *text fields*.

How It Works

UIAlertController has the ability to add a list of text fields to be displayed for user input. The result is something similar to the login alert dialogs you see in many iOS System applications. In this recipe, you will make an alert that asks for a use name and password. First, create the controller with the Alert style:

```
loginField : UITextField!
var passwordField : UITextField!

let loginAlert = UIAlertController(title: "Login",
    message: "Please enter your credentials", preferredStyle: .Alert)
```

Now you can add UITextFields to the alert. It is important to note that text fields can be used only with the Alert style. The text fields are added to the alert using the method addTextFieldWithConfigurationHandler:.

The method takes a closure with a single parameter. This closure is called when a UITextField is instantiated for the alert. Use the closure to control the behavior of the text field. Set any desired UITextField properties, such as the placeholder text and font styles.

This is also the time to set a reference to the field. Use this reference to read the values from the text field. Having to update the text-field attributes in a closure like this may seem a bit odd, but it eliminates the need to subclass UIAlertController in order to make cosmetic changes to the text fields and access the values in the text areas at a later point in the code using a reference. In the following code, a text field is added to the alert. The closure receives that new UITextField as a parameter. It sets the placeholder text and then saves a reference to the text field to be used later. It does the same for both the user name and password fields:

```
loginAlert.addTextFieldWithConfigurationHandler() { (textField) -> Void in
    textField.placeholder = "Username"
    self.loginField = textField
}

loginAlert.addTextFieldWithConfigurationHandler() { (textField) -> Void in
    textField.placeholder = "Password"
    textField.secureTextEntry = true
    self.passwordField = textField
}
```

Next add a cancel style button. For more information about adding buttons and configuring UIAlertController, see Recipe 5-7. The code for this cancel button will dismiss the alert:

```
let cancelAction = UIAlertAction(title: "Cancel", style: .Cancel) {
    (action) in
        self.dismissViewControllerAnimated(true, completion: nil)
}
loginAlert.addAction(cancelAction)
```

Use the properties loginField and passwordField to access the values of the text fields. You do this in the UIAlertAction callback:

```
let OKAction = UIAlertAction(title: "Login", style: .Default) { (action) in
    let username = self.loginField.text
    let password = self.passwordField.text
    NSLog("Username: \(username)\nPassword: \(password)")
    self.dismissViewControllerAnimated(true, completion: nil)
}
loginAlert.addAction(OKAction)
self.presentViewController(loginAlert, animated: true, completion: nil)
```

The Code and Usage

Create a single-view iOS Application in Xcode. (See Recipe 5-1.) Open the file
ViewController.swift, and replace the contents with the code in Listing 5-7. Run the
application.

Listing 5-7. Capturing user input with UIAlertController

```
import UIKit

class ViewController: UIViewController {

    var loginField : UITextField!
    var passwordField : UITextField!

    override func viewDidAppear(animated: Bool) {
        let loginAlert = UIAlertController(title: "Login",
            message: "Please enter your credentials", preferredStyle: .Alert)

        loginAlert.addTextFieldWithConfigurationHandler() { (textField) -> Void in
            textField.placeholder = "Username"
            self.loginField = textField
        }
        loginAlert.addTextFieldWithConfigurationHandler() { (textField) -> Void in
            textField.placeholder = "Password"
            textField.secureTextEntry = true
            self.passwordField = textField
        }

        let cancelAction = UIAlertAction(title: "Cancel", style: .Cancel) { (action) in
            self.dismissViewControllerAnimated(true, completion: nil)
        }
        loginAlert.addAction(cancelAction)

        let OKAction = UIAlertAction(title: "Login", style: .Default) { (action) in
            let username = self.loginField.text
            let password = self.passwordField.text
            NSLog("Username: \(username)\nPassword: \(password)")
            self.dismissViewControllerAnimated(true, completion: nil)
        }
        loginAlert.addAction(OKAction)
        self.presentViewController(loginAlert, animated: true, completion: nil)
    }
}
```

An alert will open immediately, asking for a user name and a password. When the "Login" button is tapped, the closure for OKAction will be called and the values are read into local variables. The alert then disappears from the screen in the simulator or device. In the console, you should see output similar to this:

```
Username: myUser Password: myPassword
```

5-9. Creating a UITableView

Problem

You need to display a table of values and let the user scroll and read the list.

Solution

Use UITableView to display a list of data.

How It Works

The UITableView is a cornerstone of the iOS user interface. It is used everywhere from iTunes, Contacts and Calendar to third-party apps. It can deal with small or large amounts of data. A UITableView is typically managed by a subclass of UITableViewController. It can be managed by any class as long as it conforms to the UITableViewDelegate protocol and UITableViewDataSource. The UITableViewDelegate protocol deals with the user-interaction events that occur within the UITableView. The UITableViewDataSource protocol allows the UITableView to retrieve data that will be displayed in the table.

There are three primary methods that must be implemented as part of the UITableViewDataSource protocol. The UITableView calls these methods when it requires information about the data to be displayed. Table 5-3 lists those methods and their use.

Table 5-3. Methods Used to Populate a UITableView

Method	Usage
tableView:numberOfSectionsInTableView	Returns an integer indicating the number of sections to be displayed in a UITableView. A section subdivides the table view into groups. For example, in the Apple Contacts app, the table view of contacts has a section for each letter of the alphabet. See Figure 5-9.
tableView:numberOfRowsInSection	Returns the total number of items in the dataset.
tableView:cellForRowAtIndexPath:	Returns an instance of a UITableViewCell to be used to display a row in the table view.

First, implement the `tableView:numberOfSectionsInTableView:`. In this recipe, it will be 1. A table view always has at least one section. If there is only a single section, no section header will be displayed. Create the method as follows:

```
override func numberOfSectionsInTableView(tableView: UITableView) -> Int {
    return 1
}
```

Figure 5-8 shows the Apple address book. This is an example of multiple sections. Each letter in the gray bar indicates the header of the section. The section's rows follow immediately under the header.

Figure 5-8. *The Contacts application has sections to divide the contact list alphabetically*

Next, you need a data source. Use a string array of the names of the 50 states. Then you can implement tableView:numberOfRowsInSection: and return the count of elements in the array:

```
var states = ["Alabama","Alaska","Arizona","Arkansas","California","Colorado","Connecticut",
    "Delaware","District Of Columbia","Florida","Georgia","Hawaii","Idaho",
    "Illinois","Indiana","Iowa","Kansas","Kentucky","Louisiana","Maine",
    "Maryland","Massachusetts","Michigan","Minnesota","Mississippi","Missouri",
    "Montana","Nebraska","Nevada","New Hampshire","New Jersey","New Mexico",
    "New York","North Carolina","North Dakota","Ohio","Oklahoma","Oregon",
    "Pennsylvania","Rhode Island","South Carolina","South Dakota","Tennessee","Texas",
    "Utah",
    "Vermont","Virginia","Washington","West Virginia","Wisconsin","Wyoming"]

override func tableView(tableView: UITableView, numberOfRowsInSection section:
Int) -> Int {
    return states.count
}
```

The last method required is the tableView:cellForRowAtIndexPath: method. This method returns a UITableViewCell with the proper information populated.

First, you will need to have an instance of UITableViewCell. For efficiency, UITableView performs animations that make it appear like a user is scrolling through a large number of table cells. However, it limits the number of UITableViewCell instances that need to be created. The UITableView requires only enough cells to display on screen and to create the scrolling animation. After that number of cells is created, it will then reuse those cells over and over as the user scrolls through data.

Check for a reusable cell using dequeueReusableCellWithIdentifier:. The identifier is a string used to search for a cell to reuse:

```
var cell = tableView.dequeueReusableCellWithIdentifier("Cell") as UITableViewCell?
```

If a reusable cell is not available, nil is returned. In this case, instantiate a new cell, providing a UITableViewStyle value and an identifier string. There are four built-in types of UITableViewCells. Table 5-4 lists the styles and an example of how the style appears. The example also indicates the position of text within the cell, which is dictated by the style. For this recipe, use UITableViewCellStyle.Default to create the UITableViewCell:

```
if cell == nil {
    cell = UITableViewCell(style: UITableViewCellStyle.Default,
            reuseIdentifier: "Cell")
}
```

Table 5-4. The UITableViewCellStyle Enumeration

Style	Example
Default	Title
Value1	Title Subtitle
Value2	Title Subtitle
Subtitle	Title Subtitle

You now have an instance of UITableViewCell and can populate the table cell with your data. In this recipe, you have only one field of data. There are two UILabel properties available on a UITableViewCell instance: textLabel and detailTextLabel. The placement depends on the style of the cell. Refer to table Table 5-4 to reference the locations of the labels.

The label with the text "Title" is set using the textLabel property, and the label with the text "Subtitle" is set using the detailTextLabel property. Set the text of the textLabel with the name of the state for the row indicated by the indexPath parameter. The IndexPath type has two properties, section and row. The section is the index of the section the UITableView that is being drawn. The row is the index of the row in the table view that is being drawn. In this recipe, you need only the row because there is one section. Use the row as an index of the states array:

```
cell?.textLabel?.text = states[indexPath.row]
cell?.detailTextLabel?.text = "Subtitle"
return cell!
```

Finally, return cell from the method.

The Code and Usage

For this recipe, launch Xcode and create a new iOS project, but this time, select the "Master-Detail Application" template. On the next screen, set your "Product Name" to "UITableView" and make sure "Swift" is selected as the language. Next, change the "Devices" selection to "iPhone." This template creates a working UITableView project, and restricting it to the iPhone keeps the amount of templated files to a minimum. Save your project.

The project should open automatically. In the project, there is a file named MasterViewController.swift. This contains boilerplate code for using a UITableView. To use the code in this recipe, copy all of Listing 5-8 and replace the contents of MasterViewController.swift. No other modifications are required. Run the application.

Listing 5-8. Displaying data in a UITableView

```
import UIKit

class MasterViewController: UITableViewController {

    override func viewDidLoad() {
        super.viewDidLoad()

    }

    override func tableView(tableView: UITableView,
        cellForRowAtIndexPath indexPath: NSIndexPath) -> UITableViewCell {

        var cell = tableView.dequeueReusableCellWithIdentifier("Cell") as! UITableViewCell?

        if cell == nil {
            cell = UITableViewCell(style: UITableViewCellStyle.Default, reuseIdentifier: "Cell")
        }

        cell?.textLabel?.text = states[indexPath.row]
        cell?.detailTextLabel?.text = "Subtitle"

        return cell!
    }

    var states = ["Alabama","Alaska","Arizona","Arkansas","California","Colorado","Connecticut",
        "Delaware","District Of Columbia","Florida","Georgia","Hawaii","Idaho",
        "Illinois","Indiana","Iowa","Kansas","Kentucky","Louisiana","Maine",
        "Maryland","Massachusetts","Michigan","Minnesota","Mississippi","Missouri",
        "Montana","Nebraska","Nevada","New Hampshire","New Jersey","New Mexico",
        "New York","North Carolina","North Dakota","Ohio","Oklahoma","Oregon",
        "Pennsylvania","Rhode Island","South Carolina","South Dakota","Tennessee","Texas","Utah",
        "Vermont","Virginia","Washington","West Virginia","Wisconsin","Wyoming"]

    override func tableView(tableView: UITableView, numberOfRowsInSection section: Int) -> Int {
        return states.count
    }

    override func numberOfSectionsInTableView(tableView: UITableView) -> Int {
        return 1
    }
}
```

The application will present a list of the states as they are in the states array. You can scroll the list to view all the values. On screen, the application should look something like Figure 5-9.

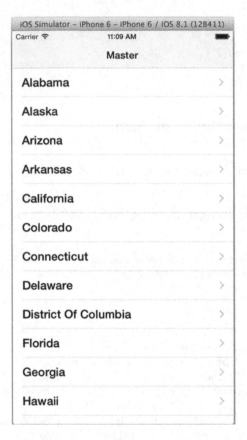

Figure 5-9. UITableView of state names

5-10. Swiping to Delete an Item from a UITableView
Problem
You would like users to be able to swipe to the left and have the option to delete a row.

Solution
Enable editing on the UITableView, and add code to remove the row from your data source.

How It Works

For this recipe, you will build upon the code from Recipe 5-9, "Creating a UITableView." The UITableView control already has the "swipe to delete" functionality built in. Activate it by implementing two methods: tableView:editingStyleForRowAtIndexPath: and tableView: commitEditingStyle:forRowAtIndexPath:. The first method indicates to the UITableView what editing options are available for each row.

Add the method tableView:editingStyleForRowAtIndexPath:. The method returns a value of UITableViewCellEditingStyle.Delete. This indicates to the table view that the row may be deleted. Without performing any checks, the table view will allow you to delete any row. If you want to protect the row from deletion, return UITableViewCellEditingStyle.None.

Note   You must implement both methods; otherwise, swiping left on a row will have no effect.

```
override func tableView(tableView: UITableView,
    editingStyleForRowAtIndexPath indexPath: NSIndexPath) -> UITableViewCellEditingStyle {
    return UITableViewCellEditingStyle.Delete
}
```

Next, implement tableView:commitEditingStyle:forRowAtIndexPath:. This method will do the work of removing the data and updating the table view to remove the row. It takes three parameters:

- tableView – The tableView that originated the method call.

- editingStyle – The UITableViewCellEditingStyle value of the action that is taking place.

- indexPath – The IndexPath corresponding to the section and row that the user acted upon.

Create the method:

```
override func tableView(tableView: UITableView,
    commitEditingStyle editingStyle: UITableViewCellEditingStyle,
    forRowAtIndexPath indexPath: NSIndexPath) {
```

When the user taps the delete button, the method is called with the proper values. The parameter editingStyle is the value UITableViewCellEditingStyle.Delete. This method is called for other editing actions, so you must check the editing style to determine what actions to take:

```
switch editingStyle
    {
        case .Delete:
```

To remove a row, first remove the value from the `states` array using `indexPath.row`. In this case, you do not need to check `indexPath.section` because there is only a single section:

```
states.removeAtIndex(indexPath.row)
```

After the row in the `tableView` has been removed, the table view and the `states` array are out of sync. The table view still contains the `UITableViewCell` for that row. To remove it, call `tableView.deleteRowsAtIndexPaths:`. The parameters are an array of `NSIndexPath` objects and an animation to use when any rows are removed. Use `UITableViewRowAnimation.Fade` and the row will fade out, and then the rows below it will close up the space:

```
        tableView.deleteRowsAtIndexPaths([indexPath], withRowAnimation:
            UITableViewRowAnimation.Fade)
```

```
Complete the remainder of
        default:
            return
    }
}
```

The Code and Usage

To work with Listing 5-9, first use Recipe 5-9 to create a project containing a `UITableView` with a list of the 50 United States and the District of Columbia. Replace the contents of `MasterViewController.swift` with the code from Listing 5-9. The `UITableView` does all the work of handling a left swipe and displaying the delete button.

The code in `tableView:commitEditingStyle:forRowAtIndexPath:` handles the removal of data and updates the interface. Run the application.

Listing 5-9. Implement swipe and delete with a UITableView

```
import UIKit

class MasterViewController: UITableViewController {
    override func tableView(tableView: UITableView,
        cellForRowAtIndexPath indexPath: NSIndexPath) -> UITableViewCell {

        var cell = tableView.dequeueReusableCellWithIdentifier("Cell") as! UITableViewCell?

        if cell == nil {
            cell = UITableViewCell(style: UITableViewCellStyle.Default, reuseIdentifier:
            "Cell")
        }

        cell?.textLabel?.text = states[indexPath.row]
        cell?.detailTextLabel?.text = "Subtitle"

        return cell!
    }
```

```swift
var states = ["Alabama","Alaska","Arizona","Arkansas","California","Colorado",
"Connecticut",
    "Delaware","District Of Columbia","Florida","Georgia","Hawaii","Idaho",
    "Illinois","Indiana","Iowa","Kansas","Kentucky","Louisiana","Maine",
    "Maryland","Massachusetts","Michigan","Minnesota","Mississippi","Missouri",
    "Montana","Nebraska","Nevada","New Hampshire","New Jersey","New Mexico",
    "New York","North Carolina","North Dakota","Ohio","Oklahoma","Oregon",
    "Pennsylvania","Rhode Island","South Carolina","South Dakota","Tennessee",
    "Texas","Utah",
    "Vermont","Virginia","Washington","West Virginia","Wisconsin","Wyoming"]

override func tableView(tableView: UITableView, numberOfRowsInSection section:
Int) -> Int {
    return states.count
}

override func numberOfSectionsInTableView(tableView: UITableView) -> Int {
    return 1
}

override func tableView(tableView: UITableView,
    editingStyleForRowAtIndexPath indexPath: NSIndexPath) -> UITableViewCellEditingStyle {
    return UITableViewCellEditingStyle.Delete
}

override func tableView(tableView: UITableView,
    commitEditingStyle editingStyle: UITableViewCellEditingStyle,
    forRowAtIndexPath indexPath: NSIndexPath) {
    switch editingStyle
    {
    case .Delete:
        states.removeAtIndex(indexPath.row)
        tableView.deleteRowsAtIndexPaths([indexPath],
            withRowAnimation:UITableViewRowAnimation.Fade)
    default:
        return
    }
}
}
```

Then swipe left on a row. A Delete button will appear as in Figure 5-10. Tap the Delete button and `tableView:commitEditingStyle:forRowAtIndexPath:` will be called to handle the delete.

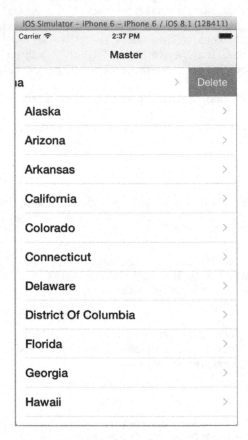

Figure 5-10. The Delete button after the user has swiped the row to the left

The row will disappear, and the surrounding rows will compress to close the space.

Chapter 6

OS X Applications

Apple has worked hard to integrate the same technologies used in iOS development into OS X applications. This allows developers to create applications that operate on the entire Apple ecosystem, including Mac, iPhone, iPad, and iPod. The OS X App Store is another potential revenue opportunity for developers. The recipes in this chapter will help you build OS X applications. The more platforms your application is available on, the more useful your application is to users. Much of OS X programming is similar to iOS; however, the primary framework—AppKit—is a different set of user-interface components and APIs. In addition, OS X applications frequently use multiple windows, toolbars, menus, and other desktop paradigms.

The recipes in this chapter cover these topics:

- Creating an OS X Application
- Adding a View to a Window
- Adding a Menu and Menu Items
- Adding a Button to a Window
- Using an NSTextField
- Displaying an Image in a Window
- Adjusting Contents When a Window Is Resized
- Implementing an NSTableView
- Sorting an NSTableView
- Handling the Selection of an NSTableView Row

6-1. Creating an OS X Application

Problem

You want to create a new OS X application.

Solution

Use the Cocoa Application template in Xcode.

How It Works

Xcode provides a number of project templates for OS X applications just like the iOS templates. Launch Xcode, and select File ➤ New ➤ Project from the menu. A dialog of project templates is displayed. A list of application categories is on the left side of the dialog. Under the "OS X" section choose "Application." Then select "Cocoa Application." See Figure 6-1.

Figure 6-1. Select the Cocoa Application template

As shown in Figure 6-2, in the next dialog you give your application a name, select Swift as the language, clear the "Use Storyboards" option, and clear the "Create Document-Based Application" option.

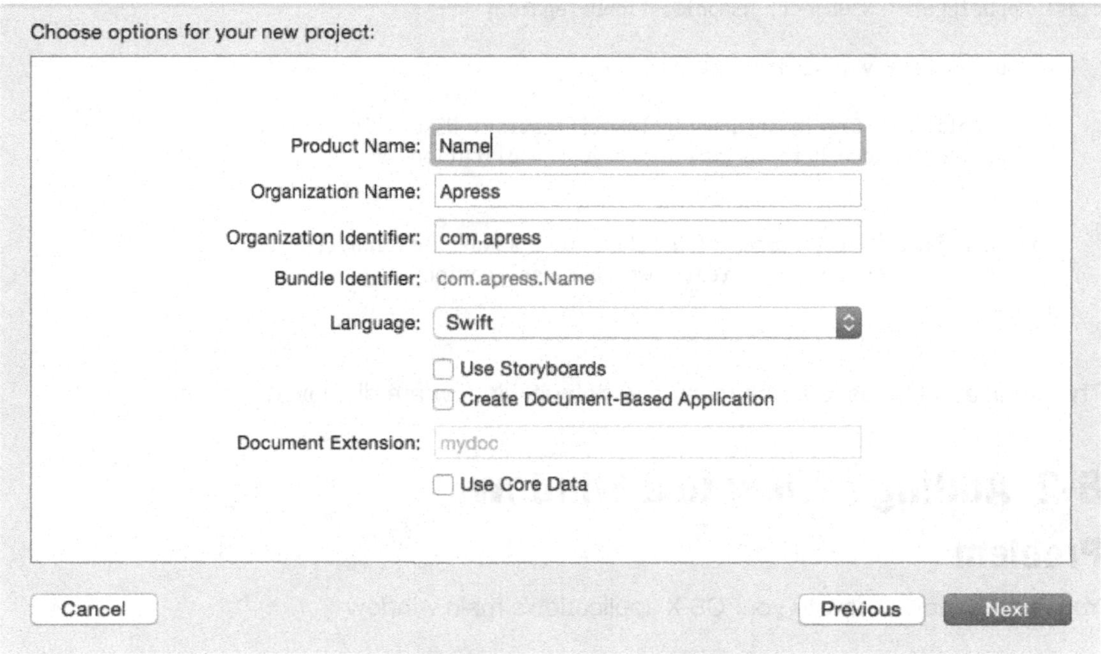

Figure 6-2. Project options dialog

The template includes some default files. The file AppDelegate.swift is the root of the application. It is the delegate's job to create the initial screens and view controllers of the application. The file named MainMenu.xib is an Interface Builder file in XML format. This xib file contains information about the windows of the application, as well as menus and additional resources. OS X applications, unlike iOS applications, are typically made up of multiple windows that can be active at once. These windows are resizable and can be positioned anywhere on the screen. iOS applications are single-window applications with multiple views displayed one at a time.

The Code and Usage

The default application template includes a single window. Listing 6-1 contains the AppDelegate class for the application. Run the application.

Listing 6-1. AppDelegate.swift

```
import Cocoa

@NSApplicationMain
class AppDelegate: NSObject, NSApplicationDelegate {

    @IBOutlet weak var window: NSWindow!

    func applicationDidFinishLaunching(aNotification: NSNotification) {
        // Insert code here to initialize your application
    }

    func applicationWillTerminate(aNotification: NSNotification) {
        // Insert code here to tear down your application
    }
}
```

The application loads, and the menu and default window are displayed.

6-2. Adding a View to a Window
Problem

You need to add a view to your OS X application's main window.

Solution

Create and add an NSView to the window's contentView property.

How It Works

The OS X user interface, like its iOS counterpart, is made up of objects derived from a view. In OS X, NSView is the equivalent of UIView in iOS. Use a CGRect to establish the x,y position and the height and width of the view. In OS X, a Cartesian coordinate system is used. The origin of the system is at the bottom left of the window or view. If you are coming from iOS, which places its origin at the top left, you can get mixed up. Apple advises that you use Cartesian coordinates, but it is possible to "flip" the coordinate system and work with a similar system as iOS. For this recipe, we will use Cartesian coordinates.

Create a new NSView with a CGRect. This view will appear in the bottom left corner of the application's window and be a 300x300 square:

```
var view = NSView(frame: CGRect(x: 10, y: 10, width: 300, height: 300))
```

If you want to make the view a blue square, you need to set the backgroundColor property. However, the NSView class does not have a property to set the background color. Instead, you can change the color of the view's layer. By default, NSView does not have layers. To set the backgroundColor, you first need a layer. To create a layer-backed NSView, set the wantsLayer property. The NSView creates a layer and manages it for you. Set the background color of the label to the blue color:

```
view.wantsLayer = true
view.layer?.backgroundColor = NSColor.blueColor().CGColor
```

Now your view is configured. An OS X window has a property named contentView. This view holds the view hierarchy displayed within the window. Add your new view as a subview:

```
self.window.contentView.addSubview(view)
```

The Code and Usage

Listing 6-2 adds an NSView to the window of a basic Cocoa application. Follow Recipe 6-1 to create a new OS X Cocoa application. Then replace the contents of AppDelegate.swift with Listing 6-2. Run the application.

Listing 6-2. AppDelegate.swift

```
import Cocoa

@NSApplicationMain
class AppDelegate: NSObject, NSApplicationDelegate {

    @IBOutlet weak var window: NSWindow!

    func applicationDidFinishLaunching(aNotification: NSNotification) {
        var view = NSView(frame: CGRect(x: 10, y: 10, width: 300, height: 300))

        view.wantsLayer = true
        view.layer?.backgroundColor = NSColor.blueColor().CGColor

        self.window.contentView.addSubview(view)
    }
}
```

You will see the application's window with a blue square in the bottom-left corner.

6-3. Adding a Menu and Menu Items

Problem

You need to add a custom menu to your application.

Solution

Create an NSMenu and then add NSMenuItems classes to create a menu.

How It Works

The items Menu, File, Edit, Format View, Window, and Help, shown in Figure 6-3, are instances of NSMenuItem. Each menu item contains an NSMenu instance. NSMenu has a collection of NSMenuItems that are displayed in the menu. In Figure 6-2, the "Menu" item is opened. The items "About Menu," "Preferences," "Services," "Hide Menu," "Hide Others," "Show All," and "Quit Menu" are menu items.

Figure 6-3. The menu bar and a menu containing NSMenuItems

First, create an NSMenuItem. The NSMenuItem initializer takes three properties:

- title – The title of the menu item to be displayed.

- action – A *Selector* that should be called when the menu item is selected by a user.

- keyEquivalent – A character to be used as the *key* of a Command-Key combination bound to this menu item.

The title parameter is the text that will appear in the menu bar. A menu item that is added to the menu bar does not need to provide an action. It will automatically display its associated menu when the user clicks on the menu. Use nil to indicate there is no related Selector.

Menu items in the main bar do not have key commands associated with them, so pass an empty string for keyEquivalent:

```
var myMenuBarItem =
    NSMenuItem(title: "My Menu", action: nil, keyEquivalent: "")
```

Then create the menu and set it as the submenu for myMenuBarItem:

```
var myMenu = NSMenu(title: "My Menu")
myMenuBarItem.submenu = myMenu
```

Next add an NSMenuItem for each option in the menu. When the menu item is selected or the user presses the Command-Key combination, it will call the Selector you provided.

Create three menu items. On the first item, use a keyEquivalent of "k." This will bind that item to Command-k. Use a selector for a function menuItemSelect: for both the first and second menu item. For the third item, use a selector for a function dontPickMe:. This menu item will be used to demonstrate how menu items can be automatically enabled and disabled based on updates in your application. This saves you the time and effort of manually managing individual menu items:

```
var mi = NSMenuItem(title: "Pick me!",
        action: Selector("menuItemSelected:"), keyEquivalent: "k")
var mi2 = NSMenuItem(title: "Them Pick Me!",
        action: Selector("menuItemSelected:"), keyEquivalent: "")
var mi3 = NSMenuItem(title: "You can't pick me",
        action: Selector("dontPickMe:"), keyEquivalent: "")
```

Add each menu item to myMenu. The order in which they are added is the order they will appear in the menu. Finally, add myMenuBarItem to the main menu. You can access the menu bar through the NSApp class variable mainMenu:

```
myMenu.addItem(mi)
myMenu.addItem(mi2)
myMenu.addItem(mi3)

NSApp.mainMenu??.addItem(myMenuBarItem)
```

Now you need to add the functions to respond when a menu item is selected. Create the functions menuItemSelected: and dontPickMe:. Each takes a single parameter of the type NSMenuItem. This is the menu item that is the source of the event. Since menuItemSelected: can be called by two different menus, print out the title of the menu item:

```
func menuItemSelected( sender : NSMenuItem ) {
    println("Menu item selected: \(sender.title)")
}

func dontPickMe( sender : NSMenuItem ) {
    println("This should not be called")
}
```

When developing applications on OS X, menu options should be enabled and disabled based on the state of the application. If an action is unavailable or does not apply to the current state, it should be disabled. By default, OS X menus are set to check with their target to determine if they should be enabled or disabled. In this recipe, the target is the same object that created the items. Your target must implement the NSUserInterfaceValidations protocol. The method validateUserInterfaceItem: has a single parameter, which is a user-interface item that conforms to the NSValidatedUserInterfaceItem protocol. NSMenuItem instances will call this method on the delegate to determine its state. Your implementation determines if the menu item being validated returns true (enabled) or false (disabled).

Since your delegate will most likely be handling multiple items, the validateMenuItem: method will need to handle each of them. In order to do so, you will need to know which user-interface element called the method. There are a number of ways to detect the source menu item. In this recipe, you will use the Selector assigned to the item. You can also use the tag property of the item. Both approaches can be used with code or the Interface Builder. Now, implement the protocol method validateMenuItem:

```
override func validateMenuItem(menuItem: NSMenuItem) -> Bool {
    if menuItem.action == Selector("dontPickMe:")
    {
        return false
    }
    return true
}
```

In our current scenario, only one menu item should ever be disabled. When a user clicks on "My Menu" in the menu bar, each menu item is validated by calling validateMenuItem:. In this recipe, the menu item titled "You can't pick me" will be disabled and the user cannot select it.

The Code and Usage

To run this code, create a new OS X Cocoa application. Then replace the contents of AppDelegate.swift with Listing 6-3. This code follows the steps provided in the recipe. It creates the menu items, adds them to the menu bar, and implements the delegate method. Run the application.

Listing 6-3. Adding a custom menu

```
import Cocoa

@NSApplicationMain
class AppDelegate: NSObject, NSApplicationDelegate {

    @IBOutlet weak var window: NSWindow!

    func applicationDidFinishLaunching(
    aNotification: NSNotification) {

        var myMenuBarItem = NSMenuItem(title: "My Menu",
            action: nil, keyEquivalent: "")
        var myMenu = NSMenu(title: "My Menu")
```

```
myMenuBarItem.submenu = myMenu

var mi = NSMenuItem(title: "Pick me!",
    action: Selector("menuItemSelected:"), keyEquivalent: "k")
var mi2 = NSMenuItem(title: "Then Pick Me!",
    action: Selector("menuItemSelected:"), keyEquivalent: "")
var mi3 = NSMenuItem(title: "You can't pick me",
    action: Selector("dontPickMe:"), keyEquivalent: "")
myMenu.addItem(mi)
myMenu.addItem(mi2)
myMenu.addItem(mi3)

NSApp.mainMenu??.addItem(myMenuBarItem)
}

func menuItemSelected( sender : NSMenuItem ) {
    println("Menu item selected: \(sender.title)")
}

func dontPickMe( sender : NSMenuItem ) {
    println("This should not be called")
}

override func validateMenuItem(menuItem: NSMenuItem) -> Bool {
    if menuItem.action == Selector("dontPickMe:")
    {
        return false
    }
    return true
}
}
```

The custom menu will be visible. Open the menu labeled "My Menu." The menu item
"Pick Me" item is disabled.

6-4. Adding a Button to a Window
Problem
You need to add a button to your application.

Solution
Create an NSButton, and add it as a subview.

How It Works

On OS X, NSButton comes with a number of options to customize its appearance. It can be a toggle, switch, radio, or normal button. Use the method NSButton.setButtonType: to set the button's type. It takes a single parameter, an NSButtonType. The NSButtonType enumeration defines values for different styles and for the interaction of a button. Table 6-1 describes the different button types and their uses. The MomentaryLightButton and MomentaryPushInButton are most commonly used to trigger user actions.

Table 6-1. *NSButtonType Enumeration*

Value	Description
MomentaryLightButton	This button becomes illuminated when the button is pressed. If the button has a border, it will push in.
PushOnPushOffButton	This button will be highlighted and appear pushed in on the first click. The second click returns the button to its original state.
ToggleButton	A toggle button changes to an alternate image or title when pressed. It maintains this state until it is clicked a second time.
SwitchButton	This button has no border. It is used like a check box and looks like the switch control in iOS.
RadioButton	The radio button works like a switch button, but is grouped with other radio buttons. When buttons are in the same group, only one can be selected at a time.
MomentaryChangeButton	When this button is pressed, an alternate image and title are displayed. When the button is released, they return to the original state.
OnOffButton	The first click of this button highlights it. The second click returns it to normal. The button does not push in.
MomentaryPushInButton	When this button is pressed it highlights. Its image or text remains the same.

Create an NSButton using a CGRect to define its frame:

```
var button = NSButton(frame: CGRect(x: 100, y: 100, width: 80, height: 30))
```

Call setButtonType: using a value from the NSButtonType enumeration. The default style is MomentaryPushInButton:

```
button.setButtonType(NSButtonType.MomentaryLightButton)
```

Set the title property to change the text displayed on the button:

```
button.title = "Click Me!"
```

The NSButton class uses the target/action pattern to indicate when the button has been clicked. Set the target to the object that is going to handle the click event. Then use a Selector to set the action property:

```
button.target = self
button.action = Selector("buttonClicked:")
```

Next, add the button to the window's contentView property:

```
self.window.contentView.addSubview(button)
```

Finally, implement the action method to handle the button click:

```
func buttonClicked( sender : NSButton ) {
    println("Button clicked")
}
```

The Code and Usage

Listing 6-4 shows the recipe code in its entirety. To use the code, follow Recipe 6-1 to create a new OS X Cocoa application. Then replace the contents of AppDelegate.swift with Listing 6-4. Run the application.

Listing 6-4. Adding an NSButton to a window

```
import Cocoa

@NSApplicationMain
class AppDelegate: NSObject, NSApplicationDelegate {

    @IBOutlet weak var window: NSWindow!

    func applicationDidFinishLaunching(aNotification: NSNotification) {
        var button =
            NSButton(frame: CGRect(x: 100, y: 100, width: 80, height: 30))

        button.setButtonType(NSButtonType.MomentaryLightButton)
        button.title = "Click Me!"
        button.target = self
        button.action = Selector("buttonClicked:")

        self.window.contentView.addSubview(button)
    }

    func buttonClicked( sender : NSButton ) {
        println("Button clicked")
    }
}
```

If you click the button, you will see the text "Button clicked" in the output window in Xcode. Try using different values for the button type to see how each looks and behaves.

6-5. Using an NSTextField

Problem

Your application needs the user to input text data.

Solution

Use an NSTextField to capture text input.

How It Works

When you need to collect user input, add an NSTextField to a window or view. The NSTextField is a single-line input control that can deal with strings as well as numeric types such as Float, Double, and Int.

In this recipe, the most common features of the NSTextField are presented, including delegate events. Changes to an NSTextField can be detected by implementing the NSTextFieldDelegate protocol. Add the protocol to the class that will implement the delegate methods:

```
class AppDelegate: NSObject, NSApplicationDelegate, NSTextFieldDelegate
```

Add an IBOutlet for the NSTextField:

```
@IBOutlet var textField : NSTextField!
```

Create a CGRect to define the position and size of the textfield. Then use it to initialize an NSTextField control:

```
var rect = CGRect(x: 10, y: window.frame.height - 20,
                width: 300.0, height: 20.0)
textField = NSTextField(frame: rect)
```

Set the delegate to self so that you can receive events when the field is updated. Finally, add the control to the window's contentView property:

```
textField.delegate = self
self.window.contentView.addSubview(textField)
```

Interacting with the NSTextField is a bit different than its iOS counterpart. NSTextField derives from NSControl. Instead of a single property to get and set the contents of the field, NSControl provides multiple properties for different types. There are properties for using String, Double, Float, and Int. The names of these methods follow the same convention. The convention for the property name is <type name>Value. For example, to set a string value in a text field, use the property stringValue:

```
textField.stringValue = "Default value"
```

You can read the value of the field at any time, but sometimes it is useful to be notified when the user has modified the field. Earlier, you indicated that your class implements the `NSTextFieldDelegate` protocol. The protocol method `controlTextDidChange:` is triggered whenever the value of the field changes. The method receives an `NSNotification` as its only parameter. It is used to determine the source control that raised the notification. This is very useful if you have a user interface with multiple fields. For this recipe, print the value of `textField.stringValue` to the console:

```
override func controlTextDidChange(obj: NSNotification) {
println("Text changed: \(textField.stringValue)")
}
```

When a user types in the field, this method will print out the value of the text field. The change event is raised for each keypress, so you will see a line for each character that you type.

The Code and Usage

To use the code, follow Recipe 6-1 to create a new OS X Cocoa application. Then replace the contents of `AppDelegate.swift` with Listing 6-5. Run the application.

Listing 6-5. Add an NSTextField to a window

```
import Cocoa

@NSApplicationMain
class AppDelegate: NSObject, NSApplicationDelegate, NSTextFieldDelegate {

    @IBOutlet weak var window: NSWindow!
    @IBOutlet var textField : NSTextField!

    func applicationDidFinishLaunching(aNotification: NSNotification) {

        var rect = CGRect(x: 10, y: window.frame.height - 50,
            width: 300.0, height: 20.0)
        textField = NSTextField(frame: rect)
        textField.delegate = self
        self.window.contentView.addSubview(textField)
}

    override func controlTextDidChange(obj: NSNotification) {
            println("Text changed: \(textField.stringValue)")
    }
}
```

An NSTextField is added to the window. Click on it to focus the text field and type a word like "recipe." You will see a line for each keypress in the console. It should look something like this:

```
Text changed: r
Text changed: re
Text changed: rec
Text changed: reci
Text changed: recip
Text changed: recipe
```

6-6. Displaying an Image in a Window

Problem

You want to display an image in your OS X application.

Solution

Use the NSImage and NSImageView classes.

How It Works

The NSImageView class is used to display images in OS X. It is similar to UIImageView on iOS. NSImage can load an image that is contained in your application bundle or accessible on the hard drive. For this recipe, you will use an image in the bundle and assume the file is in the root of the bundle. Add an image to your Xcode project. This recipe uses a photo of a ship. The image can be found in the sample code for this recipe. Add the image to the project by selecting File ➤ Add Files to [ProjectName]. You will need to tell Xcode to copy the image into the project and select the project target. If you do not, the image will not be added to the application bundle and will fail to appear. Figure 6-4 shows a screenshot of the dialog that appears when an image is added to the application.

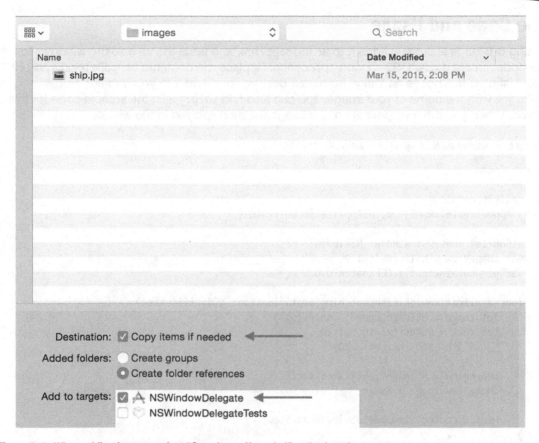

Figure 6-4. When adding images, select "Copy items if needed" and select the target

Initialize the image using NSImage(name:). Give the name of the image using a relative path. Since the image file is in the root of the bundle, use the name of the file without any path ship.jpg. If the image was in the subfolder named "images," the path would be images/ship.jpg.

```
let image = NSImage(named: "ship.jpg")
```

Now create an NSImageView sized 300x200:

```
let rect = CGRect(x: 0, y: 0,
          width: 300, height: 200)
imageView = NSImageView(frame: rect)
```

Set the image property to the image you loaded from the bundle:

```
imageView.image = image
```

Finally add it to the window's contentView property:

```
window.contentView.addSubview(imageView)
```

The image is displayed within the NSImageView.

The Code and Usage

Listing 6-6 loads an image, adds it to an `NSImageView`, and adds the view to the window. To run the code, create a new OS X Cocoa application. Replace the contents of `AppDelegate.swift` with Listing 6-6. Choose an image from your desktop, and add it to your project. Replace `ship.jpg` with the name of your image. You can also find `ship.jpg` in the sample code for this recipe. When you run the application, the image will be displayed in the window.

Listing 6-6. Adding an NSImageView to an NSWindow

```
import Cocoa

@NSApplicationMain
class AppDelegate: NSObject, NSApplicationDelegate {

    @IBOutlet weak var window: NSWindow!
    var imageView : NSImageView!
    var windowBarHeight : CGFloat = 0.0

    func applicationDidFinishLaunching(aNotification: NSNotification) {
        let image = NSImage(named: "ship.jpg")
        let rect = CGRect(x: 10, y: 10,
            width: 300, height: 200)

        imageView = NSImageView(frame: rect)
        imageView.image = image

        window.contentView.addSubview(imageView)
    }
}
```

6-7. Adjusting Contents When a Window Is Resized

Problem

OS X applications have windows that can be resized. You need to adjust the contents of windows when they are resized.

Solution

Implement the `NSWindowDelegate.windowWillResize:toSize:` protocol method.

How It Works

The `NSWindowDelegate.windowWillResize:toSize:` method is called when a window is resized. As the user drags the border of the window, this method is called multiple times as it resizes. When you are implementing your resizing logic, take performance into consideration. If you have complex drawing code, the resulting animation could become choppy as the window resizes.

In this recipe, you will create an OS X application that loads an image and resizes it as the application window is resized. Start by adding the protocol NSWindowDelegate to your AppDelegate:

```
class AppDelegate: NSObject, NSApplicationDelegate, NSWindowDelegate {
```

It is important to understand the relationship between the window and the window bar positioned at the top. The total height of the window includes the window bar. In order to properly position the image, you need to calculate the height of the window bar. If you do not take this into account, the image could extend under the window bar. Figure 6-5 illustrates the height of this window.elements.

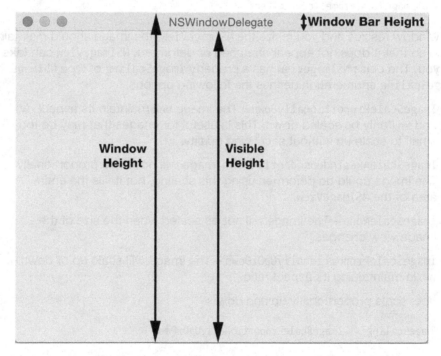

Figure 6-5. Illustration of the window, window bar, and visible area with their respective heights

Add ship.jpg to the project. See Recipe 6-6 for instructions on properly adding the image file to the project. Then define a variable for an NSImageView to display the image and a Float to hold the calculated size of the window's bar:

```
var imageView : NSImageView!
var windowBarHeight : CGFloat = 0.0
```

Calculate the height of the window bar using window.contentRectForFrameRect: The method takes a CGRect parameter. Create the CGRect with a 0,0 origin and the window's width and height. The method returns the height of the visible area in the window. See Figure 6-3 for reference. The difference between the window's height and the visible area is the height of the window bar. Make the calculation, and assign it to the `windowBarHeight` property:

```
let rect = CGRect(x: 0, y: 0,
    width: window.frame.width, height: window.frame.height)

let contentRect = window.contentRectForFrameRect(rect)
windowBarHeight = window.frame.height - contentRect.height
```

Now you can add the image to the window. Create an `NSImageView` with the `contentRect` variable:

```
imageView = NSImageView(frame: contentRect)
```

When the window resizes and you resize the `NSImageView`, the image should maintain its aspect ratio so that it does not appear stretched or deformed. `NSImageView` can take care of this for you. The class `NSImageView` has a property `imageScaling` of type `NSImageScaling`. The `NSImageScaling` enumeration defines the following options:

- `ImageScaleProportionallyDown` – The image will maintain its aspect ratio and will only be scaled down. This is useful for images that may be too small to scale up without sacrificing quality.

- `ImageScaleAxesIndependently` – The image will not scale proportionally. The image could be deformed using this scaling, but it fills the entire area of the `NSImageView`.

- `ImageScaleNone` – The image will not be scaled when the size of the image view changes.

- `ImageScaleProportionallyUpOrDown` – The image will scale up or down while maintaining its aspect ratio.

For this recipe, scale proportionally up and down:

```
imageView.imageScaling = .ImageScaleProportionallyUpOrDown
```

Create an instance of `NSImage` using the name of the image file:

```
imageView.image = NSImage(named: "ship.jpg")
```

> **Note**   If the image does not appear when you run the application, chances are the image was not found within the bundle. In addition, the file name is case sensitive, so `Ship.jpg` will not work if the name of the file is `ship.jpg` with a lowercase "s." Also, check to make sure the image is properly assigned to the target so that it will be copied to the application bundle.

Add the image view to the window:

```
window.contentView.addSubview(imageView)
```

Then assign `self` to `window.delegate`. You can also implement the `NSWindowDelegate` in a separate class, but in this recipe, the same class is used for simplicity:

```
window.delegate = self
```

Using this code, the image will appear in the window. Now you need to add code to adjust the size when the window is resized. Create the delegate method `windowWillResize:toSize:`. This method returns an `NSSize`. Use the `toSize` parameter to change the size of the `NSImage` to match the new window size. Keep the origin of the image at 0,0. The width should be the same width as the window. The height must be adjusted to account for the window bar by taking that value from the window's height:

```
func windowWillResize(sender: NSWindow, toSize frameSize: NSSize) -> NSSize {
    imageView.frame = NSRect(
        x: imageView.frame.origin.x,
        y: imageView.frame.origin.y,
        width: frameSize.width,
        height: frameSize.height - windowBarHeight)

    return frameSize
}
```

The method must return an `NSSize` value. In this situation, return the `frameSize` parameter. The value of this parameter is the height and width of the window after it was resized by the user.

In other situations, you can use this method to limit the way a window is resized. For example, if the window should not exceed 300 points high, you can return an `NSSize` with a maximum height of 300. If you want to prevent a window from resizing entirely, return `sender.frame.size`, which is the current size of the window.

The Code and Usage

Listing 6-7 calculates the proper size of the visible area of a window. Then it loads an image and will resize that image as the window is resized. To use the code, create a new OS X Cocoa application. Replace the contents of `AppDelegate.swift` with the contents of Listing 6-7. Find an image you want to use. Add that image to the project. Then change the following line to the proper file name to match this image:

```
imageView.image = NSImage(named: "ship.jpg")
```

Run the application.

Listing 6-7. Resizing an NSImageView when a window is resized

```
import Cocoa

@NSApplicationMain
class AppDelegate: NSObject, NSApplicationDelegate, NSWindowDelegate {

    @IBOutlet weak var window: NSWindow!
    var imageView : NSImageView!
    var windowBarHeight : CGFloat = 0.0

    func applicationDidFinishLaunching(aNotification: NSNotification) {
        let rect = CGRect(x: 0, y: 0,
            width: window.frame.width, height: window.frame.height)

        let contentRect = window.contentRectForFrameRect(rect)
        windowBarHeight = window.frame.height - contentRect.height

        imageView = NSImageView(frame: contentRect)
        imageView.imageScaling = .ImageScaleProportionallyUpOrDown
        imageView.image = NSImage(named: "ship.jpg")

        window.contentView.addSubview(imageView)
        window.delegate = self
    }

    func windowWillResize(sender: NSWindow, toSize frameSize: NSSize) -> NSSize {
        imageView.frame = NSRect(
            x: imageView.frame.origin.x,
            y: imageView.frame.origin.y,
            width: frameSize.width,
            height: frameSize.height - windowBarHeight)

        return frameSize
    }
}
```

A window should open and the image is displayed. Resize the window, and the image will be proportionally resized to fit the window's new size.

6-8. Implementing an NSTableView

Problem

You want to display data in a multicolumn table.

Solution

Use NSTableView to create a table of data with multiple rows and columns and the ability to sort and reorder columns.

How It Works

In this recipe, you will be using the Interface Builder to get started. The remainder of the recipe focuses on writing Swift code to implement an NSTableView delegate and data source.

Start with a new OS X Cocoa application. Follow Recipe 6-1 to create the new project. The file MainMenu.xib is part of the default template and contains a default window for the application. Open MainMenu.xib and select the window. Then drag an NSTableView from the object library onto the window. The NSTableView should be selected. Set its height and width to the dimensions of the window by clicking and dragging the resizing handles to the outer edge of the window. See Figure 6-6 for reference.

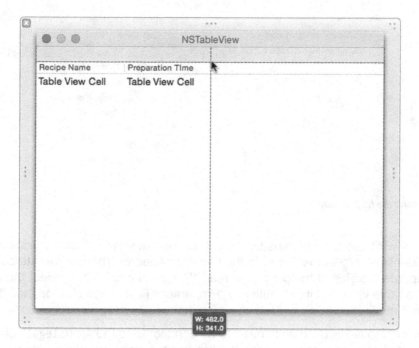

Figure 6-6. Resizing the NSTableView to fit the window

Next, select the table view from the Document Outline. Make sure you actually choose the table view. OS X items are usually embedded in scroll views and other containers. In the Interface Builder, use the left tree navigation to find and expand the NSTableView item (as shown in Figure 6-7).

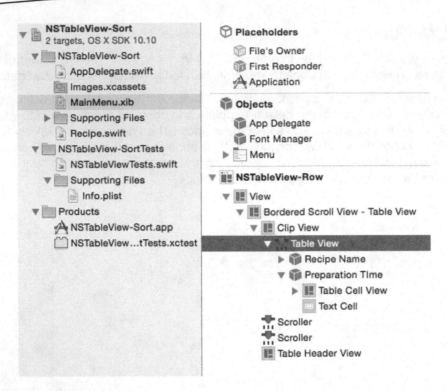

Figure 6-7. Expand the NSTableView

The table view will have two columns by default. In the tree view, select the first column. Change its identifier to "RecipeName" in the Identity inspector. Then, in the Attributes Inspector, update the Title of the column to read "Recipe Name." Next, select the second column in the table view. Set its identifier to "PreparationTime," and change the Title to "Preparation Time."

The dataSource and delegate outlets need to be connected to the AppDelegate class in order to operate properly. In the Interface Builder, use the tree view and locate the Table View. Control-Drag from the table view to the AppDelegate. (See Figure 6-8.) When you release, a pop-up menu appears. Select dataSource. Then repeat the action, but select delegate instead. This connects the table view to the AppDelegate class. NSTableView uses the dataSource outlet to retrieve information and obtain cells to be displayed within the grid.

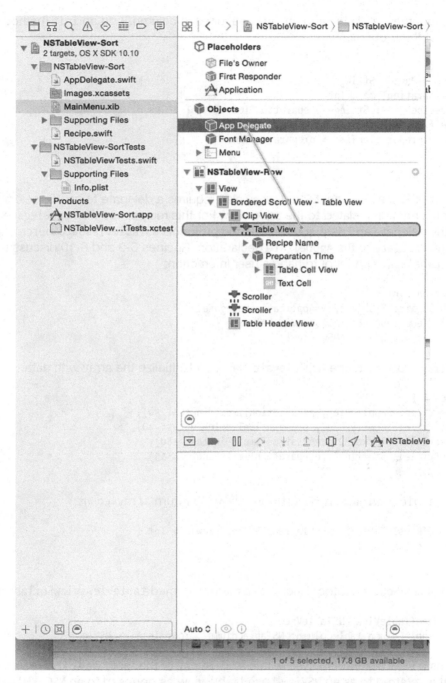

Figure 6-8. *Connect the dataSource and delegate outlets to the AppDelegate*

The data source tells the table view how many rows it contains and provides cells to be displayed inside the table view. This recipe will display a list of recipes in an NSTableView. First, you will need an array containing the recipe data. Implement a class to hold the recipe information. Create a new Swift file named Recipe.swift, and implement a Recipe class.

Add two properties, a `String` and an `Int`, one for each column. Add an `init` method to set the values of the properties:

```
class Recipe {
    var recipeName : String
    var preparationTime : Int
    init(recipeName : String, preparationTime: Int) {
        self.recipeName = recipeName
        self.preparationTime = preparationTime
    }
}
```

In addition to the data source, `NSTableView` also requires a delegate to handle selections and other user actions related to the table view. For this recipe, use the `AppDelegate` class as the delegate and data source. Add the protocols `NSTableViewDataSource` and `NSTableViewDelegate` to the `AppDelgate` declaration. Recipes 6-9 and 6-10 discuss using the `NSTableViewDelegate` protocol to handle user interaction:

```
@NSApplicationMain
class AppDelegate: NSObject, NSApplicationDelegate,
    NSTableViewDataSource, NSTableViewDelegate {
@IBOutlet weak var window: NSWindow!
```

Add an array property to the `AppDelegate` class, and initialize the array with data:

```
var recipes = [
    Recipe(title: "Apple Pie", preparationTimeInMinutes: 30),
    Recipe(title: "Cherry Pie", preparationTimeInMinutes: 30),
    Recipe(title: "Turkey", preparationTimeInMinutes: 180),
    Recipe(title: "Stuffing", preparationTimeInMinutes: 15)
]
```

Implement `tableView:numberOfRowsInTableView:` to return `array.count`:

```
func numberOfRowsInTableView(tableView: NSTableView) -> Int {
    return recipes.count
}
```

`NSTableViewDataSource` protocol includes a method named `tableView:viewForTableColumn:`

```
func tableView(tableView: NSTableView,
    viewForTableColumn tableColumn: NSTableColumn?, row: Int) -> NSView? {
```

This returns a view that is displayed within a single cell of the table view. This recipe uses what is referred to as an `NSView`-based table view as opposed to an `NSCell`-based tableView. `NSCell` is the older style of creating cells for a table view. `NSView`-based table views are now preferred. iOS has had the benefit of starting almost 10 years after OS X and its APIs, and interfaces are a bit more polished. Apple is improving and modernizing OS X to operate similarly to iOS, but be aware that sometimes the OS X AppKit API operates quite differently from its UIKit counterpart.

NSTableView is very efficient in the way it draws itself. Like UITableView, it creates only enough views to draw the visible part of the screen. It then recycles those views and gives the impression during scrolling that movement is happening. Use makeViewWithIdentifier:owner: to retrieve a reusable view:

```
var textField = tableView.makeViewWithIdentifier("TextCell",
    owner: self) as! NSTextField?
```

If a view is not available, the method returns nil. If there is not a view to reuse, create a new NSTextField. This recipe will display two columns, a String and an Int, both using NSTextField. You can use any view-based class as long as it derives from NSView. Set the width of the NSTextField to one half the width of the window. This will make both columns the same width. Alternatively, the widths can be set in the Interface Builder. You must set the width of the cell, but the height of the cell is determined by the height of the row. As a best practice, use a proper height value anyway. NSTableView calculates the actual height. After the new NSTextField is instantiated, you might also want to change the NSTextField's appearance.

Table 6-2 lists some NSTextField properties that affect the appearance and function of the field.

Table 6-2. NSTextField Properties

Property	Usage
editable : Bool	Used to determine if a user can edit the contents of the field. Defaults to true.
bordered : Bool	If false, no border will be drawn around the field. Defaults to true.
bezeled : Bool	If false, no bezel will be drawn around the field. Defaults to true. The bezel style is set using the bezelStyle property.
bezelStyle : NSTextFieldBezelStyle	SquareBezel is a rectangular bezel around the field. RoundedBezel displays a rounded rectangle.
drawsBackground : Bool	Indicates if the cell should draw its own background color. Defaults to true.

Create the NSTextField, and set any properties to change its appearance:

```
if textField == nil {
    textField = NSTextField(frame: CGRect(x: 0,y: 0,
        width: window.frame.width/2, height: 20))
    textField?.identifier = "TextCell"
    textField?.editable = false
    textField?.bordered = false
    textField?.bezeled = false
    textField?.drawsBackground = false
}
```

After the field is created or retrieved, it is time to set the contents of the field. The parameter `tableColumn` is used to determine what information you need to display in the cell. Earlier, you added an identifier to each `NSTableViewColumn`. Compare this identifier to determine the value you need to display in the view. Then assign the respective value to the `NSTextField`:

```
if let column = tableColumn {

    switch column.identifier {
        case "RecipeName":
            textField?.stringValue = recipes[row].recipeName
        case "PreparationTime":
            textField?.stringValue = "\(recipes[row].preparationTime)"
        default:
            break
    }
}
return textField
}
```

This is the bare minimum you need to implement an `NSTableView`. It doesn't do much right now except display information. Recipe 6-9 shows you how you can sort columns in the table, and Recipe 6-10 focuses on handling row-selection events.

The Code and Usage

This recipe implements an `NSTableView` using the `NSTableViewDataSource` protocol. Create a new OS X Cocoa application. Replace the contents of `AppDelegate.swift` with the code in Listing 6-8. Follow the instructions in this recipe to use Interface Builder to create the `NSTableView` and connect the outlets. Then run the application.

Listing 6-8. Implementing the NSTableViewDataSource protocol

```
import Cocoa

@NSApplicationMain
class AppDelegate: NSObject, NSApplicationDelegate, NSTableViewDataSource {
    @IBOutlet weak var window: NSWindow!

    var recipes = [
        Recipe(recipeName: "Apple Pie", preparationTime: 30),
        Recipe(recipeName: "Cherry Pie", preparationTime: 30),
        Recipe(recipeName: "Turkey", preparationTime: 180),
        Recipe(recipeName: "Stuffing", preparationTime: 15)
    ]

    func numberOfRowsInTableView(tableView: NSTableView) -> Int {
        return recipes.count
    }
```

```
func tableView(tableView: NSTableView,
    viewForTableColumn tableColumn: NSTableColumn?, row: Int) -> NSView? {

    var textField = tableView.makeViewWithIdentifier("TextCell",
        owner: self) as! NSTextField?

    if textField == nil {
        textField = NSTextField(frame: CGRect(x: 0,y: 0,
            width: window.frame.width/2, height: 20))
        textField?.identifier = "TextCell"
        textField?.editable = false
        textField?.bordered = false
        textField?.bezeled = false
        textField?.drawsBackground = false
    }

    if let column = tableColumn {

        switch column.identifier {
            case "RecipeName":
                textField?.stringValue = recipes[row].recipeName
            case "PreparationTime":
                textField?.stringValue = "\(recipes[row].preparationTime)"
            default:
                break
        }
    }
    return textField
}
}
```

You should see the data in the NSTableView as shown in Figure 6-9.

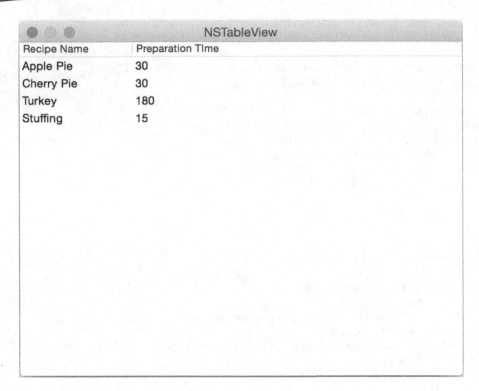

Figure 6-9. The running application

6-9. Sorting an NSTableView

Problem

When a user clicks the header of a table view, you want the data to be sorted.

Solution

Create an `NSSortDescriptor` for each column, and implement the method `tableView:sortDescriptorsDidChange:` method.

How It Works

When a user clicks on a column, you want the data to sort. If a user clicks again, you want the sort to reverse. To sort an `NSTableView`, create an `NSSortDescriptor` for each column and assign it to the `NSTableColumn.sortDescriptorPrototype` property. This recipe builds upon Recipe 6-8, which covers creating an `NSTableView`. Follow Recipe 6-8. Then you will need to make a few adjustments to the code.

NSSortDescriptor relies upon key-value-coding (KVC) to work. In the previous recipe, a class named Recipe is defined. Before implementing sorting, you must modify this class to make it KVC compliant. When Swift is used with Cocoa, there are a lot of bridges that have to be made between the Swift language and the Objective-C runtime. Swift does not support KVC by itself. In order to enable KVC, first change the Recipe class definition to inherit from NSObject:

```
class Recipe : NSObject {
```

The class now inherits the properties and methods associated with NSObject. The class is no longer a pure Swift class. Next, apply the dynamic keyword to the properties that you want to be KVC compliant:

```
dynamic var recipeName : String
dynamic var preparationTime : Int
```

In the Objective-C runtime, methods and properties are called using dynamic dispatch. In Swift, methods and properties are statically generated at compile time. A static definition and dynamic dispatch cannot be used together, which is a problem because KVC depends on dynamic dispatch. Inheriting from NSObject allows the class to run in the Objective-C runtime. Marking the properties with dynamic indicates to the compiler that these properties or methods should be called using dynamic dispatch, thus enabling KVC for the Swift class.

The next step is to create an IBOutlet in AppDelegate. This outlet is linked to the NSTableView and is used to set the sort descriptors on the table's columns.

Add the outlet to AppDelegate:

```
@IBOutlet weak var tableView : NSTableView!
```

Open MainMenu.xib, and expand the tree view until the Table View element is visible. Then Control-click on the App Delegate item, drag to the Table View, and release (as shown in Figure 6-10).

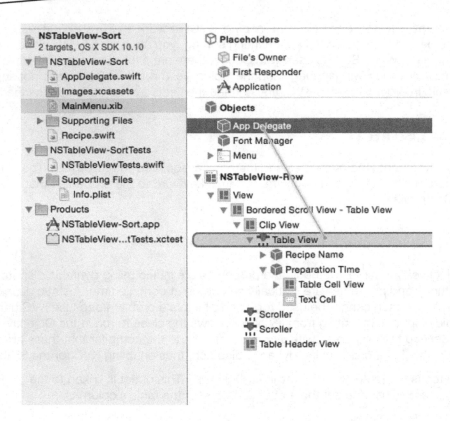

Figure 6-10. Connect the Table View outlet

In the pop-up menu, select the `tableView` outlet. The table view is now attached to the `IBOutlet` in `AppDelegate`.

The code to set up the sort descriptors will be placed in the method `applicationDidFinishLaunching:` of the `AppDelegate` class in the `AppDelegate.swift` file. Create this method if it does not exist:

```
func applicationDidFinishLaunching(aNotification: NSNotification) {
```

You must retrieve a reference to the `NSTableViewColumns` in the table view. Use `NSTableView.tableColumnWithIdentifier` to do so. The identifier is the identifier you added to the column in Interface Builder:

```
var recipeNameColumn = tableView.tableColumnWithIdentifier("RecipeName")
var preparationTimeColumn =
    tableView.tableColumnWithIdentifier("PreparationTime")
```

The `Recipe.recipeName` property is a `String`, so you can sort using a standard comparison. Create a new `NSSortDescriptor`, and assign it to `recipeNameColumn.sortDescriptorPrototype`. The `NSSortDescriptor` initializer you will use has three parameters:

- ▪ key – The name of the property on the data source to be accessed via Key Value Coding.

- ▪ ascending – A Boolean indicating if the sort should default to ascending (`true`) or descending (`false`).

- ▪ selector – A selector to use for comparison. This selector must indicate a method on the target property. Use the `String.compare:` method for this recipe.

```
recipeNameColumn?.sortDescriptorPrototype =
    NSSortDescriptor(key: "recipeName",
    ascending: true, selector: Selector("compare:"))
```

The `preparationTime` property of `Recipe` is an `Int`. The `Int` type does not have methods like the `String` class. Instead of using the same method as before, you can supply a custom `NSComparator`. This method can be used for `String` types as well. Create an `NSSortDescriptor` with `init(key:ascending:comparator:)`. The first two parameters are the same as before. The third is a closure that returns an `NSComparator`. The closure takes two parameters to compare, and both are type `AnyObject`. Since you know the two parameters will be integers, use the `integerValue` property in the comparison. The closure returns the proper `NSComparisonResult` value based on the comparison:

```
preparationTimeColumn?.sortDescriptorPrototype =
NSSortDescriptor(key: "preparationTime", ascending: true) {
    (a,b) -> NSComparisonResult in
        if a.integerValue > b.integerValue {
            return NSComparisonResult.OrderedDescending
        }
        if a.integerValue < b.integerValue {
            return NSComparisonResult.OrderedAscending
        }
        return NSComparisonResult.OrderedSame
}
```

When a user clicks on the header of a column, the method `tableView:sortDescriptorsDidChange:` is called on the delegate. Using this method, implement your sorting logic using the `NSTableView.sortDescriptors`. That property will contain the updated descriptors.

In this recipe, the data source is a Swift array. You could use the sort method, however, `NSMutableArray` has a more convenient function for this situation: `NSMutableArray.sortUsingDescriptors`. As the name suggests, this method will sort the array using the sort descriptors from the table view.

Create an `NSMutableArray` using the `recipes` array, sort the array with the descriptors, and then convert the array back to a Swift array of Recipe objects. Call `tableView.reloadData()` to refresh the table view. The rows will be sorted, and the column header will update itself to indicate the direction of the sort.

```
func tableView(tableView: NSTableView, sortDescriptorsDidChange oldDescriptors:
[AnyObject]) {
    var array = NSMutableArray(array: recipes)

    array.sortUsingDescriptors(tableView.sortDescriptors)

    recipes = array as AnyObject as! [Recipe]
        tableView.reloadData()
}
```

The Code and Usage

Listing 6-9 contains the complete code for this recipe. To run the application, first follow the instructions in Recipe 6-8. Then follow the instructions in this recipe to connect the `tableView` outlet and add the remaining code. Your `AppDelegate.swift` file should match Listing 6-8. Run the application.

Listing 6-9. Sorting an NSTableView by column

```
import Cocoa

@NSApplicationMain
class AppDelegate: NSObject, NSApplicationDelegate,
    NSTableViewDataSource, NSTableViewDelegate {
    @IBOutlet weak var window: NSWindow!
    @IBOutlet weak var tableView : NSTableView!

    var recipes = [
        Recipe(recipeName: "Apple Pie", preparationTime: 30),
        Recipe(recipeName: "Cherry Pie", preparationTime: 30),
        Recipe(recipeName: "Turkey", preparationTime: 180),
        Recipe(recipeName: "Stuffing", preparationTime: 15)
    ]

    func applicationDidFinishLaunching(aNotification: NSNotification) {
        var recipeNameColumn =
            tableView.tableColumnWithIdentifier("RecipeName")
        var preparationTimeColumn =
            tableView.tableColumnWithIdentifier("PreparationTime")

        recipeNameColumn?.sortDescriptorPrototype =
            NSSortDescriptor(key: "recipeName",
                ascending: true, selector: Selector("compare:"))
```

```
    preparationTimeColumn?.sortDescriptorPrototype =
        NSSortDescriptor(key: "preparationTime", ascending: true) {
        (a,b) -> NSComparisonResult in

        if a.integerValue > b.integerValue {
            return NSComparisonResult.OrderedDescending
        }
        if a.integerValue < b.integerValue {
            return NSComparisonResult.OrderedAscending
        }
        return NSComparisonResult.OrderedSame
    }
}

func numberOfRowsInTableView(tableView: NSTableView) -> Int {
    return recipes.count
}

func tableView(tableView: NSTableView,
    viewForTableColumn tableColumn: NSTableColumn?, row: Int) -> NSView? {

    var textField =
        tableView.makeViewWithIdentifier("TextCell", owner: self) as! NSTextField?

    if textField == nil {
        textField = NSTextField(frame: CGRect(x: 0,y: 0,
            width: window.frame.width/2, height: 20))
        textField?.identifier = "TextCell"
        textField?.editable = false
        textField?.bordered = false
        textField?.bezeled = false
        textField?.drawsBackground = false
    }

    if let column = tableColumn {

        switch column.identifier {
            case "RecipeName":
                textField?.stringValue = recipes[row].recipeName
            case "PreparationTime":
                textField?.stringValue = "\(recipes[row].preparationTime)"
            default:
                break
        }
    }
    return textField
}
```

```
func tableView(tableView: NSTableView,
    sortDescriptorsDidChange oldDescriptors: [AnyObject]) {
    var array = NSMutableArray(array: recipes)

    array.sortUsingDescriptors(tableView.sortDescriptors)

    recipes = array as AnyObject as! [Recipe]
    tableView.reloadData()
  }
}
```

Click on the "Recipe Name" header or the "Preparation Time" header. The rows will sort, and the column header will indicate the direction of the sort. The application should look like the screen depicted in Figure 6-11.

Recipe Name	∧	Preparation TIme
Apple Pie		30
Cherry Pie		30
Stuffing		15
Turkey		180

Figure 6-11. The Recipe Name column sorted in ascending order

6-10. Handling the Selection of an NSTableView Row

Problem

You want to know when a row is selected in an NSTableView.

Solution

Implement the delegate method tableViewSelectionDidChange:.

How It Works

The tableViewSelectionDidChange: delegate method is called when the selected row changes. The method has one parameter, an NSNotification. The NSNotification.object property contains the object that initiated the notification, typically the NSTableView. This recipe builds on both Recipes 6-7 and 6-8. Please follow the instructions in those recipes first. Then return to this recipe to add the ability to handle selections.

Open the AppDelegate.swift file and, at the bottom, add the delegate method tableViewSelectionDidChange:.

```
func tableViewSelectionDidChange(notification: NSNotification) {
```

NSTableView has a property selectedRow that returns the index of the selected row. Note that this method is called when the selection is cleared as well. When no rows are selected, the selectedRow property is set to -1. Check to see if a row is selected by checking if the index is zero or greater. If it is, a row is selected. Get the recipe corresponding to the selected row. Then output its name to the console.

```
        if tableView.selectedRow >= 0 {
            var recipe = recipes[tableView.selectedRow]

            println("Recipe: \(recipe.recipeName)")
        }
    }
}
```

The Code and Usage

This recipe is incremental to Recipes 6-8 and 6-9. Implement those recipes first. Then open the AppDelegate.swift file and add the function in Listing 6-10 to AppDelegate. Run the application.

Listing 6-10. Handling a row selection for an NSTableView

```
func tableViewSelectionDidChange(notification: NSNotification) {

    if tableView.selectedRow >= 0 {
        var recipe = recipes[tableView.selectedRow]

        println("Recipe: \(recipe.recipeName)")
    }
}
```

Select a row in the table. The name of the recipe in the selected row will be printed to the console. You should see a string such as:

```
Recipe: Cherry Pie
```

Chapter 7

Files and Directories

The recipes in this chapter focus on management of files and directories. The recipes can be used on both iOS and OS X. The main difference you will find between the two is that the file system on iOS is limited to the "sandbox."

The sandbox is a security and stability structure that governs and limits the access your application has to the file system and other iOS resources. The sandbox restricts file access of the application to its bundle and a set of specific directories. Applications running in iOS cannot reach outside of the sandbox, which prevents them from damaging the system and other applications. Applications can access data from other applications such as Photos, but only by using purpose-built APIs that manage access to these resources.

The following recipes are covered in this chapter:

- Locating Specialized Directories
- Checking for the Existence of a File or Directory
- Copying Files
- Creating Directories
- Deleting Files and Directories
- Getting a List of Files from a Path
- Archiving Objects to Files
- Archiving Custom Classes to Files

7-1. Locating Specialized Directories

Problem

Your application needs a place to store data created by users and your application.

Solution

Use the `NSFileManager.URLsForDirectory:inDomains:` method.

How It Works

On both iOS and OS X, there are directories intended to store particular types of data. Examples from OS X are the Photos, Music, Documents, Library, and Desktop folders. Neither OS X nor iOS place any restrictions on the type of data that can be saved in a folder. Photos and Music are for media. The Documents and Desktop folders are intended for users' personally created files. On iOS, all interaction with the file system is governed by your application, so you should take care to follow the conventions. The Documents and Library folders and the application bundle folders are the only items your application can access. The most commonly used folder applications, along with a description of the intended usage, are listed here:

- Library: The library directory is used by your application to store local data it might create, such as locally cached resources and user preferences. All files except those in the Caches folder are backed up.

- Documents: Your application should store all user-generated content in this directory. This storage is permanent and is backed up.

- Caches: A folder within the Library directory where your application should store cached files and other data that can be re-created or redownloaded later. This is transient storage. The files in this folder are not guaranteed to be persistent. The contents are not backed up, and the system might even empty the Caches folder to reclaim disk space. As a result, never assume that a file exists in this folder. Code defensively, and check for the file's existence first. The system will attempt to reclaim space or remove files only when your application is either not loaded or in a suspended state.

- Application Support: Store persistent data that your application creates or downloads in this folder. It is permanent storage, is backed up, and will not be removed for disk space by the system. A situation where you might store data here is an application that downloads video files or data required by the application to function. You want to store them until a user asks for them to be deleted. And you do not want to download them again if they are erased.

It is best practice to check for the existence of these folders before first attempting to access them. They are not guaranteed to exist. You can learn how to test for a folder's existence in Recipe 7-2. If a directory does not exist, create the directory yourself. Creating directories is covered in Recipe 7-4.

Before accessing any files, you will need to look up the path of one of these folders. To retrieve the path of these directories, use the NSFileManager class. Create a new instance of NSFileManager. There is a singleton file manager (NSFileManager.defaultManager()), but it is better to create a new instance for your own use. Call URLsForDirectory:inDomains: to retrieve the path to the desired folder. The method takes two parameters. The first is an NSSearchParthDirectory value. Table 7-1 lists the corresponding values for the folders discussed earlier and a few other common directories.

Table 7-1. Common NSSearchPathDirectory Values

Folder	NSSearchPathDirectory
Application Bundle	ApplicationDirectory
Library	LibraryDirectory
Documents	DocumentDirectory
Caches	CachesDirectory
Application Support	ApplicationSupportDirectory
Desktop (OS X)	DesktopDirectory
User Directory (OS X)	UserDirectory

The second parameter indicates where the system searches for the selected type of directories. NSSearchPathDomainMask has five options:

- UserDomainMask: The user's home directory

- LocalDomainMask: The local machine

- NetworkDomainMask: A network location

- SystemDomainMask: An Apple-specific mask

- AllDomainsMask: Includes all of the above, and it will include all future values

Most of the time, you will be using UserDomainMask. On OS X, it indicates to the system to locate the folders within a user's home directory. On iOS, it will return the path to the Documents directory. This directory will be inside the application's sandbox. The function returns an array of URLs. The path to the folder is the first element of the array. There are remote possibilities where the system could return multiple items, but when using UserDomainMask, you can take it for granted that the array will contain only one item:

```
let directories =
    NSSearchPathForDirectoriesInDomains(NSSearchPathDirectory.DocumentDirectory,
    NSSearchPathDomainMask.AllDomainsMask, true) as? [String]
```

The Code and Usage

Listing 7-1 can be run within an OS X application or a Playground. To run it as an OS X application, create a new Command Line Application in Xcode. Do this by selecting File ➤ New Project from the menu. In the next dialog, select Applications under OS X and then select Command Line Tool. Click Next, and save your project. Replace the contents of the file main.swift with Listing 7-1. Run the application.

Listing 7-1. Get the path to a user's Documents directory

```
import Foundation

let directories =
    NSSearchPathForDirectoriesInDomains(NSSearchPathDirectory.DocumentDirectory,
    NSSearchPathDomainMask.AllDomainsMask, true) as? [String]

println(directories?[0])
```

In the console, you will see a string with the file path. It should look similar to this:

```
Optional("/Users/mrogers/Documents")
```

The code can also run in a Playground, which will yield a different file path. Create a new iOS Playground, and replace the contents with Listing 7-1. In the console output and the results sidebar, you will see the path of the Documents directory. This directory is contained within a sandbox. The path will look something like this:

```
/var/folders/5m/8_xm31b51v91cffgml0s8mkc0000gp/T/com.apple.dt.Xcode.pg/containers/com.apple.
dt.playground.stub.iOS_Simulator.Listing7-1-1D78B85B-685B-44A8-A55A-343BE43FF97D/Documents
```

7-2. Checking for the Existence of a File or Directory

Problem

You need to find out if a file or directory exists on disk.

Solution

Use the NSFileManager.fileExistsAtPath: to check for a file and NSFileManager.
fileExistsAtPath:isDirectory: to check for directories.

How It Works

NSFilemanager.fileExistsAtPath: takes a string value of the path to examine. The method returns true if the file exists or false if it does not:

```
NSFileManager().fileExistsAtPath("/tmp/FindMe.txt")
```

On OS X, you can use the shortcut "~" to refer to the current user's home folder. If you do, you must expand the path using stringByExpandingTildeInPath:

```
let filepath = "~/FindMe.txt".stringByExpandingTildeInPath
NSFileManager().fileExistsAtPath(filepath)
```

To check if a directory exists, use NSFileManager().fileExistsAtPath:isDirectory:. The first parameter is the same. The second parameter is a Boolean pointer that is set by the method. The result indicates not only if the path exists, but also whether it is a directory. However, the parameter is not a Swift Boolean, it is a pointer to an Objective-C Boolean.

Define the directory path to be a directory named "recipes" in your home directory:

```
let directoryPath = "~/recipes".stringByDeletingPathExtension
```

Define the variable as an ObjCBool, and initialize it to true:

```
var isDir : ObjCBool = true
```

Now make the call to fileExistsAtPath:isDirectory:, and for the isDirectory parameter, use the & to pass the pointer:

```
if NSFileManager().fileExistsAtPath(filepath, isDirectory: &isDir){
    println("Directory exists at path \(filepath)")
} else {
    println("Directory does not exist")
}
```

The Code and Usage

Listing 7-2 checks for a file at a path and prints the results. Then it checks for a directory and prints the results. To run the code, create a new OS X Command Line Application and replace the contents of main.swift with Listing 7-2. Run the application.

Listing 7-2. Checking to see if a file exists at a file path

```
import Foundation

let filepath = "~/FindMe.txt".stringByExpandingTildeInPath

// Check for a file
if NSFileManager().fileExistsAtPath(filepath) {
    println("File exists at path \(filepath)")
} else {
    println("File does not exist")
}
```

```
// Check for a directory
let directoryPath = "~/recipes".stringByExpandingTildeInPath
var isDir : ObjCBool = true

if NSFileManager().fileExistsAtPath(directoryPath, isDirectory: &isDir){
    println("Directory exists at path \(directoryPath)")
} else {
    println("Directory does not exist")
}
```

As long as your home directory does not contain a file named FindMe.txt, you should see the following message:

```
File does not exist
```

If your home directory does not contain a directory named recipes, you will see this message:

```
Directory does not exist
```

Create a file in your home directory, and name it FindMe.txt. Run the application a second time. In the console output, you should see a message like this:

```
File exists at path /Users/mrogers/FindMe.txt
Directory does not exist
```

Create a directory named recipes in your home directory and run the application again. You will see the following output:

```
File exists at path /Users/mrogers/FindMe.txt
Directory exists at path /Users/mrogers/recipes
```

7-3. Copying Files

Problem

You need to copy a file in your application.

Solution

Use NSFileManager.copyItemAtURL:toURL:error: or copyItemAtPath:copyItemAtPath:error:.

How It Works

NSFileManager provides all the functionality you need to manipulate and retrieve information about the file system. Both copyItemAtUR:srcPath:dstPath:error: and copyItemAtPath:src Path:dstPath:error: have equivalent functionality but use different file references. Both take three parameters:

- srcPath : String or srcURL : NSURL: The path or URL of the file to be copied.

- dstPath : String or dstURL : NSURL: The path or URL of the destination. This should contain the entire path or a URL including the file name.

- error : NSErrorPointer: A pointer to an error object. If an error occurs, the pointer will be set to an actual error object containing the error information.

The method returns true if the file was successfully copied. It returns false if an error occurred. A common error is attempting to copy to a file path that already exists. If a file with the same name exists in the path or URL, the method will return an error.

The Code and Usage

Create a new OS X command-line application in Xcode. Replace the contents of main.swift with Listing 7-3. This code will get the path to your Documents directory and Desktop directory. It will print those paths to the console. Then it will attempt to copy a file (CopyMe.txt) from your Documents directory to your Desktop. If you do not have a file named CopyMe.txt in your Documents folder, the copy operation will fail and an error will be displayed. First, make sure you do not have a file named CopyMe.txt in your Documents directory. Then run the application.

Listing 7-3. Copying a file from the Documents directory to the Desktop

```
import Foundation

let documentDirs = NSSearchPathForDirectoriesInDomains(NSSearchPathDirectory.
DocumentDirectory,
    NSSearchPathDomainMask.AllDomainsMask, true) as? [String]

let desktopDirs = NSSearchPathForDirectoriesInDomains(NSSearchPathDirectory.
DesktopDirectory,
    NSSearchPathDomainMask.AllDomainsMask, true) as? [String]

if documentDirs?.count > 0 && desktopDirs?.count > 0
{
    println("Documents directory is \(documentDirs![0])")
    println("Desktop directory is \(desktopDirs![0])")

    let sourceFile = documentDirs![0].stringByAppendingPathComponent("CopyMe.txt")
    let destinationFile = desktopDirs![0].stringByAppendingPathComponent("CopyMe.txt")
```

```
    let fileManager = NSFileManager()

    var error: NSError?

    if fileManager.copyItemAtPath(sourceFile, toPath: destinationFile, error: &error) {
        println("Successfully copied \(sourceFile) to \(destinationFile).")
    }else {
        println("ERROR: \(error?.localizedDescription)")
    }
}
else
{
    println("System failed to return a valid path for the Documents or Desktop folders.")
}
```

In the console, you should see similar output to this:

```
Documents directory is /Users/mrogers/Documents
Desktop directory is /Users/mrogers/Desktop
ERROR: Optional("The file "CopyMe.txt" couldn't be opened because there is no such file.")
Program ended with exit code: 0
```

The file copy failed, and the details were returned in the NSError pointer, error. Now create a file named CopyMe.txt in your Documents folder. Then run the application again. It should successfully copy the file to your desktop. In the console output, you should see similar output to this:

```
Documents directory is /Users/mrogers/Documents
Desktop directory is /Users/mrogers/Desktop
Successfully copied /Users/mrogers/Documents/CopyMe.txt to /Users/mrogers/Desktop/CopyMe.txt.
Program ended with exit code: 0
```

Run the application a third time. This time, you will see another error because the destination file CopyMe.txt now exists on your Desktop.

7-4. Creating Directories

Problem

You need to create folders on disk to organize files.

Solution

Use NSFileManager.createDirectoryAtPath:withIntermediateDirectories:attributes:error: to create directories.

How It Works

To start, create an NSFileManager instance. Then get the path to a directory, such as the Documents directory. Call createDirectoryAtPath:withIntermediateDirectories:attributes: error: to create the directory. The method has four parameters:

- path: The full path to the directory to be created, including the new directory's name.

- withIntermediateDirectories: If true, this will create any directories specified in the path that do not yet exist. For example, if you used the path /tmp/data/downloads/pdfs and the /tmp directory was empty, the file manager will create each folder that does not exist until it gets to the end of the path. In this example, three directories will be created: data, downloads, and pdfs.

- attributes: You can specify file attributes that the system will set on the directory to be created. Attributes that can be changed include the date and time a folder was created or modified. To keep this recipe focused on creating directories, we will not use attributes.

- error: A pointer to an NSError object. If an error occurs, this pointer will point to an object containing the information about the error.

> **Note** When using withIntermediateDirectories: true and attempting to create folders that already exist, no errors will be returned. If the parameter is set to false and you attempt to create an existing folder, an error will be returned.

The Code and Usage

Create a new OS X Command Line Application. Replace the contents of main.swift with the code from Listing 7-4. Run the application.

Listing 7-4. Creating a directory

```
import Foundation

let documentDirs = NSSearchPathForDirectoriesInDomains(NSSearchPathDirectory.
DocumentDirectory,
    NSSearchPathDomainMask.AllDomainsMask, true) as? [String]

if documentDirs?.count > 0
{
    println("Documents directory is \(documentDirs![0])")

    let newDirectoryPath = documentDirs![0].stringByAppendingPathComponent("Swift/Recipes")
```

```
    let fileManager = NSFileManager()

    var error: NSError?

    if fileManager.createDirectoryAtPath(newDirectoryPath,
        withIntermediateDirectories: true, attributes: nil, error: &error) {
        println("Successfully created \(newDirectoryPath).")
    }else {
        println("ERROR: \(error?.localizedDescription)")
    }
}
else
{
    println("System failed to return a valid path for the Documents or Desktop folders.")
}
```

The folder creation should succeed, and you should see output in the console similar to this:

```
Documents directory is /Users/mrogers/Documents
Successfully created /Users/mrogers/Documents/Swift/Recipes.
Program ended with exit code: 0
```

Change the parameter withIntermediateDirectories to false. Then run the application again. An error will be returned, and your console should look similar to this:

```
Documents directory is /Users/mrogers/Documents
ERROR: Optional("The file "Recipes" couldn't be saved in the folder "Swift" because a file
with the same name already exists.")
```

7-5. Deleting Files and Directories

Problem

You need to remove a file or directory from disk.

Solution

Use NSFileManager.removeItemAtPath:error: or NSFileManager.removeItemAtURL:error:.

How It Works

NSFileManager.removeItemAtPath:error: has two parameters:

- path: This is the full path to the file or directory to be removed.

- error: A pointer to an error object. If an error occurs, an error object will be assigned to the pointer.

The method returns `true` if the file was successfully removed. If an error occurred, the error object will be populated with an `NSError` instance with details on the error. The process is the same for `removeItemAtURL:error:` except the first parameter is an `NSURL`:

```
let documentDirs = NSSearchPathForDirectoriesInDomains(NSSearchPathDirectory.
DocumentDirectory,
    NSSearchPathDomainMask.AllDomainsMask, true) as? [String]
let fileToDelete = documentDirs![0].stringByAppendingPathComponent("DeleteMe.txt")
let fileManager = NSFileManager()
var error: NSError?

fileManager.removeItemAtPath(fileToDelete, error: &error)
```

> **Caution**   The `removeItemAtPath:error:` and `removeItemAtURL:error:` methods both permanently remove the file. These methods can be used on both iOS and OS X. On OS X, these methods do not move the file to the trash; the file will be removed immediately.

If your application is running on OS X, you have the option of sending the file to the trash. If the file being removed is a user-created file, this is a safer option and allows the user to retrieve the file even after deletion. The parameters of method `trashItemAtURL:resulting ItemURL:error:` are as follows:

- url: An NSURL of the file to be moved to the trash.

- resultingItemURL: An optional NSURL pointer. The destination file name will be returned in this variable. If required to avoid file-name collisions, the file might be renamed when it is moved to the trash. The path to the renamed file is returned in this parameter. Pass `nil` if you would like to ignore the output.

- error: An optional pointer to an NSError object.

To convert a file path string to an NSURL, use `NSURL.fileURLWithPath`:

```
let urlPath = NSURL(fileURLWithPath: fileToDelete)

if fileManager.trashItemAtURL(urlPath!, resultingItemURL: &resultingURL, error: &error){
    println("Successfully moved \(fileToDelete) to the trash: \(resultingURL)")
}else {
    println("ERROR: \(error?.localizedDescription)")
}
```

The Code and Usage

Listing 7-5 creates a file path to a file to be deleted. Then it attempts to delete that file. The file is located in the user's `Documents` folder. Create a text file named `DeleteMe.txt` in your Documents directory. Then create a new OS X Command Line Application. Replace the contents of the file `main.swift` with Listing 7-5. Run the application.

Listing 7-5. Deleting a file or directory

```
import Foundation

let documentDirs = NSSearchPathForDirectoriesInDomains(NSSearchPathDirectory.DocumentDirectory,
    NSSearchPathDomainMask.AllDomainsMask, true) as? [String]
let fileToDelete = documentDirs![0].stringByAppendingPathComponent("DeleteMe.txt")
let fileManager = NSFileManager()
var error: NSError?

if fileManager.removeItemAtPath(fileToDelete, error: &error) {
    println("Successfully removed \(fileToDelete).")
}else {
    println("ERROR: \(error?.localizedDescription)")
}
```

You should see a success message indicating the file was removed:

```
Successfully removed /Users/mrogers/Documents/DeleteMe.txt.
```

Listing 7-6 is a similar program to Recipe 7-4, but instead of deleting the file, it will move the file to the trash. It will attempt to move a file named DeleteMe.txt in the current user's Documents folder to the trash. To run the following code, create a new OS X Command Line Application and copy Listing 7-6 into the main.swift file. Create a file named DeleteMe.txt in the Documents directory. Run the application.

Listing 7-6. Moving a file or directory to the trash

```
var resultingURL : NSURL?

let fileToTrash = documentDirs![0].stringByAppendingPathComponent("TrashMe.txt")
let urlPath = NSURL(fileURLWithPath: fileToTrash)

if fileManager.trashItemAtURL(urlPath!, resultingItemURL: &resultingURL, error: &error){
    println("Successfully moved \(fileToTrash) to the trash: \(resultingURL)")
} else {
    println("ERROR: \(error?.localizedDescription)")
}
```

In the output, you should see a success message similar to this:

```
Successfully moved /Users/mrogers/Documents/DeleteMe.txt to the trash: Optional(file:
///Users/mrogers/.Trash/TrashMe%2015-07-13-700.txt)
```

If you run the application a second time, without replacing a file named TrashMe.txt in the Documents folder, you will get an error indicating the file could not be removed or moved to the trash:

```
ERROR: Optional("The file "TrashMe.txt" doesn't exist.")
```

7-6. Getting a List of Files from a Path

Problem

You need to get a list of files in a directory.

Solution

Use NSFileManager.contentsOfDirectoryAtPath:error: to get an array of paths for each file and directory in the path. NSFileManager.subPathsOfDirectoryAtPath:error: will return files and paths from the specified path as well as any files contained in subdirectories.

How It Works

Let's get a list of the files in your home directory. First, create an instance of NSFileManager. Then call contentsOfDirectoryAtPath:error: with the shortcut to your home directory. If no files are found, it returns an empty array. If an error occurs, the method returns nil and the error variable will be filled with an NSError object describing the issue. If the call is successful and retrieves a list of files, an array of type [AnyObject]? is returned. If the path provided is not a directory, an error will be returned:

```
let fileManager = NSFileManager()
let path = "~/Documents/Fonts".stringByExpandingTildeInPath
var error : NSError?
let contents = fileManager.contentsOfDirectoryAtPath(path, error: &error)
```

What if you want to get more than a listing of a single directory and want to recursively traverse subdirectories? You use NSFileManager().subpathsOfDirectoryAtPath:error:. This method works similarly to contentsOfDirectoryAtPath: but will recursively traverse the file system and subdirectories, including symbolic links.

> **Note**   Traversing a deep directory is resource intensive, and the call will block the thread until it completes its traversal. You should use this typically on directory structures you know are limited in depth.

I picked a folder in my Documents folder that had only two subfolders. I suggest you do the same when you try to use subpathsOfDirectoryAtPath:error:.

The Code and Usage

Listing 7-7 outputs the list of files that are in your home directory. Don't forget that if you use the tilde (~) to start your path, you must expand the path before attempting to use it. Create a new OS X Command Line Application, and name it `ListFiles`. Copy the contents of Listing 7-7 into the `main.swift` file, replacing its contents. Run the application.

Listing 7-7.   List the files and directories in a directory path

```
import Foundation

let fileManager = NSFileManager()
let path = "~".stringByExpandingTildeInPath
var error : NSError?
let contents = fileManager.contentsOfDirectoryAtPath(path, error: &error)

if let files = contents {
    for f in files as! [String] {
        println("File: \(f)")
    }
} else {
    println("Error: \(error?.localizedDescription)")
}
```

You should see a listing of the files in your home directory. Here is an excerpt of the output from a user's home directory:

```
File: .android
File: .bash_history
File: .bash_profile
File: .CFUserTextEncoding
File: .config
File: .cups
...
File: Zapp Attack-back.jpg
File: Zapp Attack.jpg
```

Listing 7-8 traverses a directory recursively until it reaches the deepest points. This should be used on folders with a known depth, because recursion can be resource intensive. To test the code, assume you have a folder with only two subdirectories and a dozen files. You should change the path string "~/Documents/Fonts" to reference a similar directory on your computer. To run the code, create a new OS X Command Line Application and name it `DeepListFiles`. Replace the contents of `main.swift` with Listing 7-8. Don't forget to change "~/Documents/Fonts" to a directory on your computer that isn't too large or deep.

Listing 7-8. Recursively list the files and directories in a directory path and all subdirectories

```
import Foundation

let fileManager = NSFileManager()
let path = "~/Documents/Fonts".stringByExpandingTildeInPath
var error : NSError?

let deepContents = fileManager.subpathsOfDirectoryAtPath(path, error: &error)
if let files = deepContents {
    for f in files as! [String] {
        println("File: \(f)")
    }
} else {
    println("Error: \(error?.localizedDescription)")
}
```

Compare your output with the following output. Your output will be a different list of files that should correspond to the directory path you indicated in the path variable:

```
File: Proxima nova
File: Proxima nova/ProximaNova Bold.otf
File: Proxima nova/ProximaNova BoldIt.otf
...
File: Reklame
File: Reklame/ReklameScript-Regular_DEMO.otf
```

7-7. Archiving Objects to Files

Problem

You have an object that you would like to persist to disk.

Solution

Use NSKeyedArchiver to serialize the object to a file. Use NSKeyedUnarchiver to load the object into memory from a file.

How It Works

Archiving takes a code object in memory and saves it to disk. Archiving serializes primitive types as well as types such as arrays, dictionaries, and strings. For other types, such as your own classes, you can implement the protocol NSCoder on your own classes. This is discussed in Recipe 7-8. NSKeyedArchiver takes an object, serializes it to an NSData object and then saves it to disk. Archiving is a quick and easy way to persist data. However, it is slower than other methods, especially as the amount of data grows. It is very useful for storing preferences, application state, and other smaller bits of information required by your application.

For this recipe, you use an array of objects, save them to disk using NSKeyedArchiver, and then load those objects back into memory using NSKeyedUnarchiver.

Create an array, and initialize it with a list of strings:

```
var ingredients = ["Flour","Milk","Eggs","Sugar"]
```

Then use NSKeyedArchiver.archiveRootObject:toFile:. This class method will serialize the object you pass to the file indicated. The method will return true if the object was successfully archived or false it if was not. If an object fails to be archived, most frequently it is due to using an invalid path. In the following example, NSKeyedArchiver is used to save the ingredients array to a file named ingredients.bin:.

```
NSKeyedArchiver.archiveRootObject(ingredients, toFile: "ingredients.bin")
```

To load the object from disk, use NSKeyedUnarchiver.unarchiveObjectWithFile:. If the object is successfully unarchived, the return value is the object. NSKeyedUnarchiver is a member of the Foundation library and is not bridged to Swift. Therefore, the type of object it returns is AnyObject?. Cast the return value into a strongly typed object. When loading an object from disk, you must know the type of the object in order to cast it. In this recipe, the archive contains an array of strings. The array is cast to the proper type using the as? keyword:

```
var newIngredientList = NSKeyedUnarchiver.unarchiveObjectWithFile("ingredients.bin") as? [String]
```

You can check the newIngredientList variable to determine if information was loaded, and then proceed accordingly:

```
if let loadedIngredients = newIngredientList
{
    println("\(loadedIngredients.count)")
}
else
{
    println("Failed to load object")
}
```

The Code and Usage

The code in Listing 7-9 will write an array of strings to disk. Then it loads the archived object back into a different variable. To run the code, create an OS X Command Line Application in Xcode. When the project opens, replace the contents of the file main.swift with Listing 7-9. Run the application.

Listing 7-9. Using NSKeyedArchiver and NSKeyedUnarchiver

```
import Foundation

var ingredients = ["Flour","Milk","Eggs","Sugar"]
NSKeyedArchiver.archiveRootObject(ingredients, toFile: "/tmp/ingredients.bin")
```

```
var newIngredientList = NSKeyedUnarchiver.unarchiveObjectWithFile("/tmp/ingredients.bin")
as? [String]

if let loadedIngredients = newIngredientList
{
    println("\(loadedIngredients.count)")
}
else
{
    println("Failed to load object")
}
```

The array will be archived and then unarchived. If the array is successfully unarchived, the code will print the number of elements in the array (4) to the console. If it fails, the message "Failed to load object" appears. Most commonly, if an object fails to be unarchived, it is because the class has been changed and the archive data no longer matches up.

7-8. Archiving Custom Classes to Files

Problem

You want to use NSKeyedArchiver to archive a class of your own.

Solution

Implement the NSCoder protocol on your custom classes.

How It Works

The NSCoder protocol is implemented to serialize your custom classes. The NSCoder protocol defines two methods: encodeWithCoder: and initWithCoder:.

The first, encodeWithCoder:, is called when NSKeyedArchiver is serializing an object. The implementation of encodeWithCoder: saves the properties of the object to an instance of NSCoder. You do not have to archive all properties, just the ones you need persisted. The archiver then saves the data contained in the NSCoder object. The NSCoder class has a series of encoding methods.

For primitive types, the methods follow the pattern of encode[*type name*]:forKey:. For example, encodeFloat:forKey: encodes float values. For objects like NSDate, use encodeObject:forKey:. The first parameter is the value to archive. The second parameter is a string identifying the name of the property being archived. This is used to unarchive the object as well. The following code shows the implementation of encodeWithCoder:. Using an instance of NSCoder is similar to using an NSDictionary. You add the data and provide a key name for it.

In this example, the names of the fields are contained in an enumeration. It is suggested to use a strategy like this or constants so that you are not repeating the strings for the key names in code:

```
func encodeWithCoder(aCoder: NSCoder) {
    aCoder.encodeObject(date,forKey: OrderFields.Date.rawValue)
    aCoder.encodeFloat(pricePerItem, forKey: OrderFields.PricePerItem.rawValue)
    aCoder.encodeInteger(quantity, forKey: OrderFields.Quantity.rawValue)
    aCoder.encodeObject(notes,forKey: OrderFields.Notes.rawValue)
}
```

The initWithCoder: method is used to load data from an archive into your custom object. In Swift, this method is implemented as an initializer with a single parameter, NSCoder. For any complex type, use NSCoder.decodeObjectForKey:. For primitive types, the decoding methods follow the same convention as the encode methods. When decoding the value, you must cast it in order to assign it to your strongly typed properties.

The following code decodes the data from the archive back into an instance of your class. You must cast each value, because like NSDictionary, the type of value returned from decodeObjectForKey: is AnyObject:

```
required init(coder aDecoder: NSCoder) {
    date = aDecoder.decodeObjectForKey(OrderFields.Date.rawValue) as! NSDate
    pricePerItem = aDecoder.decodeFloatForKey(OrderFields.PricePerItem.rawValue)
    quantity = aDecoder.decodeIntegerForKey(OrderFields.Quantity.rawValue)
    notes = aDecoder.decodeObjectForKey(OrderFields.Notes.rawValue) as! String
}
```

After you implement the NSCoding protocol, the custom object can be persisted using NSKeyedArchiver and loaded using NSKeyedUnarchiver, which is discussed in Recipe 7-7. Instances can also be contained within objects, such as NSArray or NSDictionary, before being archived.

The Code and Usage

The code in Listing 7-10 is a command-line application that will archive an array of Order objects. The Order class is a custom class defined to illustrate archiving in this recipe.

Listing 7-11 is the implementation of the Order class that implements the NSCoding protocol. Take note of the init: and encodeWithEncoder: methods. Before the class definition in Listing 7-11, the enumeration OrderFields is defined. This enum is used to facilitate encoding and decoding. The key values used to encode and decode a property are strings. A simple misspelling between the encoding and decoding can create bugs. The enum is used for the key values in calls to the NSCoder instance. This avoids using string literals in the encoding and decoding methods. This is my preferred method. You can also use string constants or any other type of data structure to avoid using the string literals.

To use this code, create a new OS X Command Line Application in Xcode. Replace the contents of main.swift with Listing 7-10. Next create a new Swift file named Order.swift. Enter the contents of Listing 7-11 into Order.swift. Run the application.

Listing 7-10. main.swift

```swift
import Foundation

var orders : [Order] = []

orders.append(Order(date: NSDate(), pricePerItem: 2.50, quantity: 99, notes: "Trinkets"))
orders.append(Order(date: NSDate(), pricePerItem: 100.00, quantity: 2, notes: "Expensive Items"))
orders.append(Order(date: NSDate(), pricePerItem: 20000.00, quantity: 1, notes: "Car"))

NSKeyedArchiver.archiveRootObject(orders, toFile: "/tmp/orders.bin")

var loadedOrders = NSKeyedUnarchiver.unarchiveObjectWithFile("/tmp/orders.bin") as? [Order]

if let theOrders = loadedOrders
{
    for order in theOrders
    {
        println("(\(order.quantity)) \(order.notes)")
    }
}
else
{
    println("Failed to load object")
}
```

Listing 7-11. Order.swift

```swift
import Foundation

enum OrderFields : String
{
    case Date = "date",
    PricePerItem = "pricePerItem",
    Quantity = "quantity",
    Notes = "notes"
}

class Order : NSObject, NSCoding
{
    var date : NSDate
    var pricePerItem: Float
    var quantity : Int
    var notes : String
```

```
init( date : NSDate, pricePerItem : Float, quantity : Int, notes: String)
{
    self.date = date
    self.pricePerItem = pricePerItem
    self.quantity = quantity
    self.notes = notes
}

required init(coder aDecoder: NSCoder) {

    date = aDecoder.decodeObjectForKey(OrderFields.Date.rawValue) as! NSDate
    pricePerItem =
        aDecoder.decodeFloatForKey(OrderFields.PricePerItem.rawValue)
    quantity = aDecoder.decodeIntegerForKey(OrderFields.Quantity.rawValue)
    notes = aDecoder.decodeObjectForKey(OrderFields.Notes.rawValue) as! String
}

func encodeWithCoder(aCoder: NSCoder) {
    aCoder.encodeObject(date,forKey: OrderFields.Date.rawValue)
    aCoder.encodeFloat(pricePerItem, forKey: OrderFields.PricePerItem.rawValue)
    aCoder.encodeInteger(quantity, forKey: OrderFields.Quantity.rawValue)
    aCoder.encodeObject(notes,forKey: OrderFields.Notes.rawValue)
}
}
```

Three order objects are instantiated, they are added to an array, and the array is archived. The array and the three Order instances are unarchived. The code loops through the list of Orders and outputs the quantity and the notes property to the console. In the output window, you should see the following:

```
(99) Trinkets
(2) Expensive Items
(1) Car
Program ended with exit code: 0
```

Chapter 8

Concurrency

User experience is extremely dependent on responsive applications. In order to create a fluid and smooth experience for your users, asynchronous operations are required. Users expect an application to be responsive, even during long-running operations such as network access or processing-intensive operations. This chapter covers recipes about threading and concurrency using Swift. There are three approaches to threading in iOS and OS X: NSThread, Grand Central Dispatch, and NSOperationQueue. This chapter covers the following, including those approaches:

- Threading with NSThread
- Synchronizing Threads
- Using Grand Central Dispatch for Threading
- Using NSOperations and NSOperationsQueue
- Completing Tasks in the Background in iOS
- Downloading Content in the Background
- Creating Long-Running Background Tasks

8-1. Threading with NSThread

Problem

You need to perform an asynchronous operation in a new thread.

Solution

Use NSThread.detachNewThreadSelector:toTarget:withObject: to spawn a new thread.

How It Works

This method works on iOS and all versions of OS X. Calling detachNewThreadSelector: toTarget:withObject: immediately starts the thread. Threading is a means of improving performance, but it does add overhead.

Each thread consumes resources such as memory and CPU time. In addition, threading requires very structured coding to avoid race conditions, data inconsistency, and locking issues. The approximate costs of thread creation are listed in Table 8-1.

Table 8-1. Costs of Thread Creation

Item	Cost	Discussion
Kernel Data	About 1 KB	This contains information about the thread itself and its attributes. This data cannot be paged to disk.
Stack	Main Thread iOS (1 MB) Main Thread OS X (8 MB) Secondary Threads (512 KB)	The stack is set aside within your process space when the thread is created. A minimum of 16 KB can be allocated, and the stack size must be a multiple of 4 KB.
Thread Creation	About 90 microseconds	This is the time between the thread creation call and the time the entry method is called.

Let's look at an example of NSThread.detachNewThreadSelector:toTarget:withObject:. Create a class with a method call threadMethod:. This method is provided to NSThread to create a new thread. The method can take a single parameter if needed. NSThread will pass the value of the object parameter to threadMethod:. Since a Swift function is not equivalent to an Objective-C method, use the @objc attribute on the Swift class. If this is not done, at runtime you will receive an error that the selector does not exist on the class.

```
@objc class MyThreadClass {
    func threadMethod(object : AnyObject?)
    {
        for i in 1...1000
        {
            println("Thread Loop Iteration #\(i)")
        }
    }
}

class ViewController: UIViewController {

    override func viewDidLoad() {
        super.viewDidLoad()

        var myInstance = MyThreadClass()

        NSThread.detachNewThreadSelector("threadMethod:", toTarget: myInstance, withObject: nil)
    }
}
```

In this example, the thread will begin immediately. When the method specified by the selector exits, the thread is removed.

Another similar method is NSThread.initWithTarget:selector:object:. This method takes the same information; however, it does not immediately start the thread. When you want the thread to start, call start. Using this second method, you can set thread properties before the thread begins. The former method will immediately start the thread. If you need to modify thread properties such as stack size or priority, use init(target:selector:object:).

```
var thread = NSThread(target: myInstance,
    selector: "threadMethod:", object: nil)
```

Set the stackSize property in bytes:

```
thread.stackSize = 16000
```

The threadPriority property value is a number between 0.0 and 1.0. The highest priority is 1.0. Ultimately, the kernel determines priority and does not guarantee the priority will be changed:

```
thread.threadPriority = 0.75
```

To start the thread, call the start method:

```
thread.start()
```

The Code and Usage

The code in this recipe can be used in iOS or OS X. Listing 8-1 is from an iOS application. The same process can be used in an OS X application. Create a new iOS Single View Application. Replace the contents of viewController.swift with Listing 8-1. The code creates two threads. The first creates a thread with detatchNewThreadSelector:toTarget:withObject:. The second uses init(target:selector:object:). Run the application.

Listing 8-1. Creating a new thread

```
Import UIKit
import Foundation

@objc class MyThreadClass {
    func threadMethod(object : AnyObject?)
    {
        for i in 1...1000
        {
            println("Thread Loop Iteration #\(i)")
        }
    }
}
```

```
class ViewController: UIViewController {

    override func viewDidLoad() {
        super.viewDidLoad()

        var myInstance = MyThreadClass()

        // Create thread using detachNewThreadSelector:toTarget:withObject:
        NSThread.detachNewThreadSelector("threadMethod:",
            toTarget: myInstance, withObject: nil)

        // Create thread using init(target:selector:object)
        var thread = NSThread(target: myInstance,
            selector: "threadMethod:", object: nil)
        thread.stackSize = 16000
        thread.threadPriority = 0.75
        thread.start()
    }
}
```

The two threads will execute at the same time. In the output, you will see a jumble of text as each thread calls `MyThreadClass.threadMethod:`. Both threads are writing to the output buffer at the same time. Therefore, the results are mixed together:

```
TThhrread Loeoapd  ILteraotion #1
op Iteration #1
Thread Loop IteraTthiroena d# 2L
oop Iteration #2
Thread LooTph rIetaedr aLtoioopn  #3
Iteration #3
Thread Loop ItTehrraetaido nL o#o4p
 IteratiTohnr e#a4d
```

In the next recipe, Recipe 8-2, you will add a solution to this common threading problem.

8-2. Synchronizing Threads

Problem

You have a threaded application that requires synchronous access to a shared resource.

Solution

Use `objc_sync_enter` and `objc_sync_exit` to lock the resource so that only one thread at a time can access the resource.

How It Works

In the previous recipe, I discussed creating two threads that access the same resource. This approach resulted in confusing and unreadable output to the console because both threads use println to output text to the console. To solve this issue, use objc_sync_enter to create a lock before using println and release it using objc_sync_exit. This will allow the call to println in each thread to complete before the next call happens:

```
objc_sync_enter(object)
println("Loop Iteration #\(i)")
objc_sync_exit(object)
```

The object provided to objc_sync_enter and objc_sync_exit is used as the target of the lock. The same instance must be used by all threads. If the lock object is different, the two threads cannot be synchronized.

The result is output that is readable and makes sense:

```
Loop Iteration #1
Loop Iteration #1
Loop Iteration #2
Loop Iteration #2
Loop Iteration #3
Loop Iteration #3
Loop Iteration #4
Loop Iteration #4
Loop Iteration #5
Loop Iteration #5
```

The Code and Usage

To use the code in this recipe, create a new Single View Application for iOS. Replace the contents of ViewController.swift with Listing 8-2. When you are creating the threads, the instance of MyThreadClass is passed as a parameter. This object is locked to synchronize the threads. Run the application.

Listing 8-2. Synchronized threads using objc_sync_enter and objc_sync_exit

```
import UIKit

@objc class MyThreadClass {
    func threadMethod(object : AnyObject?)
    {

        for i in 1...1000
        {
            objc_sync_enter(object)
            println("Loop Iteration #\(i)")
            objc_sync_exit(object)
        }

    }
}
```

```
class ViewController: UIViewController {

    override func viewDidLoad() {
        super.viewDidLoad()

        var myInstance = MyThreadClass()

        // Create thread using detachNewThreadSelector:toTarget:withObject:
        NSThread.detachNewThreadSelector("threadMethod:",
            toTarget: myInstance, withObject: myInstance)

        // Create thread using init(target:selector:object)
        var thread = NSThread(target: myInstance,
            selector: "threadMethod:", object: myInstance)
        thread.stackSize = 16000
        thread.threadPriority = 0.75
        thread.start()
    }
}
```

You will see synchronized output from each thread:

```
Loop Iteration #1
Loop Iteration #1
Loop Iteration #2
Loop Iteration #2
Loop Iteration #3
Loop Iteration #3
```

8-3. Using Grand Central Dispatch for Threading

Problem

You want to use background threads and avoid creating and managing the threads yourself.

Solution

Use Grand Central Dispatch (GCD) to manage concurrent operations and execute tasks in the background.

How It Works

GCD is a collection of libraries and functions that support multithreaded execution. It also handles optimization of those threads using the multicore processors that are prevalent today. GCD manages a set of First In, First Out (FIFO) queues. Your application submits tasks to a queue using a closure. Then the system handles executing those tasks using a thread pool managed by the system. GCD has three types of queues:

- **Main:** Tasks run sequentially in FIFO order on the main thread of the application.

- **Concurrent:** Tasks execute in FIFO order, but run in parallel and can finish in any order.

- **Serial:** Tasks execute sequentially in FIFO order.

If you have a large number of tasks to complete, concurrent queues are the best option. If the tasks must be executed in a designated order, a serial queue is the best option. The main thread should be used for any user-interface updates. Attempting to update the user interface on a background thread will cause inconsistent behavior. GCD creates four global concurrent queues for use in your applications. Each queue is managed with a different level of priority. Use the GCD API to add tasks to individual queues. The GCD API consists of global functions.

Typically, GCD is used when you want the main thread to continue while other tasks run in parallel. Use dispatch_async to add tasks to a specified queue. It takes two parameters:

- **Queue:** The queue to push the code block

- **Block:** The code block or closure to be executed

Dispatch_async appends the closure to a queue and then returns to the calling function. The calling thread remains unblocked. You must provide a reference to a queue to dispatch a task. A reference to the main queue is retrieved using dispatch_get_main_queue(). The value reference returned from this function is passed as the first parameter to dispatch_async.

For this recipe, I will address a common situation in applications. With any network-connected application, you might need to download data and images from the Internet, local network, or mobile data network. Depending on the connection speed, the task could take a number of seconds or longer. You do not want the application to become unresponsive while this happens. The solution is to dispatch a task to a queue for asynchronous processing. A view can be loaded and displayed while the process loading the information continues in another thread. When the task completes, it can update the user interface by dispatching a task back to the main queue.

The code to add the task to the high-priority queue looks like this:

```
class ViewController: UIViewController {

    var label : UILabel!

    override func viewDidLoad() {
        super.viewDidLoad()

        label = UILabel(frame: CGRect(x: 0.0, y: 0.0, width: 200.0, height: 20.0))
        /**** CODE TO ADD AND POSITION LABEL
            HAS BEEN REMOVED FOR BREVITY ****/
```

```
    dispatch_async(dispatch_get_global_queue(
        DISPATCH_QUEUE_PRIORITY_HIGH, 0)) {
            self.longRunningTask()
    }
}
```

GCD makes four global concurrent queues available. Specify the queue using the following constants in descending order of priority:

- DISPATCH_QUEUE_PRIORITY_HIGH

- DISPATCH_QUEUE_PRIORITY_DEFAULT

- DISPATCH_QUEUE_PRIORITY_LOW

- DISPATCH_QUEUE_PRIORITY_BACKGROUND

The long-running task method performs its actions, and then dispatches a task to the main queue in order to update the user interface. In this recipe, you will update the UILabel with a message indicating the process is complete. The following method simulates a long-running task by sleeping for three seconds. It is important to note that even though this thread is currently blocked, the main thread has not been blocked and other user interaction and tasks can continue. When the processing in the task is complete, use dispatch_async to add a task to the main queue. The closure added to the queue sets the value of the UILabel to indicate the process is complete:

```
func longRunningTask() {
    sleep(3)
    dispatch_async(dispatch_get_main_queue()) {
        self.label.text = "Complete."
    }
}
```

The Code and Usage

Listing 8-3 contains the complete listing of the example outlined in this recipe. In order to use it, create a new iOS Single View Application. Replace the contents of ViewController. swift with Listing 8-3. Note that the same GCD code will run in OS X applications as well. Run the application.

Listing 8-3. Using dispatch_async to handle long-running tasks

```
import UIKit

class ViewController: UIViewController {

    var label : UILabel!

    override func viewDidLoad() {
        super.viewDidLoad()
```

```
label = UILabel(frame: CGRect(x: 0.0, y: 0.0,
    width: 200.0, height: 20.0))
label.center = self.view.center
label.text = "Loading..."
self.view.addSubview(label)

// queue a long running task
dispatch_async(
    dispatch_get_global_queue(DISPATCH_QUEUE_PRIORITY_HIGH, 0)) {
    self.longRunningTask()
}

}

func longRunningTask() {
    sleep(3)
    dispatch_async(dispatch_get_main_queue()) {
        self.label.text = "Complete."
    }
}
}
}
```

The view will load and, after three seconds, the text of the UILabel will change from "Loading..." to "Complete.":

8-4. Using NSOperations and NSOperationsQueue

Problem

You have a collection of tasks to execute asynchronously, and those tasks have dependencies that must be resolved before they can execute. You might also need to cancel, suspend, or re-use a task.

Solution

Use NSOperation with an NSOperationsQueue.

How It Works

Grand Central Dispatch, discussed in Recipe 8-3, is a lightweight approach to executing asynchronous tasks. However, managing GCD after a unit of work has been submitted to a queue requires a good deal of extra development. NSOperationsQueue provides a higher-level solution for executing tasks, managing the order in which they execute, and controlling operations after they have been added to a queue.

NSOperation and NSOperationsQueue are built on top of GCD. Apple recommends starting with this highest-level abstraction and then choosing lower levels of thread management if necessary. The reasons for this include better performance and more control over memory utilization. You will find that, for most purposes, this approach suits your needs.

In this recipe, I will illustrate a common use of NSOperation and NSOperationsQueue. In an Internet-connected application, latency is to be expected. Many applications today download media such as audio, video, and photos. Downloading data from the Internet is not something you want to do on the main thread. Doing so will interrupt the user experience. Instead, you can queue those requests and allow them to download in the background. Start by creating a new iOS Single View application. Open ViewController. swift. Add two class properties for the queues:

```swift
class ViewController: UIViewController {

    var serialQueue: NSOperationQueue?
    var mainQueue: NSOperationQueue?
```

The mainQueue will be used for user-interface updates. The serialQueue will be used for the units of work to be performed. In the viewDidLoad: method, initialize the two queues. Access the queue for your main thread with NSOperationQueue.mainQueue(). The serialQueue can be initialized normally:

```swift
mainQueue = NSOperationQueue.mainQueue()
serialQueue = NSOperationQueue()
```

Next, set the property maxConcurrentOperationCount. This property determines how many concurrent operations the queue will handle. The more concurrent operations there are, the more quickly work will be processed. However, additional overhead is required for each additional operation, so it is not infinitely scalable. Depending on your needs, limit yourself to a low number. For this recipe, we will use a max of 1:

```swift
serialQueue?.maxConcurrentOperationCount = 1
```

Next add a UIProgressView. This will display progress during the asynchronous operation:

```swift
var progress = UIProgressView(frame: CGRect(x:0,y:0,width: 200, height: 30))
progress.center = self.view.center
self.view.addSubview(progress)
```

Our asynchronous task will count up to 1,000,000, incrementing the progress view every 1,000. The entire task can be submitted as a closure. Counting to one million isn't very intensive, so the progress will move quickly:

```swift
serialQueue?.addOperationWithBlock() {

    self.mainQueue?.addOperationWithBlock() {
        progress.setProgress(0.0, animated: false)
    }

    for i in 1...1000000 {
        if i % 1000 == 0
        {
```

```
            self.mainQueue?.addOperationWithBlock() {
                var percentDone = Float(i/100000)
                progress.setProgress(percentDone, animated: true)
            }
        }
    }
}
```

> **Note**   To make user-interface updates, you always want to use NSOperationQueue.
> mainQueue(). User-interface updates cannot be made successfully on any other thread.

The Code and Usage

Listing 8-4 contains the complete listing for this recipe. To run the code, create a new iOS Single View application and replace the contents of ViewController.swift with Listing 8-4. Run the application.

Listing 8-4. Using NSOperation and NSOperationsQueue

```swift
import UIKit

class ViewController: UIViewController {

    var serialQueue: NSOperationQueue?
    var mainQueue: NSOperationQueue?

    override func viewDidLoad() {
        super.viewDidLoad()

        mainQueue = NSOperationQueue.mainQueue()
        serialQueue = NSOperationQueue()
        serialQueue?.maxConcurrentOperationCount = 1

        var progress = UIProgressView(frame: CGRect(x:0,y:0,
            width: 200, height: 30))
        progress.center = self.view.center
        self.view.addSubview(progress)

        serialQueue?.addOperationWithBlock() {

            self.mainQueue?.addOperationWithBlock() {
                progress.setProgress(0.0, animated: false)
            }
```

```
            for i in 1...1000000 {
                if i % 1000 == 0
                {
                    self.mainQueue?.addOperationWithBlock() {
                        var percentDone = Float(i/100000)
                        progress.setProgress(percentDone, animated: true)
                    }
                }
            }
        }
    }
}
```

You will see the progress bar increment up to 100% quickly.

8-5. Completing Tasks in the Background in iOS

Problem

The user or the system has moved your application to the background, but it needs to complete one or more tasks before the system suspends the application.

Solution

Use `UIApplication.beginBackgroundTaskWithName:expirationHandler:` or `UIApplication.beginBackgroundTaskWithExpirationHandler:` to ask for more time to complete the operation.

How It Works

When your application is not in use, the system moves it to the background and soon moves it to a suspended state. This is done to optimize memory, CPU, and battery life. Much of the time, an app can be moved into this state. However, it may be necessary to complete certain operations first.

iOS provides a mechanism to ask the operating system to provide extended time to process tasks in the background before it is suspended. The class method `UIApplication.beginBackgroundTaskWithName:expirationHandler:` or `UIApplication.beginBackgroundTaskWithExpirationHandler:` is used to submit background tasks that will delay the suspension of your application. When you call these methods, a unique token is generated. This token is used to notify the system when your task has completed. You can use these methods only to trigger tasks that will eventually end. If you need to continue processing or performing actions in the background, such as updating GPS or playing audio, you must use a different method. See Recipes 8-6 and 8-7 for additional options.

If your task runs too long, the system will terminate the application. You can find out how much time your task has remaining by reading the property UIApplication. backgroundTimeRemaining. When processing of the task is complete, call UIApplication. endBackgroundTask: with the token created when the job was submitted.

Start by adding code to AppDelegate.swift. To start a long-running task when your application enters the background, implement the method applicationDidEnterBackground:. Create a token to manage the long-running task. It is best practice to create an expiration handler using beginBackgroundTaskWithExpirationHandler. This handler is called if the task runs too long and the system wants to terminate the application. This is your last chance to end the task and prevent the application from being terminated.

Perform minimal work here to clean up after your task and end the task by calling endBackgroundTask: with the process token. If you want to check how long your task has before it expires, check the property UIApplication.backgroundTimeRemaining. If your application does run out of time, handling the exception and ending the task is a better solution than allowing your application to be abnormally terminated.

Create your background task token:

```
var taskToken : UIBackgroundTaskIdentifier = UIBackgroundTaskInvalid

    taskToken = application.beginBackgroundTaskWithExpirationHandler
    { () -> Void in
        application.endBackgroundTask(taskToken)
        taskToken = UIBackgroundTaskInvalid
    }
```

Now dispatch a task for asynchronous processing. In this example, the task to be performed only prints a message to the output. Normally, the tasks performed here would be something like saving data to a database, web service, or another critical task that affects the user's experience. Queue the task with Grand Central Dispatch (GCD). For more information on how to use GCD, see Recipe 8-3.

When the task has performed its work, end the task using endBackgroundTask:

```
    dispatch_async(
        dispatch_get_global_queue(DISPATCH_QUEUE_PRIORITY_DEFAULT, 0)) {
        println("Perform a long running task such as saving data")
        application.endBackgroundTask(taskToken)
        taskToken = UIBackgroundTaskInvalid
    }
}
```

The Code and Usage

To use this code, create a new iOS Single View Application. Open AppDelegate.swift and replace the default applicationDidEnterBackground: method with Listing 8-5. Run the application.

Listing 8-5. Starting a long-running task when entering background

```
func applicationDidEnterBackground(application: UIApplication) {
    var taskToken : UIBackgroundTaskIdentifier = UIBackgroundTaskInvalid

    taskToken = application.beginBackgroundTaskWithExpirationHandler
    { () -> Void in
        application.endBackgroundTask(taskToken)
        taskToken = UIBackgroundTaskInvalid
    }

    dispatch_async(
        dispatch_get_global_queue(DISPATCH_QUEUE_PRIORITY_DEFAULT, 0)) {
        println("Perform a long running task such as saving data")
        application.endBackgroundTask(taskToken)
    taskToken = UIBackgroundTaskInvalid
    }
}
```

Then tap the home button, or if you are using the simulator, use the menu option Hardware ➤ Home. The applicationDidEnterBackground: handler is called and executes the background task. You should see the following output in the debugging console:

```
Perform a long running task such as saving data.
```

8-6. Downloading Content in the Background

Problem

Your application needs to download large content files, and you would like it to do so in the background so that users can still use their phone during the download, even if the application is suspended or terminated.

Solution

Use NSURLSession to start downloads that can continue in the background.

How It Works

When you need to download files, use the class NSURLSession to start the download. It can be configured so that the system will take control of the download. If your application is suspended or terminated, the system will continue the download and notify your application when it is complete.

In this recipe, a ViewController class is used as the delegate to NSURLSession. For background downloads, you need to implement the NSURLSessionDownloadDelegate protocol.

To configure NSURLSession, create an NSURLSessionConfiguration object and set the appropriate properties. This configuration object is then used to create an NSURLSession object. First, create the configuration object using the method backgroundSessionConfigurationWithIdentifier:. The identifier used should be unique to the session. You can manage multiple download tasks using the same session.

```
var configuration =
NSURLSessionConfiguration.backgroundSessionConfigurationWithIdentifier("FileDownload")
```

Next, set the configuration with two additional settings. Set the property discretionary to true. This gives the system control over how the transfers are scheduled for optimal performance. Set the property sessionSendsLaunchEvents to true. When your application is in the background, there is always the chance that it may be suspended or terminated by the system. If your application is terminated, sessionSendsLaunchEvents tells the system to launch your application to resume the download. This is covered later on in this recipe:

```
configuration.sessionSendsLaunchEvents = true
configuration.discretionary = true
```

Create the NSURLSession. It takes three parameters: the configuration, the delegate, and the delegateQueue. Pass the configuration object with the configuration parameter. The ViewController is used for the delegate parameter. If you want NSURLSession to create its own queue, pass nil to the delegateQueue parameter. If you want to use your own queue, pass it with the delegateQueue parameter:

```
var session = NSURLSession(configuration: configuration,
    delegate: self, delegateQueue: nil)
```

Use the session to create a download task. Start the transfer by calling resume:

```
var task = session.downloadTaskWithURL(
    NSURL(string:"http://www.brainloaf.com/introduction-to-ios.mp4")!)
task.resume()
```

> **Note**   When downloading large files, you should disable the ability to download over a mobile connection or give the user a choice to use their data connection, which could incur additional costs.

Now that you can start a download task, you need to implement the protocol methods to handle the download progress, errors, and completion of the download. The methods you need to implement are these:

- URLSession:downloadTask:didFinishDownloadingToURL: When a file has completed downloading, this method is called. The file is located in a temporary location. You must move it to a permanent destination.

- URLSession:downloadTask:didWriteData: This method can be used to update the user interface to indicate progress. It is called multiple times during a download and provides updates on the amount of data that has been downloaded and how much remains to be downloaded.

- URLSession:didBecomeInvalidWithError: This method is called if an error caused the invalidation or if you call one of the methods finishTasksAndInvalidate or invalidateAndCancel:.

When the download completes successfully, move the file from its temporary location to a valid location in your application sandbox. Don't forget to check to ensure the destination file doesn't exist before moving your new download:

```
func URLSession(session: NSURLSession,
    downloadTask: NSURLSessionDownloadTask, didFinishDownloadingToURL location: NSURL) {

    println("Temporary file path: \(location)")
    var fileManager = NSFileManager()
    var err : NSError?
    var destination = NSSearchPathForDirectoriesInDomains(.DocumentDirectory,
        .UserDomainMask, true).first?.stringByAppendingString("/introduction-to-ios.mp4")
        as String!

    if fileManager.moveItemAtURL(location,
        toURL: NSURL(fileURLWithPath: destination)!, error: &err) {
        println("File downloaded to \(destination)")
    } else {
        println("Failed to save \(err?.description)")
    }
}
```

The method URLSession:downloadTask:didWriteData: has three parameters: bytesWritten, totalBytesWritten, and totalBytesExpectedToWrite. You can use these values to update your interface. For example, you can update a progress bar to indicate status:

```
func URLSession(session: NSURLSession,
    downloadTask: NSURLSessionDownloadTask, didWriteData bytesWritten: Int64,
    totalBytesWritten: Int64, totalBytesExpectedToWrite: Int64) {
        println("Wrote an additional \(bytesWritten) bytes")
        println ("total \(totalBytesWritten) bytes) out \(totalBytesExpectedToWrite)
        total bytes.")
}
```

URLSession:didCompleteWithError: tells the delegate that the download for that task is complete. If an error occurred, the error parameter is populated with an NSError object:

```
func URLSession(session: NSURLSession,
    task: NSURLSessionTask, didCompleteWithError error: NSError?) {
    if error == nil {
        println("Download completed")
    } else {
        println("Download failed with error \(error?.description)")
    }
}
```

This code is sufficient to handle downloads that happen while your application is running. If the system suspends or terminates your application, the downloads will continue.

When the download completes, the system will launch your application and notify it of the task's completion. The application delegate method `application:handleEventsForBackg roundURLSession:completionHandler:` is called. Complete handling the download in your implementation of this method. Two things are required to resume the session you created before the application was suspended or terminated.

First, create a new `NSURLSession` instance using the same identifier and configuration settings. The system will reconnect the session to this new session. Second, after you have completed handling the task, call the `completionHandler`. This tells the system your work is done and the interface can be updated.

In this recipe, when the application is reactivated by the system, the root `ViewController` reconnects the `NSURLSession`. If your application starts the session at a different point of time, you will need to reinstantiate the session and delegate to handle the events in the appropriate spot. For example, if your download is started in a view controller that is not visible when the application resumes or is relaunched, you need to decide if you handle the download in your `AppDelegate` or return the application to the proper state so that the session can be reconnected.

To complete this recipe, add a public property to the `AppDelegate` class called `completionHandler`. This property is used to hold a reference to the `completionHandler` parameter:

```
var completionHandler: (() -> Void)?
```

Then add the implementation of `application:handleEventsForBackgroundURLSession:compl etionHandler:`. This method is always called before the delegate methods for `NSURLSession`. This ensures that the `completionHandler` can be accessed from anywhere within your application:

```
func application(application: UIApplication,
        handleEventsForBackgroundURLSession identifier: String, completionHandler: () -> Void) {
    self.completionHandler = completionHandler
}
```

In `ViewController.swift`, add code to the `URLSession:task:didCompleteWithError:` method. If the application has been launched by the system to handle a background download task, this calls the completion handler. If the `appDelegate.completionHandler` is not `nil`, it has been set during the launch of the application:

```
var appDelegate = UIApplication.sharedApplication().delegate as! AppDelegate

if let complete = appDelegate.completionHandler {
    complete()
        appDelegate.completionHandler = nil
}
```

The Code and Usage

To use this code, create a new iOS Single View Application. Replace the contents of AppDelegate.swift with Listing 8-6. Then replace the contents of ViewController.swift with Listing 8-7. The application will start a download of a large video file on a web server. Run the application.

Listing 8-6. AppDelegate.swift

```swift
import UIKit

@UIApplicationMain
class AppDelegate: UIResponder, UIApplicationDelegate {

    var window: UIWindow?
    var completionHandler: (() -> Void)?

    func application(application: UIApplication,
        didFinishLaunchingWithOptions launchOptions: [NSObject: AnyObject]?) -> Bool {
        // Override point for customization after application launch.
        return true
    }

    func application(application: UIApplication,
        handleEventsForBackgroundURLSession identifier: String, completionHandler: () ->
        Void) {
        self.completionHandler = completionHandler

    }
}
```

Listing 8-7. ViewController.swift

```swift
import UIKit

class ViewController: UIViewController, NSURLSessionDownloadDelegate {

    override func viewDidLoad() {
        super.viewDidLoad()

        var configuration =
NSURLSessionConfiguration.backgroundSessionConfigurationWithIdentifier("FileDownload")

        configuration.sessionSendsLaunchEvents = true
        configuration.discretionary = true

        var session =
            NSURLSession(configuration: configuration, delegate: self, delegateQueue: nil)

        var task =
            session.downloadTaskWithURL(NSURL(string:"http://www.brainloaf.com/introduction-
            to-ios.mp4")!)
        task.resume()
    }
```

```
func URLSession(session: NSURLSession,
    didBecomeInvalidWithError error: NSError?) {
    println("Session is invalid: \(error?.description)")
}

func URLSession(session: NSURLSession,
    downloadTask: NSURLSessionDownloadTask, didFinishDownloadingToURL location: NSURL) {

    println("Temporary file path: \(location)")
    var fileManager = NSFileManager()
    var err : NSError?
    var destination =
        NSSearchPathForDirectoriesInDomains(.DocumentDirectory, .UserDomainMask,
        true).first?.stringByAppendingString("/introduction-to-ios.mp4") as String!

    if fileManager.moveItemAtURL(location,
        toURL: NSURL(fileURLWithPath: destination)!, error: &err) {
        println("File downloaded to \(destination)")
    } else {
        println("Failed to save \(err?.description)")
    }
}

func URLSession(session: NSURLSession,
    downloadTask: NSURLSessionDownloadTask, didWriteData bytesWritten: Int64,
    totalBytesWritten: Int64, totalBytesExpectedToWrite: Int64) {
        println("Wrote an additional \(bytesWritten) bytes")
        println("total \(totalBytesWritten) bytes) out \(totalBytesExpectedToWrite)
        total bytes.")
}

func URLSession(session: NSURLSession, task: NSURLSessionTask,
    didCompleteWithError error: NSError?) {
    if error == nil {
        println("Download completed")
    } else {
        println("Download failed with error \(error?.description)")
    }
    var appDelegate =
        UIApplication.sharedApplication().delegate as! AppDelegate

    if let complete = appDelegate.completionHandler {
        complete()
        appDelegate.completionHandler = nil
    }
}
}
```

In the console, you will see the status of the download as parts of the file are written to disk. Click the home button; the application will move to the background. In the console output, you will see the progress as the download continues.

> **Note**   Background downloading will continue only if the system terminates your application. If the user force quits an application, all download tasks will be canceled.

8-7. Creating Long-Running Background Tasks
Problem

Your application is designed to play audio, perform navigation, download content, or perform tasks that provide utility to your users. You need these tasks to continue running if your application is moved to the background.

Solution

In iOS, you can take advantage of long-running background tasks by declaring specific capabilities for your application.

How It Works

Your application must declare the background modes it requires. The available background modes are listed in Table 8-2 along with descriptions of the usage.

Table 8-2. UIBackgroundModes Values

UIBackgroundModes Value	Description
Audio	Indicates your application plays audio while in the background. The user will be prompted for permission for apps that need the microphone prior to use.
location	The app updates the user's GPS location and provides updates based on the location.
voip	The application is used to make Internet phone calls.
newsstand-content	Your app downloads content such as periodicals.
external-accessory	You application interacts with a hardware accessory that provides updates via the External Accessory Framework.
bluetooth-central	Your application works with a Bluetooth accessory that provides updates via the Core Bluetooth framework.
bluetooth-peripheral	Your application acts as a Bluetooth LE accessory. User permission is required to use this mode.
fetch	Your app regularly checks for small amounts of content and downloads it, such as email.
remote-notification	Your app will download content when a push notification arrives.

On the Capabilities tab in Xcode, select the modes your application requires. Select your application's target, and then choose "Capabilities" from the tab bar. Switch Background Modes to "On," and select each capability your application requires. Figure 8-1 shows where the BackgroundModes section is located.

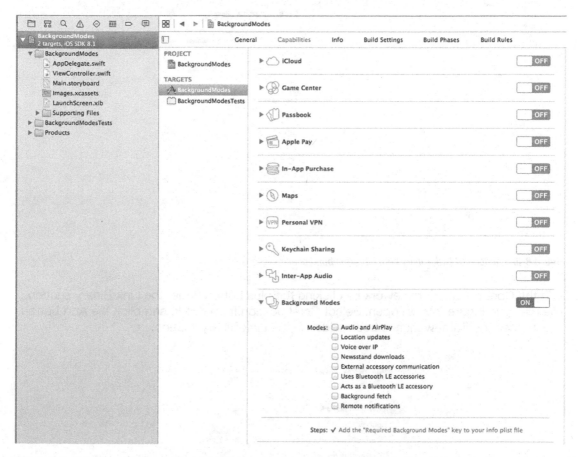

Figure 8-1. Selecting BackgroundModes in Xcode

This recipe outlines an application that uses location updates in the background.

After you set the background mode for Location Updates, the CLLocationManager class is allowed to run in the background and the system will not suspend or terminate your application. Please note, this example uses a very accurate GPS reading and continually gets updates. As a result, it is not power friendly and will drain the battery quickly.

The first step to use the Core Location services is to add the framework to your project. Follow these instructions and reference Figure 8-2 for clarification. Select your project under the project navigator. (In Figure 8-2, the project is BackgroundModes.) Then select the target of your application (in Figure 8-2, the target is BackgroundModes) and click on the Build Phases tab. Expand the Link Binary With Libraries section.

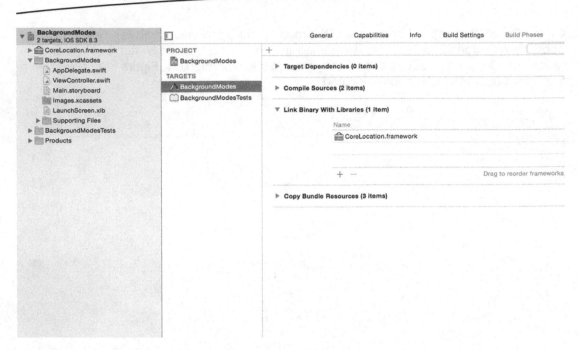

Figure 8-2. Location of Link Binary With Libraries build phase settings

Add the Core Location framework by clicking the plus button under the Link Binary section. The dialog in Figure 8-3 will open. Select CoreLocation.framework, and click the Add button. You will see the framework has been added in the Link Binary section.

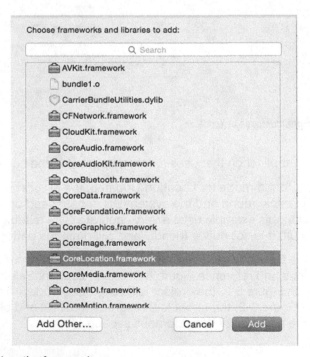

Figure 8-3. Add the Core Location framework

Then add a custom property with the key in the target properties of your target application. This string value is included in the dialog shown to the user when the system asks to allow use of the geolocation services. For example, your custom text could read: "This app requires access to your location to provide updates." See Figure 8-4 as an example of this text in the permission dialog.

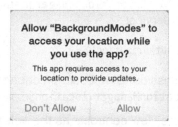

Figure 8-4. Example of custom text in a geolocation permission dialog

Add the key by selecting the project in the project navigator, selecting the application target, and then selecting the Info tab as shown in Figure 8-5.

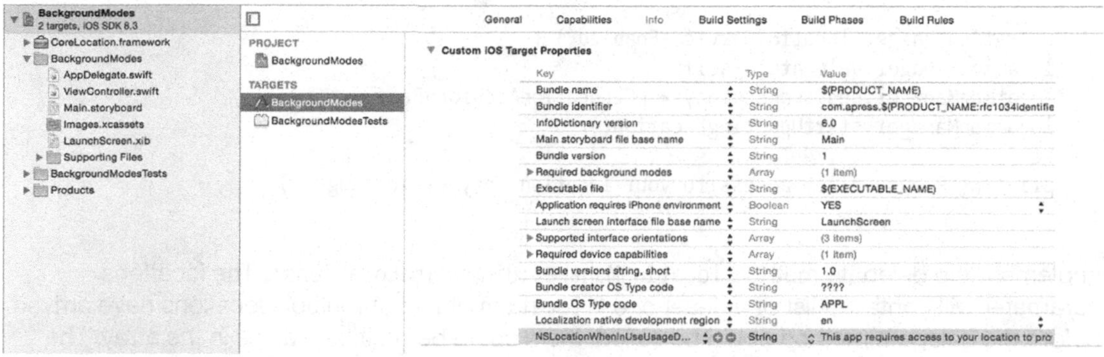

Figure 8-5. The Info tab

Expand the Custom iOS Target Properties. A list of keys, types, and values is shown. Roll over any of the lines and two buttons will appear, a plus sign and a minus sign. Click the plus sign. Enter the name of the key as "NSLocationWhenInUseUsageDescription". Give it a string to be displayed.

> **Note**   If this key is not added, the location services will not work and the user will never be prompted to give permission for the location services.

Next, indicate that your `ViewController` implements the `CLLocationManager` protocol and create a property to store a reference to the location manager:

```
class ViewController: UIViewController, CLLocationManagerDelegate {
var locationManager : CLLocationManager!
```

In the `viewDidLoad` method, create a `CLLocationManager` instance and then request user authorization to use the location services:

```
locationManager.requestWhenInUseAuthorization()
```

If the user does not provide permission, Core Location cannot be used. Check to see if you received permission using `CLLocationManager.locationServicesEnabled()`:

If you received permission, set the view controller as the delegate, set the desired accuracy to `kCLLocationAccuracyBest`, and then start updating the location. This tells the location manager to use fine-grained GPS positioning. It will call its delegate method more frequently to report position updates. The delegate method `locationManager:didUpdateLocations:` is called to provide position updates. If permission is not obtained, indicate this to the user and direct them to the settings app to change their settings:

```
if CLLocationManager.locationServicesEnabled() {
    locationManager.delegate = self
    locationManager.desiredAccuracy = kCLLocationAccuracyBest
    locationManager.startUpdatingLocation()
} else {
    println("Please allow access to your location in your settings.")
}
```

Implement the delegate method `locationManager:didUpdateLocations:`. The locations parameter will contain a list of at least one `CLLocation` object. If multiple locations have arrived before the delegate method could be called, there could be multiple values in the array. The most recent update is at the end of the array. When the location is obtained, process the data:

```
func locationManager(manager: CLLocationManager!,
    didUpdateLocations locations: [AnyObject]!) {
    var lastLocation = locations.last as? CLLocation

    if let location = lastLocation {
        println("Location Updated to: \(location.coordinate.latitude) Lat.,")
        println("\(location.coordinate.longitude) Long.")
    }
}
```

The Code and Usage

To use this code, create a new iOS Single View Application. Add the CoreLocation framework. Enable the Location Updates Background mode for your application's target. See Figure 8-1 for the location of the Background Modes in Xcode. Then under the "Info" tab, add a custom property with the key "NSLocationWhenInUseUsageDescription" and set the value to a string that will be displayed to the user when iOS asks the user for permission to access the location services.

Replace the contents of ViewController.swift with the contents of Listing 8-8. Run the application.

Listing 8-8. Geolocation updates background task

```swift
import UIKit
import CoreLocation

class ViewController: UIViewController, CLLocationManagerDelegate {

    var locationManager : CLLocationManager!

    override func viewDidLoad() {
        super.viewDidLoad()

        locationManager = CLLocationManager()
        locationManager.requestWhenInUseAuthorization()

        if CLLocationManager.locationServicesEnabled() {
            locationManager.delegate = self
            locationManager.desiredAccuracy = kCLLocationAccuracyBest
            locationManager.startUpdatingLocation()
        } else {
            println("Please allow access to your location in your settings.")
        }
    }

    func locationManager(manager: CLLocationManager!,
        didUpdateLocations locations: [AnyObject]!) {
        var lastLocation = locations.last as? CLLocation

        if let location = lastLocation {
            println("Location Updated to: \(location.coordinate.latitude) Lat.,")
            println("\(location.coordinate.longitude) Long.")
        }
    }
}
```

Authorize the use of location services. If you are running on the simulator, you can have the simulator generate location updates. In the simulator's Debug menu, select Debug ➤ Location ➤ Freeway Drive. This will simulate a car driving on a freeway and will provide location updates often. You should see output similar to this:

```
Location Updated to: 37.5015348 Lat.,-122.32888352 Long.
Location Updated to: 37.50165151 Lat.,-122.32922148 Long.
Location Updated to: 37.50177946 Lat.,-122.32955407 Long.
```

Then tap the home button. The application will continue providing updates. As of iOS 8, there will also be a blue bar (as shown in Figure 8-6) displayed in the status bar area indicating that an application is using the location services in the background.

Figure 8-6. Blue status bar indicates your application is using the location services

Web Services

It is difficult to build an application today without connecting to at least one web server or API. This chapter covers recipes that can be used to connect to those services, parse the information that is returned, and deal with things like checking network connectivity.

The topics covered in this chapter are

- Parsing JSON
- Parsing XML
- Making HTTP Calls
- Checking for Network Connectivity
- Calling a REST API
- Posting Data to a REST API

9-1. Parsing JSON

Problem

You need to parse JSON data to use it in your application.

Solution

Use the class NSJSONSerialization to parse JSON.

How It Works

JSON is a common format used in web services and APIs today. *JSON* stands for "JavaScript Object Notation." JSON is a common data interchange format that consists of name/value pairs of data. The following is an example of JSON that defines a recipe. The object has three name/value pairs, which represent the properties of a recipe: its name, how many people it serves, and how long it takes to prepare. It is simple, compact, and human readable:

```
{
    "name" : "Pot Pie",
    "serves" : 1,
    "preparation-time" : 60
}
```

JSON could represent any type of object, and Swift is a strongly typed language. How can you safely handle parsing an unknown format into a strongly typed instance? NSJSONSerialization returns a parsed JSON document as arrays and dictionaries of data. The preceeding JSON example would be returned as an NSDictionary populated with the name/value pairs. The name value, or the value to the left of the colon, is used as the key for the dictionary. The value to the right of the colon is stored in the dictionary using that key.

The JSON format also allows arrays of objects. Assume you have a String variable named data that contains the JSON string shown previously and contains an array of objects. NSJSONSerialization parses the string into an NSArray of NSDictionary. Each element in the array becomes an instance of NSDictionary. All the elements are returned in an NSArray. This is how you use NSJSONSerialization to parse the JSON contained in the data variable:

```
var parsedObject : AnyObject? = NSJSONSerialization.JSONObjectWithData(data, options: nil, error: &error)
```

Once the JSON is parsed, you need to know the structure of data in order to work with it. You can access the values using the NSArray or NSDictionary instances returned. However, this can be code heavy, as each call to index an array or retrieve a value from a dictionary could be nil. As a result, you can end up with dozens of nested nil checks. If you wanted to retrieve the name of a recipe from the paredObject variable, you would have to do the following:

```
if let recipes = parsedObject as? NSArray {
    if let firstRecipe = recipes[0] as? NSDictionary {
        if let name = firstRecipe["name"] as? String {
            println("Name: \(name)")
        }

    }
}
```

It would be easier if you could accomplish the same thing with a single line like this:

```
println(recipes[0]?["name"]?.stringValue)
```

You will be shown the code needed to accomplish this in the following section.

The Code and Usage

The code in this recipe includes an example of a JSON parsing class that uses NSJSONSerialization and adds features to eliminate the need for the nested nil checks. The parser requires an NSData to contain JSON text, such as a response from a web service or local file. For this recipe, we will be using a file located in the application bundle.

First, get the file path from the bundle and create an NSData instance using the file path:

```
var fileError, jsonError : NSError?

var jsonData =
    NSData(contentsOfFile:NSBundle.mainBundle().pathForResource("Recipes",ofType:"json")!,
    options: nil, error: &fileError)
if let err = fileError {
    println("Error: Could not load JSON file: \(fileError?.localizedDescription)")
    return
}
```

Listing 9-1 is a class, JSONParser, used in this recipe. JSONParser has a single class method. Pass the jsonData variable to JSONParser.parseJsonData:error:. If the JSON data provided cannot be parsed, the error parameter will be populated with an NSError object containing the error details. Otherwise, this method returns an optional JSON instance. JSON is a class that contains the parsed data and provides methods for accessing the data without all of those nested if statements. The listing for JSON.swift can be found in Listing 9-2.

Listing 9-1. JSONParser.swift

```
import Foundation

class JSONParser {

    class func parse(data : NSData, inout error: NSError?) -> JSON? {

        var parsedObject : AnyObject? =
            NSJSONSerialization.JSONObjectWithData(data, options: nil, error: &error)

        if let obj: AnyObject = parsedObject {
            return JSON( parsedObject: obj )
        }

        return nil // error state
    }

}
```

Listing 9-2. JSON.swift

```swift
import Foundation

public class JSON
{
    public var error : NSError?

    private var parsedObject : AnyObject

    init ( parsedObject : AnyObject ) {
        self.parsedObject = parsedObject
    }

    subscript(index : Int) -> JSON? {
        if let item = parsedObject as? NSArray {
            return JSON(parsedObject: item[index])
        }
        else { return nil }
    }

    subscript(key : String) -> JSON? {
        if let item = parsedObject as? NSDictionary {
            if item[key] != nil {
                return JSON(parsedObject: item[key]!)
            }
        }
        return nil
    }

    var stringValue : String { get { return parsedObject as! String } }

    var intValue : Int { get { return parsedObject as!  Int } }
}
```

The JSONParser class is used as follows:

```swift
var jsonError : NSError?
var json = JSONParser.parse(jsonData!, error: &jsonError)

if let j = json {
    println(j[0]?["name"]?.stringValue)
    println(j[0]?["serves"]?.intValue)
} else {
    println("Error: Could not parse JSON. \(jsonError?.localizedDescription)")
}
```

The previous code parses a JSON string and returns a JSON class instance. If the return value is nil, the error parameter should contain an NSError object with details.

If the JSON string is successfully parsed, a new JSON class instance is created with the parsed data.

The JSON class holds the original data in a private variable named parsedObject. There are two subscript properties defined: one for String values and one for Int values. For additional data types, you can extend this class. The following code is the subscript that handles string values. When it is used, the method will treat the private variable parsedObject as an NSDictionary. If this downcast fails, nil will be returned. If it is successful, a new JSON instance is returned. By doing this, you can chain together a sequence of subscript calls, making the code more readable:

```
subscript(key : String) -> JSON?
{
    if let item = parsedObject as? NSDictionary {
        if item[key] != nil {
            return JSON(parsedObject: item[key]!)
        }
    }
    return nil
}
```

Accessing the subscript will recursively move down the tree of JSON data stored in the parsedObject variable. In each subsequent recursive call, the code moves one more level down.

Consider this JSON. It is an array of two objects that each represents information about a recipe:

```
[ { "name" : "Pot Pie", "serves" : 1, "preparation-time" : 60 },
  { "name" : "Pizza", "serves" : 6, "preparation-time" : 20 } ]
```

If you wanted to retrieve the name of the first recipe, you could use the instance of a JSON class returned from JSONParser.parseData:error:

```
println(recipes[0]?["name"]?.stringValue)
```

This chained call creates a series of calls to the subscript method. The first call, recipes[0], attempts to get the first object from the array. If it is unsuccessful because the type of the data contained in the private variable parsedObject is not an NSArray, nil is returned. If it is an NSArray, the subscript will return the value of the array at the index via a new instance of JSON.

In the preceding line of code, recipes[0] returns a new JSON object representing the first object in the array. The private variable parsedObject of this new instance now contains an NSDictionary. The second subscript uses the string to retrieve a value from this dictionary. The returned value is contained in a JSON object. Calling the property stringValue casts string and returns the parsedObject variable as a String:

```
var stringValue : String? { get { return parsedObject as? String } }
```

Use the JSONParser and JSON classes when you need to parse JSON files and the structure of the data is known. You can then access the data by chaining calls to subscripts to retrieve your data. To run the example code, create a new iOS Single View Application using Xcode. Create three new files: two Swift files, named JSONParser.swift and JSON.swift, and one plain text file named `Recipes.json`. Copy Listing 9-1 to `JSONParser.swift`, Listing 9-2 to `JSON.swift`, and Listing 9-3 to `Recipes.json`. Then replace the contents of the existing `ViewController.swift` file with the contents of Listing 9-4. Run the application.

Listing 9-3. Recipes.json

```
[ { "name" : "Pot Pie", "serves" : 1, "preparation-time" : 60 },
  { "name" : "Pizza", "serves" : 6, "preparation-time" : 20 } ]
```

Listing 9-4. ViewController.swift

```
import UIKit

class ViewController: UIViewController {

    override func viewDidLoad() {
        super.viewDidLoad()

        var fileError, jsonError : NSError?

        var jsonData =
            NSData(contentsOfFile:NSBundle.mainBundle().pathForResource("Recipes",
            ofType:"json")!,
            options: nil, error: &fileError)
        if let err = fileError {
            println("Error: Could not load JSON file: \(fileError?.localizedDescription)")
            return
        }

        var json = JSONParser.parse(jsonData!, error: &jsonError)

        if let j = json {
            println(j[0]?["name"]?.stringValue)
            println(j[0]?["serves"]?.intValue)
        } else {
            println("Error: Could not parse JSON. \(jsonError?.localizedDescription)")
        }
    }
}
```

You will see the following output in the console:

```
Optional("Pot Pie")
Optional(1)
```

Try changing the subscript values used in the code to output a different property value, object in the array, or nonexisting value. If you choose a nonexisting value, you will see the value returned is `nil`.

9-2. Parsing XML

Problem

You need to parse XML in an application.

Solution

Use a library like SMXMLDocument to parse the XML.

How It Works

There are two ways to parse XML. One is using a SAX (Simple API for XML) parser. The second is using a DOM (Document Object Model) parser. While a SAX parser can be useful for large amounts of data, a DOM parser is easier to use. A SAX parser requires the developer to manage state and store information as the parser moves through the document. A DOM parser, on the other hand, parses the entire document into memory. While this may not be optimal in some cases, a DOM parser will work for most circumstances and provides a friendlier API for accessing the document.

In this recipe, you will use an open source parser that can be found on GitHub at https://github.com/nfarina/xmldocument. The library is maintained by Nick Farina, an iOS developer. The library is distributed under the MIT license. In order to abide by the license, make sure to include the copyright comments listed in the source code when you add the code to your project.

To get started, use git to clone the repository, or just download a .zip file of the code. The use of git is outside the scope of this recipe; however, you can quickly download the code in a .zip file by clicking the Download Zip button as shown in Figure 9-1.

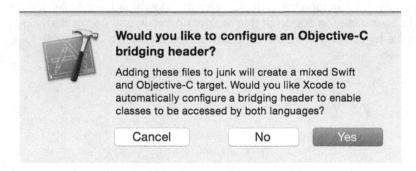

Figure 9-1. Downloading as a .zip from GitHub

This recipe assumes you have downloaded the code. There are two files you need: SMXMLDocument.h and SMXMLDocument.m. Add them to your project. After you add them, Xcode will recognize that you have added Objective-C code and will prompt you to optionally add an Objective-C bridging header. Click Yes. See Figure 9-2.

Figure 9-2. Xcode prompt to add a bridging header

This bridging header file is used to enable Objective-C classes to be accessed in both languages. One additional thing to note, in your target's build settings, under "Swift Compiler – Code Generation" (shown in Figure 9-3), the path to the bridging header is added by Xcode. You should not need to modify this unless you are removing the header.

▼ Swift Compiler - Code Generation	
Setting	⚡ XMLParsing
Install Objective-C Compatibility Header	Yes ◇
Objective-C Bridging Header	**XMLParsing/XMLParsing-Bridging-Header.h**

Figure 9-3. Swift Compiler – Code Generation section of target Build Settings

In order to use the SMXMLDocument class, open the bridging header file and add the following:

```
#import "SMXMLDocument.h"
```

This line will make the SMXMLDocument class available in your Swift code. The first step is to get your XML-formatted data into an NSData variable. The quickest way to do so is to use NSData.withContentsOfFile:. Get the path to your file using the bundle. In this recipe, we will use a file named recipes.xml containing a list of recipe data in XML format:

```
var xml = NSData(contentsOfFile: NSBundle.mainBundle().pathForResource("recipes",
ofType: "xml")!)
```

Instantiate an SMXMLDocument and assign it to a variable named doc. Pass the xml variable and a pointer to an NSError object. If a parsing error occurs, the error pointer will point to a valid NSError object with details about the error:

```
var error : NSError?
var doc = SMXMLDocument(data: xml, error: &error)
```

If parsing is successful, the variable doc will contain the parsed contents of the XML file. It is important to know the structure of the file, as you will need to ask for nodes and attributes using a string that matches the markup. For example, loop through the list of recipes and output the three fields that are contained in each recipe:

```
if error == nil {
        for recipe in doc.childrenNamed("recipe") {
        var name = recipe.valueWithPath("name")
        var serves = recipe.valueWithPath("serves")
        var preparationTime = recipe.valueWithPath("preparation-time")

        println("Recipe name: \(name)")
        println("Serves: \(serves)")
        println("Preparation Time: \(preparationTime)")
    }

} else {
    println("Error parsing xml: \(error?.localizedDescription)")
}
```

The Code and Usage

Listing 9-5 contains the complete code of this recipe. It will load an XML file of recipe data. Listing 9-6 contains a short XML file to be used for testing. To use the code, create a new Single View iOS application. Download and add the SMXMLDocument.h and SMXMLDocument.m files to the project according to the previous instructions. Create a new file recipes.xml. Copy the contents of Listing 9-6 into this file. Create all files at the root of the project.

This code will open the recipes.xml file and parse it using SMXMLDocument. If there are no errors, it will loop through the results and print the recipe name, serving, and preparation time information.

Listing 9-5. ViewController.swift

```swift
import UIKit

class ViewController: UIViewController {

    override func viewDidLoad() {
        super.viewDidLoad()
        // Do any additional setup after loading the view, typically from a nib.
        var xml = NSData(contentsOfFile: NSBundle.mainBundle().pathForResource("recipes",
        ofType: "xml")!)

        var error : NSError?

        var doc = SMXMLDocument(data: xml, error: &error)

        if error == nil {

            for recipe in doc.childrenNamed("recipe") {
                var name = recipe.valueWithPath("name")
                var serves = recipe.valueWithPath("serves")
                var preparationTime = recipe.valueWithPath("preparation-time")

                println("Recipe name: \(name)")
                println("Serves: \(serves)")
                println("Preparation Time: \(preparationTime)")
            }

        } else {
            println("Error parsing xml: \(error?.localizedDescription)")
        }
    }
}
```

Listing 9-6. recipes.xml

```xml
<?xml version="1.0"?>
<recipes>
    <recipe>
        <name>Pot Pie</name>
        <serves>1</serves>
        <preparation-time>60</preparation-time>
    </recipe>
    <recipe>
        <name>Pizza</name>
        <serves>6</serves>
        <preparation-time>20</preparation-time>
    </recipe>
</recipes>
```

9-3. Making HTTP Calls

Problem

You need to download data from a resource using a URL.

Solution

Use `NSURLSession` to get a resource using a URL.

How It Works

Chapter 8 discussed using `NSURLSession` in Recipe 8-6. In this recipe, we will focus on retrieving the contents of a web page. All web services or APIs are built using HTTP, the HyperText Transfer Protocol. The `NSURLSession` class will make an HTTP request to a web server, providing information via the URL or some data that is posted. It then expects a response back. Typically, web services use either JSON or XML formats to communicate.

In Recipes 9-1 and 9-2, you can find solutions for parsing JSON and XML data. In order to make a request to a web service, you can make a GET or POST request. The difference between a GET and a POST is how data in the form of a request is sent to the server. GET requests encode data on the URL itself. POST requests encode the data and deliver it to the web server after the connection has been made using the URL. For this recipe, we will perform a GET and retrieve the Google home page.

Start by creating an `NSURL`:

```
let url = NSURL(string: "http://www.google.com")
```

Next, you will create the NSURLSession. Use the dataTaskWithURL: method. It takes an NSURL as the first parameter. The second parameter is a closure for the completion handler. The completion handler takes the following parameters:

- data – The data received from the specified URL.

- response – An NSURLResponse containing the metadata related to the HTTP response.

- error – An optional NSError object. If an error occurred, the object will be populated with details of the error.

dataTaskWithURL: returns an NSDataTask object. The connection will not be initiated until you call task.resume():

```
let task = NSURLSession.sharedSession().dataTaskWithURL(url!)
{
    (data, response, error) in
        println(NSString(data: data, encoding: NSUTF8StringEncoding))
}

task.resume()
```

The Code and Usage

Create a new iOS Single View Application in Xcode. Replace the contents of ViewController.swift with Listing 9-7. Run the application.

Listing 9-7. Retrieving a web page using NSURLSession

```
import UIKit

class ViewController: UIViewController {

    override func viewDidLoad() {
        super.viewDidLoad()

        let url = NSURL(string: "http://www.google.com")

        let task = NSURLSession.sharedSession().dataTaskWithURL(url!) {
            (data, response, error) in
                println(NSString(data: data, encoding: NSUTF8StringEncoding))
        }
        task.resume()
    }
}
```

When you run the application, it will connect to Google's web server and get the contents of the home page. This will be printed to the console. What you should see is the HTML of the Google home page.

9-4. Checking for Network Connectivity

Problem

You need to know if your application is connected to the Internet and whether it is using a WiFi connection or a mobile data connection.

Solution

Use the Reachability class provided by Apple.

How It Works

Most iOS applications today use the Internet for backup, downloading data, or sharing information. You want to make sure that you know if the application has a network connection. In order to create user-friendly applications, you should provide notification if your network-connected app is offline. If your application downloads large files, it is important to warn the user and ask them for permission when downloading via a mobile data connection.

Apple provides a class called Reachability to be used for this purpose. Interestingly, it is not part of the SDK. It is a class and headerfile that you must download and include in your project. The files can be downloaded from https://developer.apple.com/library/ios/samplecode/Reachability/Introduction/Intro.html. Add Reachability.h and Reachability.m to your project. You may be prompted to create a bridging header. You must do so. If you have trouble, read Recipe 9-2, which includes information on using Objective-C code in your Swift applications.

Assume that you are adding this check for Internet access in the first view controller that is displayed. In the viewDidLoad: method, create an instance of Reachability using Reachability.reachabilityForInternetConnection:

```
let reach = Reachability.reachabilityForInternetConnection()
```

Apple created an enum NetworkStatus to define the three network states:

■   NotReachable – The Internet cannot be reached.

■   ReachableViaWiFi – The device is connected to a WiFi network.

■   ReachableViaWWAN – The device is connected to a wireless data network.

To get the current connection status, call Reachability.currentReachabilityStatus. This will return a NetworkStatus value. Use this information to make the appropriate updates in your application.

Since users are constantly on the go, it is not sufficient to check the network just once. The Reachability class can publish a notification each time the status of the network connection changes. It does so through the NSNotificationCenter. The constant kReachabilityChangeNotification is used to subscribe to those notifications. In your viewDidLoad: method, add an observer to the NSNotificationCenter:

```
NSNotificationCenter.defaultCenter()
.addObserver(self, selector:"checkForReachability:",
name: kReachabilityChangedNotification, object: nil)
```

Then activate the Reachability notifications with the method startNotifier(). In most cases, you will want to do this early in your application startup so that it is available as soon as the app launches:

```
reach.startNotifier()
```

The checkForReachability: function will handle the notifications sent by the Reachability class. The function needs to handle the three possibilities: no connection, a WiFi connection, or a wireless connection. If the change in the network affects the user's experience, you should modify any application features or screens to indicate that the connection has changed. Add this function to your view controller:

```
func checkForReachability( notification : NSNotification )
{
    switch reach.currentReachabilityStatus().value
    {
        case ReachableViaWiFi.value:
            println("Connected to WiFi")
        case ReachableViaWWAN.value:
            println("Connected via Wireless Data")
        case NotReachable.value:
            println("No Connection")
        default:
            println("No Connection")
    }
}
```

The Code and Usage

To see this code in action, start by adding the Reachability.h and Reachability.m files to a new iOS Single View Application project. Remember, since the Reachability class is implemented in Objective-C, you will need to add a bridging header as discussed in Recipe 9-2. Then replace the contents of ViewController.swift with Listing 9-8. This code will create an instance of the Reachability class, subscribe to the notifications, and handle those notifications when network conditions change. Messages will be printed to the console. Run the application.

Listing 9-8. Responding to network connectivity changes

```
import UIKit

class ViewController: UIViewController {

    private var reach : Reachability!

    override func viewDidLoad() {
        super.viewDidLoad()
        reach = Reachability.reachabilityForInternetConnection()

        NSNotificationCenter.defaultCenter()
            .addObserver(self, selector:"checkForReachability:",
                name: kReachabilityChangedNotification, object: nil)

        reach.startNotifier()
    }

    func checkForReachability( notification : NSNotification )
    {
        switch reach.currentReachabilityStatus().value
        {
            case ReachableViaWiFi.value:
                println("Connected to WiFi")
            case ReachableViaWWAN.value:
                println("Connected via Wireless Data")
            case NotReachable.value:
                println("No Connection")
            default:
                println("No Connection")
        }
    }
}
```

You may notice, right after the class is instantiated; there is a call to checkForReachability. The first time you run the application, it is unlikely that a network change has happened. When your application first starts, it is a good idea to call the checkForReachability method to get the current network status. Then rely on the notifications. Once you are running, if you are on WiFi, turn the WiFi connection off. You will see the network update results printed to the console. If you are not connected to WiFi, connect and watch the results. This recipe should be used in any Internet-connected application you may create.

9-5. Calling a REST API

Problem

You need to make calls to a REST API.

Solution

Use a combination of NSURLSession and NSJSONSerialization to perform an HTTP GET and parse the results.

How It Works

In this recipe, we will build upon Recipe 9-1 and Recipe 9-3. Recipe 9-1 deals with parsing JSON into a data structure that allows for easy access of the data. Recipe 9-3 deals with making HTTP calls. You will combine these classes to create a client for calling REST APIs. Start by following Recipes 9-1 and 9-3, and familiarize yourself with the elements and how they work. You will use the classes JSONParser and JSON from Recipe 9-1 for this recipe. Start by following Recipe 9-1.

You need the RestClient class to fetch a URL and download its content. Then it will attempt to parse the contents to a JSON object and return the results via a callback. Start by defining the RestClient class. Our first method will be named Get. To keep the code simple, make the Get method a class method. The following is the complete listing of the RestClient class. Add this class to RestClient.swift, and add it to the root of the project. This method performs an HTTP call using a GET. The first method parameter is a string for the URL. The second parameter is a required completion callback.

```
import Foundation

public class RestClient {

    public class func Get(url : String, callback : (JSON?, NSError?)->()) {
        let url = NSURL(string: url)

        let task = NSURLSession.sharedSession().dataTaskWithURL(url!) {
            (data, response, error) in

            if let err = error {
                callback(nil, err)
            }

            // attempt to parse
            var parseError : NSError?

            var parsedData = JSONParser.parse(data, error: &parseError)
            if let err = parseError {
                callback(nil, err)
            }
```

```
            callback ( parsedData, nil)
        }
        task.resume()
    }
}
```

The following discusses the implementation of the Get method. The first thing in this method is to instantiate a new NSURL object:

```
let url = NSURL(string: url)
```

Using NSURLSession, create a new task and start it:

```
let task = NSURLSession.sharedSession().dataTaskWithURL(url!) {
        // COMPLETION HANDLER CODE WILL GO HERE
}
task.resume()
```

If the task is successful, the NSURLSession calls the completion handler you supply. The completion handler has three parameters:

- data – The information returned from the dataTaskWithURL: method.

- response – The NSURLResponse object associated with this data task.

- error – An NSError object pointer that will point to a valid object if there were errors with the data task.

In the completion handler, first check for errors. If the error parameter is not nil, an error occurred. The Get method's second parameter is a callback with two parameters. The first is an optional JSON instance. The second is an optional NSError pointer.

In the case of an error with the connection, return nil and the error object returned by NSURLSession:

```
(data, response, error) in

    if let err = error {
        callback(nil, err)
    }
```

Next, attempt to parse the results from the HTTP call. Then check for parsing errors. If there were errors, return nil for the data and the error object from the parser:

```
var parseError : NSError?

var parsedData = JSONParser.parse(data, error: &parseError)
if let err = parseError {
    callback(nil, err)
}
```

Finally, if no errors have occurred, the JSON was successfully parsed. Return the JSON object and `nil` for the error:

```
callback (parsedData, nil)
```

Thanks to the `RestClient` class, REST API calls can now be made with a single line of code and a completion handler. OpenLibrary.org is an open library catalog with a REST API that returns JSON. The URL `https://openlibrary.org/works/OL11315329W.json` is the record for Julia Child's "Mastering the Art of French cooking." To use the `RestClient`, add the URL into a call to the `Get` method:

```
RestClient.Get("https://openlibrary.org/works/OL11315329W.json")
```

Then create a completion handler to handle either an error state or the success state where the JSON has been successfully parsed:

```
{
        (json, error) -> Void in

            if let err = error {
                println("Error: \(error?.localizedDescription)")
                return
            }

            if let j = json {

                var title = j["title"]?.stringValue
                var revision = j["revision"]?.intValue

                println("Title: \(title!)")
                println("Revision: \(revision!)")
            }
}
```

The Code and Usage

This recipe combines two other recipes: Recipe 9-1 and Recipe 9-2. Listing 9-9 is the full code for the `RestClient` class. To use this code, you can include the classes `RestClient`, `JSONParser` (Listing 9-1), and `JSON` (Listing 9-2) in your own applications. To test the code here, create a new iOS Single View Application. Add these three classes to the project. Then replace the contents of `ViewController.swift` with Listing 9-10. This sample application will use the `RestClient` class to fetch the JSON data and parse it into a usable object. Run the application.

Listing 9-9. Rest API client

```
import Foundation

public class RestClient {

    public class func Get(url : String, callback : (JSON?, NSError?)->()) {
        let url = NSURL(string: url)

        let task = NSURLSession.sharedSession().dataTaskWithURL(url!) {
            (data, response, error) in

            if let err = error {
                callback(nil, err)
            }

            // attempt to parse
            var parseError : NSError?

            var parsedData = JSONParser.parse(data, error: &parseError)
            if let err = parseError {
                callback(nil, err)
            }

            callback ( parsedData, nil)
        }
        task.resume()
    }
}
```

Listing 9-10. Using the RestClient class

```
import UIKit

class ViewController: UIViewController {

    override func viewDidLoad() {
        super.viewDidLoad()

        RestClient.Get("https://openlibrary.org/works/OL11315329W.json")
        { (json, error) -> Void in

            if let err = error {
                println("Error: \(error?.localizedDescription)")
                return
            }
```

```
        if let j = json {

            var title = j["title"]?.stringValue
            var revision = j["revision"]?.intValue

            println("Title: \(title!)")
            println("Revision: \(revision!)")
        }
    }
  }
}
```

You should see output similar to the following in the console:

```
Title: Mastering the Art of French Cooking
Revision: 6
```

9-6. Posting Data to a REST API

Problem

You need to make a POST call to a REST API.

Solution

Use a combination of `NSURLSession` and `NSJSONSerialization` to make an HTTP POST call and parse the response.

How It Works

This recipe builds upon Recipe 9-5. Start with Recipe 9-5, which builds the foundation for making a GET call to a REST API and parses the response. Recipe 9-5 defines a class `RestClient`. In this recipe, you will add a method that uses the POST method to send data to an API. In order to test the code, you will need a server that can accept the posted data. The web site `http://www.jsontest.com/` is a tool for testing API code. It will accept a POST and return a preset response that you define via URL parameters. Try it yourself. Enter this URL in your browser:

```
http://echo.jsontest.com/status/OK
```

You should see the following JSON as a result:

```
{"status": "OK"}
```

When posting data to the API, you need to encode that data as JSON. The method
NSJSONSerialization. dataWithJSONObject:options:error: will encode your data properly.
Put the data into a [String,AnyObject] dictionary containing your name/value pairs. For
example, a list of recipe data could be defined this way:

```
var data: [String: AnyObject] = ["name" : "Pea Soup",
    "Ingredients" : "Split Peas, Water, Chicken Broth, Milk, Salt, Onions"]
```

Create a call to the RestClient object for a Post. It will work similarly to the Get method
from Recipe 9-5 except it will need one more parameter for the data. Note the URL we are
posting to is a test URL on JSONTest.com. This URL will return a JSON response with a single
name/value pair "Status"/"OK".

```
RestClient.Post("http://echo.jsontest.com/status/OK", data: data)
        { (json, error) -> Void in

            if let err = error {
                println("Error: \(error?.localizedDescription)")
                return
            }

            if let j = json {
                var status = j["status"]?.stringValue

                println("Status: \(status!)")
            }
        }
```

Start implementing the Post method by starting with the same definition as the Get method,
and then add another parameter for the data dictionary. The callback method will be the
same:

```
public class func Post(url : String, data : [String: AnyObject], callback :
(JSON?, NSError?)->()) {
        let url = NSURL(string: url)
```

In order to handle the POST request, we will use an NSMutableURLRequest instance to define
the URL, method, headers, and data. Instantiate the request with the url parameter:

```
var request = NSMutableURLRequest(URL: url!)
```

In order to inform the server that the information being posted is formatted as JSON, and set
the HTTP headers for the Content-type and Accept. The server will also want to know the
length of the data you are posting. The NSURLSession class handles this for you:

```
request.HTTPMethod = "POST"
request.addValue("application/json", forHTTPHeaderField: "Content-type")
request.addValue("application/json", forHTTPHeaderField: "Accept")
```

Now encode the dictionary to an NSData object, and assign it to the HTTPBody property of the request. If you decode it and then print the results, you will see the JSON that will be posted to the server:

```
var paramError : NSError?
     var paramData = NSJSONSerialization.dataWithJSONObject(data,
         options: NSJSONWritingOptions.allZeros, error: &paramError)

     request.HTTPBody = paramData

     println("POST DATA")
     println(NSJSONSerialization.JSONObjectWithData(paramData!, options: nil, error: nil)!)
```

This time, use dataTaskWithRequest to create the task that will post the data. The approach from there is basically the same as using the Get method. Check for errors in the callback, parse the JSON, and call the completion handler with the results:

```
let task = NSURLSession.sharedSession().dataTaskWithRequest(request) {
    (data, response, error) in

    if let err = error {
        callback(nil, err)
    }

    // attempt to parse
    var parseError : NSError?

    var parsedData = JSONParser.parse(data, error: &parseError)
    if let err = parseError {
        callback(nil, err)
    }

    callback ( parsedData, nil)
}
task.resume()
```

The Code and Usage

This recipe depends on Recipe 9-5. Start by following Recipe 9-5, and then continue adding the following code. Copy the contents of Listing 9-11, and replace the contents of RecipeClient.swift. Listing 9-11 is the full code of the class RecipeClient, including the Get and Post methods that you can use to call REST APIs. Then replace the ViewController.swift contents with Listing 9-12. Run the application.

Listing 9-11. RestClient with Post method

```swift
import Foundation

public class RestClient {

    public class func Get(url : String, callback : (JSON?, NSError?)->()) {
        let url = NSURL(string: url)


        let task = NSURLSession.sharedSession().dataTaskWithURL(url!) {
            (data, response, error) in

            if let err = error {
                callback(nil, err)
            }

            // attempt to parse
            var parseError : NSError?

            var parsedData = JSONParser.parse(data, error: &parseError)
            if let err = parseError {
                callback(nil, err)
            }

            callback ( parsedData, nil)
        }
        task.resume()
    }

    public class func Post(url : String, data : [String: AnyObject], callback :
    (JSON?, NSError?)->()) {
        let url = NSURL(string: url)

        var request = NSMutableURLRequest(URL: url!)
        request.HTTPMethod = "POST"
        request.addValue("application/json", forHTTPHeaderField: "Content-type")
        request.addValue("application/json", forHTTPHeaderField: "Accept")

        var paramError : NSError?
        var paramData = NSJSONSerialization.dataWithJSONObject(data,
            options: NSJSONWritingOptions.allZeros, error: &paramError)

        request.HTTPBody = paramData

        println("POST DATA")
        println(NSJSONSerialization.JSONObjectWithData(paramData!, options: nil,
        error: nil)!)
```

```swift
        let task = NSURLSession.sharedSession().dataTaskWithRequest(request) {
            (data, response, error) in

            if let err = error {
                callback(nil, err)
            }

            // attempt to parse
            var parseError : NSError?

            var parsedData = JSONParser.parse(data, error: &parseError)
            if let err = parseError {
                callback(nil, err)
            }

            callback ( parsedData, nil)
        }
        task.resume()
    }
}
```

Listing 9-12. ViewController.swift

```swift
import UIKit

class ViewController: UIViewController {

    override func viewDidLoad() {
        super.viewDidLoad()

        var data: [String: AnyObject] = [ "name" : "Pea Soup",
            "Ingredients" : "Split Peas, Water, Chicken Broth, Milk, Salt, Onions" ]

        RestClient.Post("http://echo.jsontest.com/status/OK", data: data)
        { (json, error) -> Void in

            if let err = error {
                println("Error: \(error?.localizedDescription)")
                return
            }

            if let j = json {
                var status = j["status"]?.stringValue

                println("Status: \(status!)")
            }
        }
    }
}
```

When you run the application, a call will be made to JSONTest.com, so make sure you are connected to the Internet when trying this recipe. Just before it posts your data, the JSON version of your data is printed to the console so that you can see what it looks like. JSONTest.com will return a JSON string with a single name/value pair. RestClient.Post prints the JSON data that is posted to the URL. The test API server will return a JSON string like this:

```
{"status": "OK"}
```

The completion handler will print out the status value. You should see output like this in the console:

```
POST DATA
{
    Ingredients = "Split Peas, Water, Chicken Broth, Milk, Salt, Onions";
    name = "Pea Soup";
}
Status: OK
```

Chapter 10

Core Data

Core Data is at the heart of many data-driven iOS and OS X applications. It can be used for storage, syncing information across the web and devices, as well as providing fast access to large data sets. It is optimized to work with iOS and OS X, works directly with iCloud, and provides Object Relation Mapping between data storage and your class objects.

Each recipe in this chapter builds upon the previous recipe. Core Data involves a number of different components, and those parts are presented in recipe format. The first time through this chapter, you should follow it chronologically to understand the overview of Core Data and Swift. After that, this chapter serves as a great reference.

In this chapter, you will build a helper class, `CoreDataHelper`, that can be reused in other Core Data projects you create. The approaches in this class should be applicable to many applications. Use `CoreDataHelper` to jumpstart your own applications.

The topics covered in this chapter are

- Creating a Data Model
- Creating Model Classes
- Creating a Data Store
- Creating a Managed Object Context
- Adding a New Entity
- Creating an `NSFetchRequest`
- Populating a `UITableView` with a Fetched Results Controller
- Deleting an Item
- Searching for Entities

10-1. Creating a Data Model

Problem

You want to design the entities you will persist using Core Data.

Solution

Create a data model.

How It Works

Core Data uses a Data Model to determine how to map an entity class to the underlying data storage. An *entity* is a class that is mapped to data storage. In a relational database for example, an entity class is mapped to a table and each property in the entity is mapped to a column in the table. The model includes information detailing the name of the entity classes, the data types of the entity properties, and relationships. The recipes in this chapter focus on an SQLite based solution, which is the most common storage provider that developers use.

The first step is to add the Core Data framework to a project. Create a new iOS Master-Detail Application, and save it. After the project opens in Xcode, add the Core Data Framework. As shown in Figure 10-1, select the application target "Core Data" and the "Build Phases" tab. Then, under "Link Binary With Libraries," click the plus button. A dialog with a list of frameworks will open. Select "CoreData.framework" from the list, and click Add.

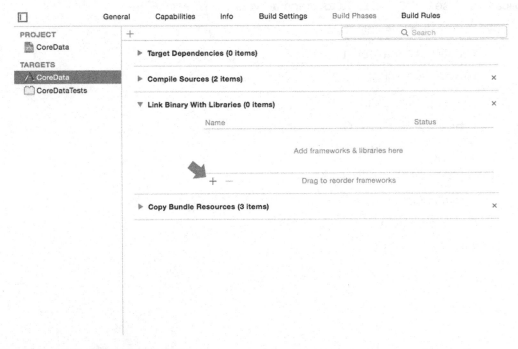

Figure 10-1. Add the CoreData framework

Next, add a new file to your project. Under the "Core Data" section in the new file dialog, choose "Data Model." Save the new file as RecipeBook.

The data model will appear in the project navigator. Click to open the data model. You will see the Data Model editor in Xcode. Add a new entity by clicking "Add Entity" near the bottom of the window as indicated in Figure 10-2.

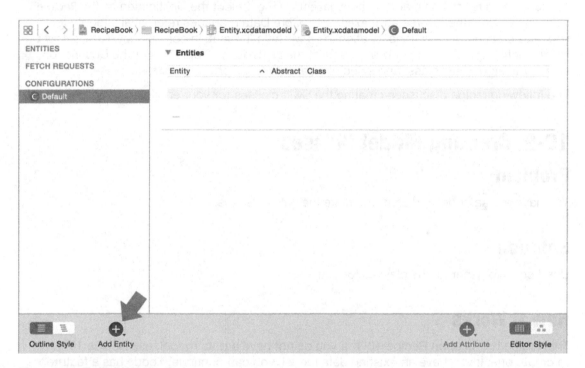

Figure 10-2. The Data Model editor

Rename the entity by double-clicking on the name. Call it Recipe. This will define an entity named Recipe that will be mapped to the database. When you select Recipe under the "Entities" section, the entity properties will appear. There is a section for Attributes, Relationships, and Fetched Properties. The Attributes will map the property names to the storage type. The Relationships are used to design the Object-Oriented relations to other objects. These mappings do not have knowledge of the actual underlying storage mechanism. Core Data uses SQLite by default, and that is what this recipe uses. The idea to keep in mind is that you do not need to create a relational model like a database; you should focus on a proper Object-Oriented design. Core Data will take care of the rest.

Now imagine the properties of a recipe. The recipe may have a name, the number of people it serves, a list of ingredients, and a description. Create a new attribute by clicking the plus sign under the "Attributes" section. You may need to expand the section by clicking the small gray triangle to the left. Create three attributes.

Add the name attribute, and select the corresponding type, String. Create the serves attribute with the type of Integer 32. Then add recipeDescription and set the type to String.

Under the "Relationships" section, click the plus button and you will add a relationship named ingredients. The Recipe entity will need a list of ingredients. Right now, you are defining only the relationship. This name is also the name of the collection in the Recipe entity.

Create a new entity, and name it Ingredient. Create two attributes: measurement, which is an Int16, and ingredient, which is a String. Add them to the entity. Then in the "Relationship" section, add a relationship and name it parentRecipe. Select the Destination as the Recipe class, and select the inverse as ingredients. Core Data manages referential integrity for you, and creating bi-directional relationships will help it maintain consistency. Now select the Recipe entity again. You must now complete the ingredients relation. For the Destination, select the Ingredient class, and select the parentRecipe property for the inverse.

The following recipe discusses creating the Swift classes for your entities.

10-2. Creating Model Classes

Problem

You have a data aodel and want to create the entity classes.

Solution

Use Xcode to generate the classes for you.

How It Works

This recipe builds upon Recipe 10-1. If you do not have a data model, use Recipe 10-1 to create one. If you have an existing data model, you can continue. Xcode has a feature that will generate the entity code using a Core Data model. Open the data model, and you will be looking at the editor. In the Menu bar, select the menu option Editor ➤ Create NSManagedObject Subclass.

As you can see in Figure 10-3, a dialog will open and ask you to select the data model to use. Make sure RecipeBook is selected, and then click Next.

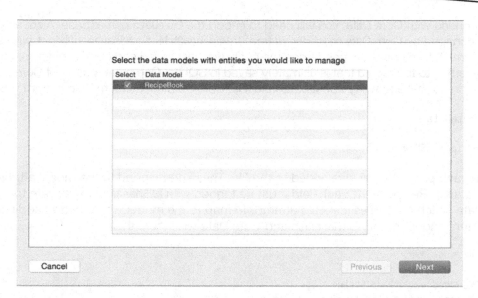

Figure 10-3. Select the Data Model RecipeBook

Then a list of the entities in your model is displayed. (See Figure 10-4.) Select Recipe and Ingredient, and click Next.

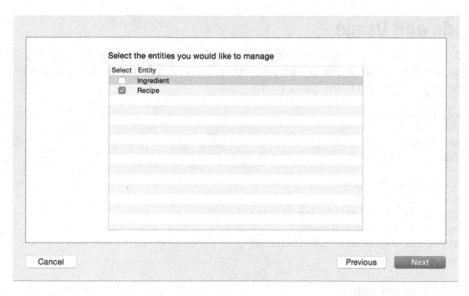

Figure 10-4. Select the Recipe and Ingredient entities

Check to make sure that Swift is selected as the language. Finally, select the location for your classes to be saved.

You will end up with two Swift files, one for each entity. Open Recipe.swift.

When working with Core Data, you will need to import the `CoreData` namespace. Also, any class that is managed by Core Data must derive from `NSManagedObject`. `NSManagedObject` will keep track of which fields have changed since the entity was last saved and contains information to map the entity to the record that is ultimately saved in SQLite. One great feature of Core Data is that you do not have to worry about database IDs. Core Data keeps them hidden from you:

```
import CoreData

class Recipe: NSManagedObject
```

Look at each property that was added to the file. These correspond to the model attributes you created in Recipe 10-1. Each field must be tagged with @NSManaged to indicate to Core Data which properties it should attempt to map to the model. You can add additional parameters and functions to this class and Core Data will ignore them:

```
{

    @NSManaged var name: String
    @NSManaged var recipeDescription: String
    @NSManaged var serves: NSNumber
    @NSManaged var ingredients: NSOrderedSet

}
```

The Code and Usage

Listing 10-1 and Listing 10-2 show the code for the entities `Recipe` and `Ingredient`. They are both subclasses of the `NSManagedObject` class. This will allow Core Data to access and persist the data contained in the class properties.

Listing 10-1. The Recipe entity

```
import Foundation
import CoreData

class Recipe: NSManagedObject {
    @NSManaged var name: String
    @NSManaged var recipeDescription: String
    @NSManaged var serves: NSNumber
    @NSManaged var ingredients: NSOrderedSet
}
```

Listing 10-2. The Ingredient entity

```
import Foundation
import CoreData

class Ingredient: NSManagedObject {
    @NSManaged var ingredient: String
    @NSManaged var measurement: NSNumber
    @NSManaged var parentRecipe: Recipe
}
```

10-3. Creating a Data Store

Problem

You need to create or open an existing data store.

Solution

Instantiate an NSManagedObjectModel and an NSPersistentStoreCoordinator.

How It Works

This recipe builds upon Recipe 10-2. Start with that recipe and then proceed. In this recipe, you will create a reusable helper class that will initialize the Core Data storage and handle creating or updating the data store file.

Create a new file named CoreDataHelper.swift. This will contain the helper class. Define the class and initializer. You will need two string properties, one for the model name and one for the name of the data file. Set up the initializer to set the value of these properties:

```
import Foundation
import CoreData

public class CoreDataHelper {

    var modelName : String
    var datastoreFileName : String

    init( modelName : String, datastoreFileName : String)
    {
        self.modelName = modelName
        self.datastoreFileName = datastoreFileName
    }
```

Next you will add code to create instances of the NSManagedObjectModel and the NSPersistentStoreCoordinator. The NSManagedObjectModel class reads a data-model file and loads it into memory. This class is then used in conjunction with NSPersistentStoreCoordinator to create a new data store or open an existing one. The NSPersistentStoreCoordinator class is middleware that sits between your application and the data-storage mechanism. First create a property for the NSManagedObjectModel. This property will use the contents of RecipeBook.xcdatamodeld.

In Swift, instead of declaring variables and then instantiating them within another method, you can use a lazy-loaded property with an inline initializer. Since loading the object model is a one-time thing, it lends itself to this pattern. Define the property with the lazy keyword, and specify its type. Then add an immediately invoked closure to initialize it. Since the property is marked as lazy, the actual initialization is deferred until the first time it is accessed. As soon as you access the property, it will invoke the closure and return a new NSManagedObjectModel. Creating the instance requires only the path to the data-model file in your bundle:

```
lazy var managedObjectModel: NSManagedObjectModel = {
    let modelURL = NSBundle.mainBundle().URLForResource("RecipeBook", withExtension: "momd")!
    return NSManagedObjectModel(contentsOfURL: modelURL)!
}()
```

The managed object model is required to create the persistent store coordinator. Start creating that lazy property like this:

```
lazy var persistentStoreCoordinator: NSPersistentStoreCoordinator? = {
```

The coordinator is an optional type since there are a number of reasons why a coordinator could fail to initialize. A couple of common reasons for this include a problem with the existing store file and it cannot be read, or your device is out of memory and the new file cannot be written.

Instantiate the persistent store coordinator:

```
var coordinator: NSPersistentStoreCoordinator? =
    NSPersistentStoreCoordinator(managedObjectModel: self.managedObjectModel)
```

Then build a URL path to the persistent store data file. Name the file RecipeBook.sqlite:

```
let documentsDirectory : NSURL =
    NSFileManager.defaultManager().URLsForDirectory(.DocumentDirectory,
        inDomains: .UserDomainMask).last as! NSURL

let url = documentsDirectory.URLByAppendingPathComponent(self.datastoreFileName)
```

The next step is to create the data store using the method addPersistentStoreWithType: configuration:url:options:error:. The parameters to this method indicate options, such as which type of data store to use, and configuration information, which can include database migrations or other versioning code to be used when upgrading the application:

- type – The type of data store to be used. There are a number of items available. The most commonly used option is NSSQLiteStoreType. This recipe uses this store type. For other options, reference the online iOS Developer Library, "Store Types," located under the NSPersistentStoreCoordinator class reference.

- configuration – The name of a configuration contained in the managed object model. If the configuration is nil, no other configurations are allowed.

- url – The URL path to the data file.

- options – A dictionary of key value pairs defining options for the particular type of data store. Options for the data store as well as migration options can be passed this way. See "Store Options" in the NSPersistentStoreCoordinator class reference for details about the store options. In order to manage migrations, you should use the key NSInferMappingModelAutomaticallyOption and a value of true. The persistent store coordinator will automatically attempt to update the data store using model version information.

- error – A pointer to an NSError variable. If there is an error, this variable will be populated with an NSError instance describing the issue. Handle this error and then provide the user with direction. If the data store cannot open, at this point, the file may be corrupt, or there was a problem migrating it.

Define the NSError variable as well as the options dictionary. Add the NSMigratePersistentStoresAutomaticallyOption and NSInferMappingModelAutomaticallyOption keys to the dictionary, both with a value of true. NSMigratePersistentStoresAutomaticallyOption will attempt to upgrade the store by using any migrations you define as part of the data model. NSInferMappingModelAutomaticallyOption can still attempt to update the data store if only simple changes are made, such as adding a new attribute or entity. Changes to existing entities and attributes require the use of a data-model migration:

```
var error: NSError? = nil
let options = [NSMigratePersistentStoresAutomaticallyOption: true,
    NSInferMappingModelAutomaticallyOption: true]
```

Call addPersistentStoreWithType:configuration:url:options:error: and check the result. If it returns nil, an error has occurred. Errors at this point are fatal. Handle the error by providing some sort of action for the user to take to recover from the error. Most likely, the user will need a new data-storage file. Do not remove the existing file, because it will still contain data. If a migration failed to execute, you can still repair the existing file, but that would need to be done outside of the application. As the developer, you would need to manually edit the SQLite database and fix the information. An open source tool named "SQLite Database Browser for OS X" can open and edit SQLite files. The end user will be required to get you the .sqlite file. Enabling support for iTunes file sharing allows the user to retrieve the file via iTunes. The user can then email it to you for repair. The file is replaced using iTunes file sharing. See "UIFileSharingEnabled" in Apple's developer documentation for the "Information Property List Reference."

If an error occurred, wrap the error in an NSError instance with a custom domain specific to your application. If there was no error, return coordinator:

```
if coordinator!.addPersistentStoreWithType(NSSQLiteStoreType,
    configuration: nil, URL: url,
    options: options, error: &error) == nil {

    coordinator = nil
    // Report any error we got.
    var dict = [String: AnyObject]()
```

```
dict[NSLocalizedDescriptionKey]
    = "Failed to initialize the application's saved data"
dict[NSLocalizedFailureReasonErrorKey]
    = "There was an error creating or loading the application's saved data."
dict[NSUnderlyingErrorKey] = error
error = NSError(domain: "com.apress.recipebook", code: 9999, userInfo: dict)
// Replace this with code to handle the error appropriately.
NSLog("Unresolved error \(error), \(error!.userInfo)")
abort()
}

return coordinator
}()
```

The helper class is complete for this recipe. In order to use it, you instantiate the helper with the model name (but with no file extension) and the name of the data file to use. Just use the file name, not the entire path. Add this code to the end of the viewDidLoad: method in MasterViewController.swift:

```
var helper = CoreDataHelper(modelName: "RecipeBook", datastoreFileName: "RecipeBook.sqlite")
let coordinator = helper.persistentStoreCoordinator
```

The Code and Usage

Listing 10-3 contains the entire CoreDataHelper class. In order to test it out, create a new iOS Single View Application. Do NOT select the Core Data box. You can do this in future cases, but for now, you do not want all the extra template code. Add the CoreData library to the project.

Then create a new Swift file and name it CoreDataHelp.swift. Copy the contents of Listing 10-3 into the file. Add the following to the end of the viewDidLoad: method in ViewController.swift. This code will instantiate the helper and then access the persistentStoreCoordinator property. This will trigger the lazy-loading code and create the new RecipeBook.sqlite file:

```
var helper = CoreDataHelper(modelName: "RecipeBook", datastoreFileName: "RecipeBook.sqlite")
let coordinator = helper.persistentStoreCoordinator
```

Listing 10-3. CoreDataHelper.swift

```
import Foundation
import CoreData

public class CoreDataHelper {

    var modelName : String
    var datastoreFileName : String
```

```
init( modelName : String, datastoreFileName : String)
{
    self.modelName = modelName
    self.datastoreFileName = datastoreFileName
}

// MARK: Core Data
lazy var managedObjectModel: NSManagedObjectModel = {
    let modelURL =
        NSBundle.mainBundle().URLForResource(self.modelName, withExtension: "momd")!
    return NSManagedObjectModel(contentsOfURL: modelURL)!
    }()

lazy var persistentStoreCoordinator: NSPersistentStoreCoordinator? = {
    // Create the coordinator and store
    var coordinator: NSPersistentStoreCoordinator? =
        NSPersistentStoreCoordinator(managedObjectModel: self.managedObjectModel)
    let documentsDirectory : NSURL =
        NSFileManager.defaultManager().URLsForDirectory(.DocumentDirectory,
            inDomains: .UserDomainMask).last as! NSURL

    let url = documentsDirectory.URLByAppendingPathComponent(self.datastoreFileName)
    println("DEBUG: path to data file \(url)")
    var error: NSError? = nil
    let options = [NSMigratePersistentStoresAutomaticallyOption: true,
        NSInferMappingModelAutomaticallyOption: true]
    if coordinator!.addPersistentStoreWithType(NSSQLiteStoreType, configuration: nil,
        URL: url, options: options, error: &error) == nil {

            coordinator = nil
            // Report any error we got.
            var dict = [String: AnyObject]()
            dict[NSLocalizedDescriptionKey]
                = "Failed to initialize the application's saved data"
            dict[NSLocalizedFailureReasonErrorKey]
                = "There was an error creating or loading the application's saved data."
            dict[NSUnderlyingErrorKey] = error
            error = NSError(domain: "com.apress.recipebook", code: 9999, userInfo: dict)
            // Replace this with code to handle the error appropriately.
            NSLog("Unresolved error \(error), \(error!.userInfo)")
            abort()
    }

    return coordinator
}()

lazy var managedObjectContext: NSManagedObjectContext? = {
    let coordinator = self.persistentStoreCoordinator
    if coordinator == nil {
        return nil
    }
```

```
    var managedObjectContext =
        NSManagedObjectContext(concurrencyType: .MainQueueConcurrencyType)

    managedObjectContext.persistentStoreCoordinator = coordinator
    return managedObjectContext
}()
```

If you do not receive an exception and the application doesn't quit, it was successful. In the console, you will see a path to the file. It will be long and look like this:

```
file:///Users/mrogers/Library/Developer/CoreSimulator/Devices/CBD5DF93-6E34-47EA-905E-
3E76BFB58E42/data/Containers/Data/Application/0BF9D411-57DB-4B71-9030-BCE612188237/
Documents/RecipeBook.sqlite
```

Copy everything from /Users up to /Documents to the clipboard. Switch to the finder, and select Go ➤ Go to Folder. Paste the path, and click Go. A finder window will open, and you should see the data files that were created.

10-4. Creating a Managed Object Context

Problem

You need to work with a collection of managed objects.

Solution

Create an instance of NSManagedObjectContext.

How It Works

The NSManagedObjectContext manages an object's life cycle. It is responsible for communicating between the managed objects and the data store. This recipe builds upon Recipe 10-3 and adds the NSManagedContext to the CoreDataHelper class.

Create a lazy-load property named managedObjectContext:

```
lazy var managedObjectContext: NSManagedObjectContext? = {
```

Access the persistentStoreCoordinator property. If it has not been loaded yet, it will be. If it is nil, something has failed to initialize. Creating the managed object context depends on the persistentStoreCoordinator:

```
let coordinator = self.persistentStoreCoordinator
if coordinator == nil {
    return nil
}
```

Instantiate an NSManagedObjectContext. The initializer has a parameter named concurrencyType. If you are using the context to populate the user interface, the concurrency type to use is NSManagedObjectContextConcurrencyType.MainQueueConcurrencyType. There are two other values that can be used:

- NSConfinementConcurrencyType – This is the default context. It exists for backward compatibility. Apple recommends that an NSManagedObject always be instantiated with one of the other explicit types.

- NSPrivateQueueConcurrencyType – This creates and uses a private queue. If this type of concurrency is used, you must dispatch requests to the queue using performBlock: or performBlockAndWait:.

Dispatching messages is not required with MainQueueConcurrencyType as long as those messages originate within the main queue, such as controllers or UI elements:

```
var managedObjectContext = NSManagedObjectContext(concurrencyType: .MainQueueConcurrencyType)
managedObjectContext.persistentStoreCoordinator = coordinator
return managedObjectContext
}()
```

In this chapter, you are creating an application that will display a list of recipes, so the managed object context is tied to the main queue because it will be used by the user interface. When you continue to Recipe 10-5, you'll see that it uses the context to add an object to the database.

The Code and Usage

Listing 10-4 is the code that should be added to CoreDataHelper.swift. Add this code to the project you created in Recipe 10-3, and then continue to Recipe 10-5.

Listing 10-4. A lazy property used to create a managed object context

```
lazy var managedObjectContext: NSManagedObjectContext? = {
    let coordinator = self.persistentStoreCoordinator
    if coordinator == nil {
        return nil
    }
    var managedObjectContext = NSManagedObjectContext(
        concurrencyType: NSManagedObjectContextConcurrencyType.MainQueueConcurrencyType)
    managedObjectContext.persistentStoreCoordinator = coordinator
    return managedObjectContext
}()
```

10-5. Adding a New Entity

Problem

You need to create a new entity and save it.

Solution

Use NSEntityDescription.insertNewObjectForEntityForName:inManagedObjectContext: to create a new managed object. Use NSManagedObjectContext.saveContext to save the data to the database.

How It Works

NSEntityDescription.insertNewObjectForEntityForName:inManagedObjectContext: creates a new instance of a managed object. It takes two parameters:

- entityName – A String that matches the name of an entity in the model.

- inManagedObjectContext – The managed object context instance that will manage this entity.

Create a function named newEntity in the CoreDataHelper class. It takes one parameter, a String named name. It returns an optional NSManagedObject:

```
func newEntity( named : String ) -> NSManagedObject? {
```

If the managedObjectContext is nil, return nil. You cannot create an object without it:

```
if managedObjectContext == nil {
    return nil
}
```

Attempt to create the new object using NSEntityDescription.insertNewObjectForEntityForName:inManagedObjectContext:

```
        var newManagedObject =
            NSEntityDescription.insertNewObjectForEntityForName(named,
                inManagedObjectContext: managedObjectContext!) as? NSManagedObject

    return newManagedObject
}
```

Once the object has been created, it will need to be saved to persist the data to the data store. Create a saveContext method:

```
func saveContext() {
```

The NSManagedObjectContext.save: method takes a pointer to an NSError variable. The method returns true or false if the object was saved. If the method returns false, the error variable will contain an NSError object with the information:

```
    var error: NSError? = nil
    if managedObjectContext?.save(&error) != nil {
        // You must handle the error properly in a graceful way.
        // abort() may be used for development, but should not be used in a
        // production quality appliction
        println("Unresolved error \(error), \(error?.userInfo)")
        abort()
    }
}
```

Now, open MasterViewController.swift. The line of code let coordinator = helper. persistentStoreCoordinator was added in a previous recipe. Remove this line, and replace it with a call to CoreDataHelper.newEntity:

```
var recipe = helper.newEntity("Recipe") as? Recipe
```

Then, if the creation was successful, set some properties. Then call helper.saveContext() to write the recipe to the database:

```
if let r = recipe {
    r.name = "Apple Pie"
    r.serves = 8
    r.recipeDescription = "A summer tradition."

    helper.saveContext()
}
```

The Code and Usage

Listing 10-5 contains two methods to be added to CoreDataHelper.swift based on this recipe. Listing 10-6 is code that should be added to the end of the viewDidLoad: method. After you add this code, run the application.

Listing 10-5. Methods to add and save Core Data entities

```
func newEntity( named : String ) -> NSManagedObject? {
    if managedObjectContext == nil {
        return nil
    }
    var newManagedObject =
        NSEntityDescription.insertNewObjectForEntityForName(named,
            inManagedObjectContext: managedObjectContext!) as? NSManagedObject

    return newManagedObject
}
```

```
func saveContext() {
    let context = self.managedObjectContext!
    var error: NSError? = nil
    if !context.save(&error) {
        // You must handle the error properly in a graceful way.
        // abort() may be used for development, but should not be used in a
        // production quality appliction
        println("Unresolved error \(error), \(error?.userInfo)")
        abort()
    }
}
```

Listing 10-6. Code to be added to the end of the viewDidLoad function

```
var recipe = helper.newEntity("Recipe") as? Recipe

if let r = recipe {
    r.name = "Apple Pie"
    r.serves = 8
    r.recipeDescription = "A summer tradition."

    helper.saveContext()
}
```

If no errors occur, the entity was created and saved successfully. In the next recipe, you will look at retrieving those results. The code will print out the path to the file `RecipeBook.sqlite`:

```
DEBUG: path to data file file:///Users/mrogers/Library/Developer/CoreSimulator/
Devices/3F8DD1EC-E1DA-4CF6-A343-401A435DB191/data/Containers/Data/Application/A22A4514-A9D5-
4F34-9395-0F68D08C250C/Documents/RecipeBook.sqlite
```

10-6. Creating an NSFetchRequest

Problem

You need to retrieve entities from a Core Data persistent store.

Solution

Create an `NSFetchRequest` and execute it.

How It Works

The `NSFetchRequest` object is used by a managed object context to retrieve objects from a Core Data data source. It can also handle tasks like sorting and searching. In this recipe, you will retrieve all of the results in the database and output them. Later recipes deal with sorting and searching. This recipe builds on Recipe 10-5. Follow that recipe before continuing.

Start by opening `MasterViewController.swift`. Instantiate a new `NSFetchRequest` object at the end of the `viewDidLoad:` method. Leave all existing code:

```
let fetchRequest = NSFetchRequest()
```

Set the `NSFetchRequest.entity` property to indicate the type of entity to retrieve:

```
let entity =
    NSEntityDescription.entityForName("Recipe",
        inManagedObjectContext: helper.managedObjectContext!)
fetchRequest.entity = entity
```

Call `NSManagedObjectContext.executeFetchRequest:` to attempt to retrieve the results. Cast the results to an optional array of Recipe objects:

```
var error : NSError?
var results = helper.managedObjectContext?.executeFetchRequest(fetchRequest, error: &error)
    as? [Recipe]
```

If the results variable contains values, loop through the results and print the name of the recipe to the console:

```
if let recipes = results {
    for r in recipes {
        println("Name: \(r.name)")
}
```

If the query failed, the error variable will contain details about the error.

The Code and Usage

Listing 10-7 contains additional code to add to the end of the `viewDidLoad:` function in `MasterViewController.swift`. Add this code and then run the application.

Listing 10-7. NSFetchRequest code

```
let fetchRequest = NSFetchRequest()

let entity =
    NSEntityDescription.entityForName("Recipe",
        inManagedObjectContext: helper.managedObjectContext!)
fetchRequest.entity = entity

var error : NSError?
var results = helper.managedObjectContext?.executeFetchRequest(fetchRequest, error: &error)
as? [Recipe]

if let recipes = results {
    for r in recipes {
        println("Name: \(r.name)")
    }
}
```

The NSFetchRequest is used to get the objects from the database and will then loop through them. Since there is only one recipe, you should see a single item output in the console:

```
Name: Apple Pie
```

If you run the application multiple times, it will continue to create the same object each time and save it, creating duplicates that will then be listed out:

```
Name: Apple Pie
Name: Apple Pie
Name: Apple Pie
```

10-7. Populating a UITableView with a Fetched Results Controller

Problem

You want to display the contents of a Core Data database in a UITableView.

Solution

Implement an NSFetchedResultsController.

How It Works

The NSFetchedResults controller is designed for use in conjunction with the UITableViewController. The two are tightly integrated and, as a result, provide an extremely efficient and performant solution. This recipe builds upon Recipe 10-6. Complete Recipe 10-6 and then continue with this recipe.

NSFetchedResultsController utilizes a delegate to indicate to the table view when certain data events happen. Add the NSFetchedResultsControllerDelegate to the MasterViewController class:

```
class MasterViewController: UITableViewController, NSFetchedResultsControllerDelegate
```

Start by adding a private variable and a property to MasterViewController.swift. Make both an NSFetchedResultsController. The variable should be an optional type. When the computed property is accessed, if the controller has already been created and stored in the private variable, return the existing controller:

```
var _fetchedResultsController: NSFetchedResultsController? = nil

var fetchedResultsController: NSFetchedResultsController {
    if _fetchedResultsController != nil {
        return _fetchedResultsController!
    }
```

A fetched results controller needs an NSFetchRequest object to get the list of objects to display. Create the request as specified in Recipe 10-6. In addition, you will set the fetchBatchSize property. This property will fetch up to the number of objects specified in fetchBatchSize. This is done to improve efficiency. The UITableView is optimized to draw only as many cells as needed for it to display and animate on screen. Setting the batch size creates a similar effect. As you scroll the UITableView, the NSFetchedResultsController is being used to populate the table. If it decides it needs more records to display, it will load them in batches. This way, a very large database does not need to be kept in memory to scroll. Only small pieces are loaded to keep the memory footprint small:

```
let fetchRequest = NSFetchRequest()

let entity = NSEntityDescription.entityForName("Recipe",
    inManagedObjectContext: self.managedObjectContext!)
fetchRequest.entity = entity
fetchRequest.fetchBatchSize = 20
```

A fetched results controller requires at least one NSSortDescriptor to order the results. The property NSFetchedResultsController.sortDescriptors is an array of sort descriptors. Sorting is straightforward. The NSSortDescriptor takes two parameters. The first is a string that must match the name of a property on the entity. The second attribute is a Boolean that indicates if the sort order is ascending. If you want to sort by multiple fields, multiple sort descriptors are added to the array:

```
let sortDescriptor = NSSortDescriptor(key: "name", ascending: true)
let sortDescriptors = [sortDescriptor]
fetchRequest.sortDescriptors = [sortDescriptor]
```

Create the controller. The controller takes four parameters:

- fetchRequest – An NSFetchRequest object that is used to get the results.
- managedObjectContext – The context used to access the data.
- sectionNameKeyPath – The name of a property on the retrieved object to be used for grouping records into table-view sections.
- cacheName – The cache is used to store precomputed section information on disk. Use nil to prevent caching. Using the cache avoids the overhead of computing the section and index information.

  ```
  let aFetchedResultsController = NSFetchedResultsController(fetchRequest:
  fetchRequest,
      managedObjectContext: self.managedObjectContext!,
      sectionNameKeyPath: nil, cacheName: nil)
  ```

Set the delegate property to self, and then set the private variable:

```
aFetchedResultsController.delegate = self
_fetchedResultsController = aFetchedResultsController
```

Perform the fetch using the controller method `performFetch`. If the fetch fails, something seriously wrong happened. At this point, it could be a memory error or some bad data. Determine the cause of the error, and handle it properly based on your application's needs:

```
var error: NSError? = nil
if !_fetchedResultsController!.performFetch(&error) {
    println("Unresolved error \(error), \(error?.userInfo)")
    abort()
}
```

If the fetch succeeds, return the controller and end the function:

```
    return _fetchedResultsController!
}
```

To display the data in the `UITableView`, you need to implement three `UITableViewDelegate` methods: `numberOfSectionsInTableView:`, `tableView:numberOfRowsInSection:`, and `tabl eView:cellForRowAtindexPath:`. The fetched results controller supplies all the necessary information. Use the `sections` property to get the number of sections. The `sections` property is an optional type. Use a ternary operator to guard against the case where `sections` is nil:

```
override func numberOfSectionsInTableView(tableView: UITableView) -> Int {
    return self.fetchedResultsController.sections?.count ?? 0
}
```

The number of rows in a section requires getting an `NSFetchedResultsSectionInfo` object containing that information:

```
override func tableView(tableView: UITableView, numberOfRowsInSection section: Int) -> Int {
        let sectionInfo = self.fetchedResultsController.sections![section] as!
        NSFetchedResultsSectionInfo
        return sectionInfo.numberOfObjects
}
```

The last required method is the `tableView:cellForRowAtIndexPath:`. The fetched results controller makes it very easy to get an object based on the `indexPath`. The method `objectAtIndexPath` will return the object. Create the method to get a reusable cell, retrieve the object from the fetched results controller, and set up the table cell:

```
override func tableView(tableView: UITableView,
    cellForRowAtIndexPath indexPath: NSIndexPath) -> UITableViewCell {

    let cell = tableView.dequeueReusableCellWithIdentifier("Cell",
        forIndexPath: indexPath) as! UITableViewCell

    let recipe = self.fetchedResultsController.objectAtIndexPath(indexPath) as! Recipe
    cell.textLabel!.text = recipe.name

    return cell
}
```

The Code and Usage

The code added in this recipe will display records contained in the Core Data database. The application adds a record for an Apple Pie recipe each time you run the application. If you run the application three times, there will be three records displayed. Listing 10-8 contains the complete `MasterViewController.swift`. Replace the contents of `MasterViewController.swift` with the contents of Listing 10-8. Run the application.

Listing 10-8. MasterViewController.swift

```swift
import UIKit
import CoreData

class MasterViewController: UITableViewController, NSFetchedResultsControllerDelegate {

    var helper : CoreDataHelper!

    override func awakeFromNib() {
        super.awakeFromNib()
    }

    override func viewDidLoad() {
        super.viewDidLoad()
        // Do any additional setup after loading the view, typically from a nib.
        self.navigationItem.leftBarButtonItem = self.editButtonItem()

        let addButton = UIBarButtonItem(barButtonSystemItem: .Add, target: self,
        action: "insertNewObject:")
        self.navigationItem.rightBarButtonItem = addButton

        helper = CoreDataHelper(modelName: "RecipeBook", datastoreFileName:
        "RecipeBook.sqlite")
        var recipe = helper.newEntity("Recipe") as? Recipe

        if let r = recipe {
            r.name = "Apple Pie"
            r.serves = 8
            r.recipeDescription = "A summer tradition."

            helper.saveContext()
        }

        let fetchRequest = NSFetchRequest()

        let entity = NSEntityDescription.entityForName("Recipe",
            inManagedObjectContext: helper.managedObjectContext!)
        fetchRequest.entity = entity

        var error : NSError?
        var results =
            helper.managedObjectContext?.executeFetchRequest(fetchRequest, error: &error)
            as? [Recipe]
```

```swift
        if let recipes = results {
            for r in recipes {
                println("Name: \(r.name)")
            }
        }
}

// MARK: - Fetched results controller
var _fetchedResultsController: NSFetchedResultsController? = nil

var fetchedResultsController: NSFetchedResultsController {
    if _fetchedResultsController != nil {
        return _fetchedResultsController!
    }

    let fetchRequest = NSFetchRequest()

    let entity =
        NSEntityDescription.entityForName("Recipe",
            inManagedObjectContext: helper.managedObjectContext!)
    fetchRequest.entity = entity
    fetchRequest.fetchBatchSize = 20

    let sortDescriptor = NSSortDescriptor(key: "name", ascending: true)
    let sortDescriptors = [sortDescriptor]
    fetchRequest.sortDescriptors = [sortDescriptor]

    let aFetchedResultsController = NSFetchedResultsController(fetchRequest: fetchRequest,
        managedObjectContext: helper.managedObjectContext!,
        sectionNameKeyPath: nil, cacheName: nil)
    aFetchedResultsController.delegate = self
    _fetchedResultsController = aFetchedResultsController

    var error: NSError? = nil
    if !_fetchedResultsController!.performFetch(&error) {
        println("Unresolved error \(error), \(error?.userInfo)")
        abort()
    }

    return _fetchedResultsController!
}

override func numberOfSectionsInTableView(tableView: UITableView) -> Int {
    return self.fetchedResultsController.sections?.count ?? 0
}

override func tableView(tableView: UITableView, numberOfRowsInSection section: Int) ->
Int {
    let sectionInfo =
        self.fetchedResultsController.sections![section] as! NSFetchedResultsSectionInfo
    return sectionInfo.numberOfObjects
}
```

```
override func tableView(tableView: UITableView,
    cellForRowAtIndexPath indexPath: NSIndexPath) -> UITableViewCell {
    let cell = tableView.dequeueReusableCellWithIdentifier("Cell",
        forIndexPath: indexPath) as! UITableViewCell

    let recipe = self.fetchedResultsController.objectAtIndexPath(indexPath) as! Recipe
    cell.textLabel!.text = recipe.name

    return cell
  }
}
```

All the objects currently in the database will be listed in the UITableView.

10-8. Deleting an Item

Problem

You need to delete an entity.

Solution

Use NSManagedObjectContext.deleteObject to remove an object from Core Data.

How It Works

This recipe builds upon Recipe 10-7. Complete everything up to that recipe before continuing with this recipe. The managed object contents will deal with deleting an object for you. In this recipe, you will leverage the UITableView's editing capabilities to call the delete functionality. Open MasterViewController.swift. First, add the delegate method to enable editing:

```
override func tableView(tableView: UITableView, canEditRowAtIndexPath indexPath:
NSIndexPath) -> Bool {
    return true
}
```

This will display the edit button in the navigation bar, and it will display the delete button when you swipe to the left on a table row. When the user taps the delete button, the delegate method tableView:commitEditingStyle:forRowAtIndexPath: is called. If the editing style is Delete, you want to remove the object corresponding to that row. Get the context, and call deleteObject. The parameter is the object at the current indexPath. Commit the changes to the database by calling the CoreDataHelper.saveContext method:

```
override func tableView(tableView: UITableView,
    commitEditingStyle editingStyle: UITableViewCellEditingStyle,
    forRowAtIndexPath indexPath: NSIndexPath) {
```

```
        if editingStyle == .Delete {
            let context = self.fetchedResultsController.managedObjectContext
context.deleteObject(self.fetchedResultsController.objectAtIndexPath(indexPath) as!
NSManagedObject)

        helper.saveContext()
    }
}
```

After the object is removed from the database, the table view needs to be updated.
Implement the NSFetchedResultsController method controllerDidChangeContent: method.
In this method, reload the tableView:

```
func controllerDidChangeContent(controller: NSFetchedResultsController) {
    // In the simplest, most efficient, case, reload the table view.
    self.tableView.reloadData()
}
```

If you run the application, you can now delete any of the rows in the UITableView.

The Code and Usage

The code in Listing 10-9 should be added to MasterViewController.swift. Run the
application, and swipe to the left on a row; then click delete. The row should be removed
from the table view.

Listing 10-9. Additions to MasterViewController.swift

```
// MARK: Enable Editing
override func tableView(tableView: UITableView, canEditRowAtIndexPath indexPath:
NSIndexPath) -> Bool {
    return true
}

override func tableView(tableView: UITableView,
    commitEditingStyle editingStyle: UITableViewCellEditingStyle,
    forRowAtIndexPath indexPath: NSIndexPath) {
    if editingStyle == .Delete {
        let context = self.fetchedResultsController.managedObjectContext
        context.deleteObject(self.fetchedResultsController.objectAtIndexPath(indexPath) as!
        NSManagedObject)

        helper.saveContext()
    }
}

func controllerDidChangeContent(controller: NSFetchedResultsController) {
    // In the simplest, most efficient, case, reload the table view.
    self.tableView.reloadData()
}
```

10-9. Searching for Entities

Problem

You want to search a collection of objects in a Core Data database.

Solution

Use an NSPredicate to define the search criteria. Then set the NSFetchedResults.predicate property.

How It Works

This recipe builds on Recipe 10-8. Complete that recipe first, and then continue with this recipe. To illustrate using a predicate, you will search for all Recipe entities that serve more than two people. Open MasterViewController.swift, and go to the fetchedResultsController property. Right after the line fetchRequest.sortDescriptors = [sortDescriptor], add the following code to create a predicate. In this example, the predicate is created using a string format and the values will be substituted. Here the string is the property name, operand, and value formatter. In this example, the predicate is serves > 2. Predicates can be used with most types of dates, strings, and relations, and they provide many types of comparisons. The best reference for all the possibilities is the "Predicate Programming Guide" from Apple.

```
let statusPredicate = NSPredicate(format: "serves > %d", 2)
fetchRequest.predicate = statusPredicate
```

After you have added the code, run the application. The results will appear in the table view. No records have been filtered out because the Apple Pie recipe serves 8. Now change the comparison to be less than 2 and run the application again. The table view will be empty since no results are found in the Core Data database where the serves field has a property less than 2.

```
let statusPredicate = NSPredicate(format: "serves < %d", 2)
```

NSPredicate is a very powerful class and provides simple or complex search capabilities for your apps.

The Code and Usage

Listing 10-10 contains the updated property fetchedResultsController. The code includes the addition of the NSPredicate. Replace the existing property code in MasterViewController.swift. Run the application.

Listing 10-10. The fetchedResultsController property

```
var fetchedResultsController: NSFetchedResultsController {
        if _fetchedResultsController != nil {
            return _fetchedResultsController!
        }

        let fetchRequest = NSFetchRequest()

        let entity = NSEntityDescription.entityForName("Recipe",
            inManagedObjectContext: helper.managedObjectContext!)
        fetchRequest.entity = entity
        fetchRequest.fetchBatchSize = 20

        let sortDescriptor = NSSortDescriptor(key: "name", ascending: true)
        let sortDescriptors = [sortDescriptor]
        fetchRequest.sortDescriptors = [sortDescriptor]

        let statusPredicate = NSPredicate(format: "serves < %d", 2)
        fetchRequest.predicate = statusPredicate

        let aFetchedResultsController = NSFetchedResultsController(fetchRequest:
        fetchRequest,
            managedObjectContext: helper.managedObjectContext!, sectionNameKeyPath: nil,
            cacheName: nil)
        aFetchedResultsController.delegate = self
        _fetchedResultsController = aFetchedResultsController

        var error: NSError? = nil
        if !_fetchedResultsController!.performFetch(&error) {
            println("Unresolved error \(error), \(error?.userInfo)")
            abort()
        }

        return _fetchedResultsController!
}
```

No records will be displayed in the table view. The code in Listing 10-10 will search the database for Recipes where the `serves` property has a value of less than 2. Try using different comparisons and properties to create additional searches.

Chapter **11**

Advanced iOS 8 Features

iOS 8 added many advanced features to the ecosystem. This chapter will cover some of those and present Swift-based recipes you can integrate into your own applications.

The topics covered in this chapter are

- Creating a Today Extension
- Creating a Custom Keyboard Extension
- Creating a Sharing Extension
- Creating an Action Extension
- Creating a WatchKit Application

11-1. Creating a Today Extension

Problem

You would like to make information available to users to display in the Today screen.

Solution

Create a Today extension.

How It Works

The Today extension is added to your application and allows a user to choose to display information from your application on the Today screen. Currently, Today extensions can be distributed only as part of an application. In this recipe, you will create a boilerplate application, add the extension, and present a solution for obtaining data and then presenting it in your widget.

Start with a Single View iOS application. Name it `RecipeWidget`. You actually won't need to do anything with this application. Once that project is open in Xcode, select the menu item File ➤ New ➤ Target. Select "Application Extension" under iOS. Then select "Today Extension" from the list of options that appears to the right. (See Figure 11-1 for an example of what this selection should look like.) Then click Next and give your target a name such as "RandomRecipe." This recipe presents an extension that selects a random recipe to be displayed on your Today view.

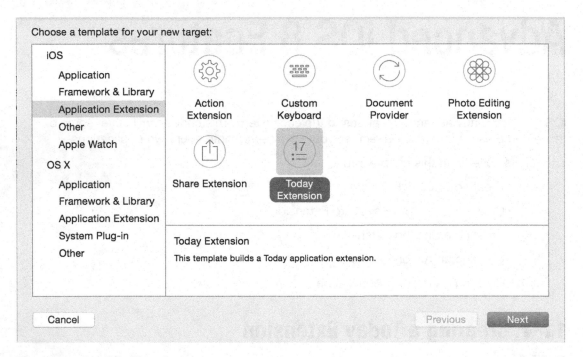

Figure 11-1. *New Today Extension target*

Xcode will ask if you would like to activate the scheme. Confirm you would like to activate it. Run the application. The dialog in Figure 11-2 is displayed. Select Today, and click Run to view your widget.

Figure 11-2. Select an application

The iOS Simulator application opens, and the Today view appears. Click the "Edit" button (shown in Figure 11-3).

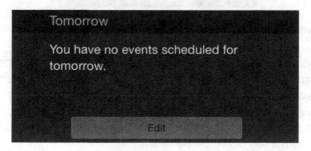

Figure 11-3. Edit widgets button

Then, click the plus (see Figure 11-4) button to add the RandomRecipe widget.

Figure 11-4. Add the RandomRecipe widget

A section titled "RandomRecipe" is now visible in the Today view.

Now that the widget is visible on the Today view, take a look at the structure of the project. A new group named "RandomRecipe" was added to the project. A view controller and storyboard were added to the group. This view controller controls the extension, otherwise known as a "widget." The storyboard contains the user interface for the widget. Open the storyboard and examine it. It contains a single view with a single label. You will use the label to display the name of the random recipe. You may have noticed the text "Hello World" is positioned slightly to the right. You will fix this next. All widgets in the Today screen have a default left margin. That is why the "Hello World" label appears to be oddly positioned. Fix this by adding a protocol method from NCWidgetProvidingProtocol in the TodayViewController.swift file under the RandomRecipe group:

```
func widgetMarginInsetsForProposedMarginInsets
    (defaultMarginInsets: UIEdgeInsets) -> (UIEdgeInsets) {
    return UIEdgeInsetsZero
}
```

Resetting the margin insets to zero removes the default and positions the label where you would expect it to be. In the storyboard, set the label's text alignment to left. In order to do this, select the MainInterface.storyboard file under the RandomRecipe group. Then select the label with the text "Hello World" in the storyboard. In the Attributes inspector, change the text alignment to left aligned. Then set the offset of the label's leading space constraint to 40. This will align the text with the title of the widget on the Today view. Run the application again. It should look something like Figure 11-5.

Figure 11-5. The Today screen with the RandomRecipe widget

Now you want to display the name of a random recipe in the widget. Since the widget will be sharing code with your application, you have a number of options. If the same information will be used in both your application and the widget, create a new Swift file named RecipeService.swift. This method will deliver the information to be displayed in the widget or the application. Open the file, and create the RecipeService class. Add a string array property to the class with a list of recipe names:

```
import Foundation

class RecipeService {

    var recipes = [
        "Grilled Fish",
        "Fajitas",
        "Chicken Stir Fry",
        "Hamburger",
        "Fried Chicken",
        "Miso Soup",
```

```
        "Lo Mein",
        "Tofu and Rice",
        "Spaghetti and Meatballs",
    ]
```

Complete the class with a function to return one of the recipe names at random:

```
    func randomRecipe() -> String {
        return recipes[ Int(arc4random_uniform(UInt32(recipes.count))) ]
    }
}
```

Now add an outlet from the label on the storyboard to the TodayViewController class. Name the outlet recipeName. Then in the viewDidLoad: method of TodayViewController.swift, add the following code to set the widget to display a random recipe name:

```
var service = RecipeService()
recipeName.text = service.randomRecipe()
```

Run the application. When the widget displays, it will display a random recipe name.

The Code and Usage

Listing 11-1 contains the complete code of the widget's view controller. Listing 11-2 is an example RecipeService class that will return a random name of a recipe. To use the code, create a Single View iOS application. Once that project is open in Xcode, select the menu item File ➤ New ➤ Target. Select Application Extension under iOS. Then select "Today Extension" from the list of options that appears to the right. (See Figure 11-1 for an example of what this selection should look like.) Then click Next and give your target a name such as RandomRecipe. Replace the contents of TodayViewController.swift with Listing 11-1. Create a new swift file named RecipeService.swift. Under the "File Inspector" tab, make sure the file is selected for both "RecipeWidget" and "RandomRecipe" under "Target Membership." Run the application.

Listing 11-1. TodayViewController.swift

```
import UIKit
import NotificationCenter

class TodayViewController: UIViewController, NCWidgetProviding {

    @IBOutlet weak var recipeName: UILabel!
    override func viewDidLoad() {
        super.viewDidLoad()
        var service = RecipeService()
        recipeName.text = service.randomRecipe()
    }
```

```swift
    override func didReceiveMemoryWarning() {
        super.didReceiveMemoryWarning()
        // Dispose of any resources that can be recreated.
    }

    func widgetPerformUpdateWithCompletionHandler(completionHandler: ((NCUpdateResult) ->
Void)!) {
        // Perform any setup necessary in order to update the view.

        // If an error is encountered, use NCUpdateResult.Failed
        // If there's no update required, use NCUpdateResult.NoData
        // If there's an update, use NCUpdateResult.NewData

        completionHandler(NCUpdateResult.NewData)
    }

    func widgetMarginInsetsForProposedMarginInsets
        (defaultMarginInsets: UIEdgeInsets) -> (UIEdgeInsets) {
            return UIEdgeInsetsZero
    }
}
```

Listing 11-2. RecipeService.swift

```swift
import Foundation

class RecipeService {

    var recipes = [
        "Grilled Fish",
        "Fajitas",
        "Chicken Stir Fry",
        "Hamburger",
        "Fried Chicken",
        "Miso Soup",
        "Lo Mein",
        "Tofu and Rice",
        "Spaghetti and Meatballs",
    ]

    func randomRecipe() -> String {
        return recipes[ Int(arc4random_uniform(UInt32(recipes.count))) ]
    }
}
```

You should see the RandomRecipe widget as it appears in Figure 11-5. Don't forget to add the extension as detailed in the previous "How It Works" section.

11-2. Creating a Custom Keyboard Extension

Problem

You want to create a custom keyboard.

Solution

Create a keyboard extension.

How It Works

As of iOS 8, Apple has finally introduced a way to create custom keyboards. A custom keyboard can be used within any application as long as the user has it installed and activated. In this recipe, you will create a keyboard that has some features that would be of value to coders. The standard keyboard on iOS hides a lot of the necessary punctuation and characters that are frequently used when programming. Custom keyboards open up a lot of new possibilities for developers. However, you should be aware of the limitations:

- The keyboard does not have access to the text in a text control. For example, you cannot select text. In addition, the keyboard does not have access to the Copy, Cut, or Paste functions.

- A custom keyboard cannot provide input to a secure text input or a phone pad input.

- Elements of the keyboard cannot extend past the borders of the view, like Apple Keyboards do on the top row of keys.

A custom keyboard is an Application Extension in iOS 8. Open an existing application, or create a new Single View iOS Application. Then add a "Custom Keyboard" extension using File ➤ New ➤ Target and then select "Custom Keyboard" from the "Application Extensions" list that appears. Open the file Info.plist. The Info.plist file includes a couple of useful settings:

- PrefersRightToLeft – Used for languages that require an alternate direction.

- RequestsOpenAccess – Indicates that the keyboard requires network access to operate.

Keyboards need to be installed in iOS 8 before they can be used. Compile your project, and run it on the simulator. At this point, the keyboard has been deployed to the simulator, but it is not yet accessible. On the simulator, open Settings ➤ General ➤ Keyboard ➤ Keyboards ➤ Add New Keyboard. Select the name of your keyboard under the "Third Party Keyboards" section. Then back in your application, tap in a text box. Click the world button that switches to the next keyboard. All keyboards must have a Next button for users to change keyboards.

In this recipe, you will create a custom keyboard using an XIB file. Using an XIB file makes the layout and design of keyboards very easy, especially since you should be using Auto Layout to make your layout adaptable. Add a new View (XIB) to your keyboard project group. Select File ➤ New ➤ File. From the iOS User Interface Group, choose View and click Next. Save the XIB as `CodeKeyboard.xib`.

Open `KeyboardViewController.swift`. Note that the `KeyboardViewController` inherits from `UIInputViewController`. You will use some of the properties and methods later on in the recipe. The XIB is loaded in the `viewDidLoad` method. Add this code to the method to load the XIB:

```
override func viewDidLoad() {
    super.viewDidLoad()

    var xib = NSBundle.mainBundle().loadNibNamed("CodeKeyboard", owner: self, options: nil)

    var keyboardView = xib[0] as! UIView
    keyboardView.setTranslatesAutoresizingMaskIntoConstraints(false)
    view.addSubview(keyboardView)

    nextKeyboardButton.addTarget(self, action: "advanceToNextInputMode",
    forControlEvents: .TouchUpInside)
}
```

It is important to set the `View.translatesAutoresizingMaskIntoConstraints` to false to allow for Auto Layout of the buttons. Open the XIB file. You can now add the buttons to the layout. This recipe focuses on a single keyboard size using Auto Layout. Other size classes can be added after the fact.

Select the view, and open the Attributes Inspector. Set the size to Freeform and the Status Bar to None. Change to the Size Inspector, and set the size to 320 wide by 160 high.

Drag a button onto the view. Set the size to 30 wide by 34 high. The keyboard will have an even spacing of 4 points around the outer edge of the keyboard. It will have four rows separated by 5 points. The first three rows will have 10 buttons. The bottom row will have three. The bottom border will be 5 points. Create your XIB file so that it looks like Figure 11-6.

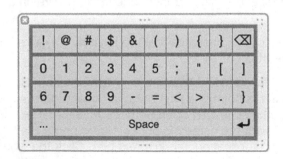

Figure 11-6. Custom keyboard layout

Create 10 copies of the button in the first row. Add a "Leading Space" constraint to the superview of 4 points. Separate each button from the other with "Leading Space" of a single point. Set the "Trailing Space" constraint to 4. Set the width of the first nine buttons to the width of the tenth. Select all the buttons in the first row, add a "Top Constraint" of 4 to the top of the superview, and set the height of the buttons to 34.

Repeat the process for rows two and three. However, set the "Top Constraint" to 5 points.

The fourth row has three buttons. Create the first and last buttons like you did for the first three rows. Set the width of the first to the width of the button above it. Do the same for the last button. Add the space button, and set a "Leading Constraint" and "Trailing Constraint" of 1 point to the Space button.

For the new line button and the backspace, I used Unicode characters. While in Xcode, put your cursor in the title of a button and press Control+Command+Space. The character viewer will open. You can then find the characters for those keys.

Now create outlets and actions to handle the keyboard buttons. Open the Assistant Editor. Control+Drag the "Next Keyboard" button to the `KeyboardViewController`, and create an outlet named `nextKeyboardButton`. Control+Drag the new line key to the class, and create an action named `newline`. Do the same for the backspace key, and name the action `backspace`. Select all the remaining buttons at the same time. Then Control+Drag them and create an action named `keyUp`.

In the file `KeyboardViewController.swift`, in the `newline` action method, add the following code to insert a new line character. The `textDocumentProxy` property of the `UIInputViewController` is the object to use to insert characters and send editing commands:

```
(textDocumentProxy as! UITextDocumentProxy).insertText("\n")
```

Add the next line to the `backspace` action:

```
(textDocumentProxy as! UITextDocumentProxy).deleteBackward()
```

In the file `KeyboardViewController.swift`, the `keyUp` method will handle all the character keys, as well as the space bar. The code inserts the title of the button into the text input. This way, when you change the character on the button, no code updates are required. However, for the space bar, that will not work. If the title of the button is "Space," a space is inserted instead:

```
var proxy = textDocumentProxy as! UITextDocumentProxy

var button = sender as? UIButton

if let input = button?.titleLabel?.text as String? {
    if input == "Space"
    {
        proxy.insertText(" ")
        return
    }
    proxy.insertText(input)
}
```

The Code and Usage

Listing 11-3 contains the complete code for the keyboard controller. To use this code, add a Keyboard Extension target to a project. Then create a CodeKeyboard.xib file with the keyboard's design. Connect the IBOutlets and IBActions, and run the application. You will need to install the keyboard the first time it runs before you can use it.

Listing 11-3. KeyboardViewController

```
import UIKit

class KeyboardViewController: UIInputViewController {

    @IBOutlet var nextKeyboardButton: UIButton!

    @IBAction func newLine (sender: AnyObject) {
        (textDocumentProxy as! UITextDocumentProxy).insertText("\n")
    }

    @IBAction func backspace(sender: AnyObject) {
        (textDocumentProxy as! UITextDocumentProxy).deleteBackward()
    }
    @IBAction func keyUp(sender: AnyObject) {
        var proxy = textDocumentProxy as! UITextDocumentProxy

        var button = sender as? UIButton

        if let input = button?.titleLabel?.text as String? {
            if input == "Space"
            {
                proxy.insertText(" ")
                return
            }
            proxy.insertText(input)
        }
    }

    override func viewDidLoad() {
        super.viewDidLoad()

        var xib = NSBundle.mainBundle().loadNibNamed("CodeKeyboard", owner: self,
        options: nil)

        var keyboardView = xib[0] as! UIView
        keyboardView.setTranslatesAutoresizingMaskIntoConstraints(false)
        view.addSubview(keyboardView)

        nextKeyboardButton.addTarget(self, action: "advanceToNextInputMode",
    forControlEvents: .TouchUpInside)
    }
}
```

11-3. Creating a Sharing Extension

Problem

You want to give users another option to use the global Sharing Sheet in iOS 8.

Solution

Create a share extension.

How It Works

Share extensions are part of the new extensibility framework in iOS 8. Previously, developers had to wait for Apple to add new social networks or external applications to the build in Share tools. Now the systemwide Share Sheets can be customized and developers can package their custom sharing functions within a Sharing Extension for use in any application. The results are up to the developer. You could make a sharing extension that posts to multiple social networks, or share a photo on your custom web application. There isn't any restriction on where content can be posted.

In this recipe, you will create a share extension that displays a dialog, allows the user to add some additional information, and then outputs that content to the console. For actual use in your applications, you will need to add the code to handle the content. Typically, applications will use web APIs or some other method of sharing the content. The details of executing the share are not the focus of this recipe. This recipe will focus on how to create a Share Extension, add it to an application, and get data about the content to be shared from the host application.

Share extensions are embedded within an application. First create a Single View iOS application. Then, to add a Share Extension to an application, choose File ➤ New Target and then select "Share Extension." For this recipe, name the extension ShareRecipe. This adds a new target to your project. Two files are added to the project under a new group. ShareViewController.swift is used to implement the Share Extension. It is a subclass of SLComposeServiceViewController. Refer to Figure 11-7 to see the default share extension interface. This view contains a UITextView that can be used to capture user input. In this recipe, you will use this default view. You can alternatively use your own view designed as an XIB or a Storyboard. The SLComposeServiceViewController does have features that allow for customization. Where possible, use this mechanism to save time and maintain a consistent user experience.

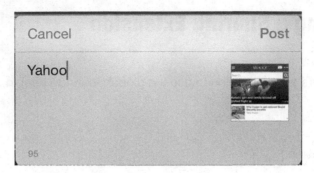

Figure 11-7. *The* `SLComposeServiceViewController` *default view*

There are three methods included in the default code template for the
`SLComposeServiceViewController`. They are `isContentValid`, `didSelectPost`, and
`configurationItems`:

- `isContentValid` – This method is called each time changes are made in
  the compose view. If you return `false`, the "Post" button is disabled. In
  addition, you can update the characters remaining within this function.
  The number of characters remaining is displayed below the text area.

- `didSelectPost` – When the user taps the "Post" button, this method is
  called. In this method, perform the actions required for the actual share.
  You can connect to a server, post to a web service, or do something
  locally. The `didSelectPost:` method executes on the main thread, so
  create an alternate thread in order to avoid locking the main thread.

- `configurationItems` – The `configurationItems` collection is used to
  add additional items to the bottom of the compose view. The items
  are added in a table view. Typically, these items are used for activities
  such as selecting a social network account, collecting additional data
  to be shared, or other options related to sharing the content. These are
  optional.

In this recipe, you will implement all of these methods. You will create a `configurationItem`
that will display a new view allowing a user to provide a star rating. To test the Share
Extension, select the `ShareRecipe` scheme from the list of Schemes in the toolbar. Then
click Run. Xcode will ask you to select an application to run. Select Safari. Safari will launch.
Browse to a URL, and then click the share icon in the toolbar at the bottom of the screen.
The Share Extension will not be available to select yet. The first row of icons contains share
extensions, and the second row contains Action extensions. Click the "More" button in the
first row. A list of extensions is displayed and should include `ShareRecipe`. Tap the toggle
switch to on, and click done.

> **Note**   In some versions of Xcode, when you run the extension again for testing, it will not appear in the list of Sharing icons. However, when you click more, the list of Activities shows the extension as on. This must be a bug of some sort. Toggle the extension off and then on again, and then click Done. The extension will appear.

Click the icon for your ShareRecipe extension. The default compose view is displayed. The next step is to add validation code. Open ShareViewController.swift. In the isContentValid method, add the following code. This code will check the length of the message and update the character count. If true is returned, the "Post" button will be enabled. If false is returned, the "Post" button is disabled:

```
override func isContentValid() -> Bool {
    var messageLength =
        count(self.contentText)

    var charactersRemaining = 100 - messageLength;
    self.charactersRemaining = charactersRemaining;

    if charactersRemaining >= 0 {
        return true;
    }

    return false;
}
```

Finally, to complete the extension, update the method didSelectPost to contain the following code. In this method, you will print the user's message to the console and then notify the host application that sharing is complete. In your own applications, this is where you will post the information to a website or to an API, or to send it via a messaging mechanism. You can handle it any way you prefer. However, these methods do run on the main thread, so keep any blocking activities you run in a separate thread. Then notify the host application that the sharing activity is complete:

```
override func didSelectPost() {
    println("Message: \(self.contentText)")
    self.extensionContext!.completeRequestReturningItems([],
        completionHandler: nil)
}
```

The method configurationItems is used to add additional items such as social account selection or custom input. To complete this recipe, you will add a view and display a list of five buttons for the user to rate the content being shared. You can create a custom view using an XIB or Storyboard. In this recipe, you will create a simple view programmatically. If you use code or an XIB/Storyboard, it is advisable to use Auto Layout so that the view is adaptable to different devices.

Add two properties to the ShareViewController class. One is the
SLComposeSheetConfigurationItem you will create and add to the default view. The second is
a constant for the Unicode glyph ★:

```
var userRating : SLComposeSheetConfigurationItem!
let star : Character = "\u{2605}"
```

Fill in the body of the configurationItems method. This method will create a new view
controller, add five buttons with stars to it, and set constraints to display them properly in
AutoLayout. This method creates a single SLComposeSheetConfigurationItem stored in the
property userRating. You will use that property later to update the view, indicating how many
stars the user selected. Return the userRating property wrapped in an array. If you want to
add multiple configuration items, add them to the array before it is returned.

The constraints added to the buttons will evenly distribute them horizontally
across the screen. Once the view controller is set up, display it using
pushConfigurationViewController. The share view adds your view controller using a
navigation controller and then transitions to your view:

```
override func configurationItems() -> [AnyObject]! {
    // To add configuration options via table cells at the bottom of the sheet, return an
    array of SLComposeSheetConfigurationItem here.
    userRating = SLComposeSheetConfigurationItem()

    userRating.title = "Rating"
    userRating.value = ""

    userRating.tapHandler = {
        SLComposeSheetConfigurationItemTapHandler in

        var starsSelection = UIViewController()
        //starsSelection.view.setTranslatesAutoresizingMaskIntoConstraints(false)
        var s1 = self.createStarButton(1)
        var s2 = self.createStarButton(2)
        var s3 = self.createStarButton(3)
        var s4 = self.createStarButton(4)
        var s5 = self.createStarButton(5)
        var views = ["s1":s1,"s2":s2,"s3":s3,"s4":s4,"s5":s5]

        starsSelection.view.addSubview(s1)
        starsSelection.view.addSubview(s2)
        starsSelection.view.addSubview(s3)
        starsSelection.view.addSubview(s4)
        starsSelection.view.addSubview(s5)

        starsSelection.view.addConstraints(
            NSLayoutConstraint.constraintsWithVisualFormat(
                "H:|-[s1(s2)]-[s2(s3)]-[s3(s4)]-[s4(s5)]-[s5]-|",
                options: NSLayoutFormatOptions(0), metrics: nil, views: views))
        starsSelection.view.addConstraints(
            NSLayoutConstraint.constraintsWithVisualFormat("V:|-[s1(30)]",
                options: NSLayoutFormatOptions(0), metrics: nil, views: views))
```

```
    starsSelection.view.addConstraints(
        NSLayoutConstraint.constraintsWithVisualFormat("V:|-[s2(30)]",
            options: NSLayoutFormatOptions(0), metrics: nil, views: views))
    starsSelection.view.addConstraints(
        NSLayoutConstraint.constraintsWithVisualFormat("V:|-[s3(30)]",
            options: NSLayoutFormatOptions(0), metrics: nil, views: views))
    starsSelection.view.addConstraints(
        NSLayoutConstraint.constraintsWithVisualFormat("V:|-[s4(30)]",
            options: NSLayoutFormatOptions(0), metrics: nil, views: views))
    starsSelection.view.addConstraints(
        NSLayoutConstraint.constraintsWithVisualFormat("V:|-[s5(30)]",
            options: NSLayoutFormatOptions(0), metrics: nil, views: views))
    self.pushConfigurationViewController(starsSelection)

    }

    return [userRating]
}
```

Also add the `createStarButton` method that sets up a button's properties. Since the constraints are added in the code, you must disable `translatesAutoresizingMaskIntoConstraints`:

```
func createStarButton(value : Int ) -> UIButton {
    var button = UIButton()
    button.setTitle("\(star)", forState: UIControlState.Normal)
    button.addTarget(self, action: "buttonTapped:", forControlEvents:
    UIControlEvents.TouchUpInside)
    button.setTranslatesAutoresizingMaskIntoConstraints(false)
    button.tag = value
    return button
}
```

In the `createStarButton:` method, the target is set to the `ShareViewController` and the target is `buttonTapped:`. This method will handle all button clicks. Using the value set in the `tag` property of the button, it will set the rating and use the method `popConfigurationViewController` to return to the share view:

```
func buttonTapped(sender : AnyObject?) {
    println("#\(sender!.tag) tapped")
    var rating : Int = sender!.tag as Int

    var stars = ""
    for i in 1...rating {
        stars += "\(star)"
    }
    userRating.value=stars
    self.popConfigurationViewController()
}
```

Finally, add the following line to the `didSelectPost` method. It will output the number of stars the user selected:

```
println("Rating: \(count(userRating.value)) Stars")
```

The Code and Usage

Listing 11-4 contains the complete listing of the `ShareViewController`. Use this code to quickly create a Share Extension for your applications. To use the code, add a new Share Extension Target to any iOS application. Replace the contents of the `ShareViewController` with this code. Select the "Share Extensions Scheme" from the menu, and run the extension with Safari. Try sharing the web page using your extension. When you click the "Post" button, the console should output the text you entered and the rating if you selected a rating.

Listing 11-4. ShareViewController

```swift
import UIKit
import Social

class ShareViewController: SLComposeServiceViewController {

    var userRating : SLComposeSheetConfigurationItem!
    let star : Character = "\u{2605}"

    override func isContentValid() -> Bool {
        var messageLength =
            count(self.contentText)

        var charactersRemaining = 100 - messageLength;
        self.charactersRemaining = charactersRemaining;

        if charactersRemaining >= 0 {
            return true;
        }

        return false;
    }

    override func didSelectPost() {
        println("Message: \(self.contentText)")
        println("Rating: \(count(userRating.value)) Stars")
        self.extensionContext!.completeRequestReturningItems([], completionHandler: nil)
    }

    override func configurationItems() -> [AnyObject]! {
        // To add configuration options via table cells at the bottom of the sheet
        // return an array of SLComposeSheetConfigurationItem here.
        userRating = SLComposeSheetConfigurationItem()

        userRating.title = "Rating"
        userRating.value = ""
```

```
        userRating.tapHandler = {
            SLComposeSheetConfigurationItemTapHandler in

            var starsSelection = UIViewController()
            //starsSelection.view.setTranslatesAutoresizingMaskIntoConstraints(false)
            var s1 = self.createStarButton(1)
            var s2 = self.createStarButton(2)
            var s3 = self.createStarButton(3)
            var s4 = self.createStarButton(4)
            var s5 = self.createStarButton(5)
            var views = ["s1":s1,"s2":s2,"s3":s3,"s4":s4,"s5":s5]

            starsSelection.view.addSubview(s1)
            starsSelection.view.addSubview(s2)
            starsSelection.view.addSubview(s3)
            starsSelection.view.addSubview(s4)
            starsSelection.view.addSubview(s5)

            starsSelection.view.addConstraints(
                NSLayoutConstraint.constraintsWithVisualFormat(
                    "H:|-[s1(s2)]-[s2(s3)]-[s3(s4)]-[s4(s5)]-[s5]-|",
                    options: NSLayoutFormatOptions(0), metrics: nil, views: views))
            starsSelection.view.addConstraints(
                NSLayoutConstraint.constraintsWithVisualFormat("V:|-[s1(30)]",
                    options: NSLayoutFormatOptions(0), metrics: nil, views: views))
            starsSelection.view.addConstraints(
                NSLayoutConstraint.constraintsWithVisualFormat("V:|-[s2(30)]",
                    options: NSLayoutFormatOptions(0), metrics: nil, views: views))
            starsSelection.view.addConstraints(
                NSLayoutConstraint.constraintsWithVisualFormat("V:|-[s3(30)]",
                    options: NSLayoutFormatOptions(0), metrics: nil, views: views))
            starsSelection.view.addConstraints(
                NSLayoutConstraint.constraintsWithVisualFormat("V:|-[s4(30)]",
                    options: NSLayoutFormatOptions(0), metrics: nil, views: views))
            starsSelection.view.addConstraints(
                NSLayoutConstraint.constraintsWithVisualFormat("V:|-[s5(30)]",
                    options: NSLayoutFormatOptions(0), metrics: nil, views: views))
            self.pushConfigurationViewController(starsSelection)

        }

        return [userRating]
    }

    func createStarButton(value : Int ) -> UIButton {
        var button = UIButton()
        button.setTitle("\(star)", forState: UIControlState.Normal)
        button.addTarget(self, action: "buttonTapped:", forControlEvents:
        UIControlEvents.TouchUpInside)
        button.setTranslatesAutoresizingMaskIntoConstraints(false)
        button.tag = value
        return button
    }
```

```
func buttonTapped(sender : AnyObject?) {
    println("#\(sender!.tag) tapped")
    var rating : Int = sender!.tag as Int

    var stars = ""
    for i in 1...rating {
        stars += "\(star)"
    }
    userRating.value=stars
    self.popConfigurationViewController()
}
}
```

11-4. Creating an Action Extension

Problem

You want to make a feature from your application available to other applications.

Solution

Create an Action extension.

How It Works

Action extensions are part of iOS 8's extensibility functions. Actions are displayed along with sharing options. However, they are meant for a different purpose. Sharing extensions are about distributing content to others. Actions are about acting on the content. You could create an Action extension that puts a mustache on a picture or turns a photo into black and white. When the action is complete, the information can be returned to the application using the extension.

In this recipe, you will create an Action extension that captures a URL from a browser. An action like this could be used to create a bookmarking application that bookmarks your favorite recipes. What happens to the information once it is stored is up to your imagination. This recipe will focus on the mechanics of creating the Action extension, receiving data from the application using the extension, and returning a confirmation message about the status of the action. If you were building a bookmarking application, you could add the URL to a Core Data database for access at a later time.

Create a Single View iOS Application. Then add an Action extension target to the project by selecting File ➤ New ➤ Target. Then choose "Action Extension." Name the extension Bookmarker. This recipe will create an Action extension that will capture the URL from a web page as if you were building an app that bookmarks favorite recipes. It will then notify the host application to display a confirmation message.

The Action extension template adds a new group to your project along with the new target. This extension will work only with URLs. You can specify this in the Info.plist file contained in the Bookmarker group under "Supporting Files."

> **Note**   Make sure you pick the `Info.plist` file for the extension and not the Application.

Click on `Info.plist`. Under NSExtension ➤ NSExtensionAttributes ➤ NSExtensionActivationRule, there could be a number of options. These all indicate to the operating system what types of content your extension can work with. Delete everything except the entry `NSExtensionActivationSupportsWebURLWithMaxCount`. Set its value to 1. This simple action will handle one URL at a time. Descriptions of the other options can be found in Apple's "App Extension Programming Guide" in the section "Declaring Supported Data Types for a Share or Action extension." As the title implies, you can configure a Sharing Extension like Recipe 11-3 the same way.

In the project under the `Bookmarker` group, there is a file named `Action.js`. This contains the JavaScript code that will be running in the host app browser. This JavaScript file is required to export a variable `ExtensionPreprocessingJS` that contains the functions that make up both sides of the integration. The `run` method is triggered when a user clicks on the Action extension button in the Share Screen. The `finalize` function is used to receive information back from the extension. This function will be discussed shortly:

```
var Action = function() {}

Action.prototype = {

    run: function(arguments) {
        arguments.completionFunction({ "currentUrl" : document.URL })
    }
}

var ExtensionPreprocessingJS = new Action
```

The `run` function takes the URL and adds it to a JSON object. This JSON object is sent to the Action extension to be processed.

The `ActionRequestHandler` class is what handles the action. The class implements the `NSExtensionRequestHandling` protocol. The method `beginRequestWithExtensionContext` gets the data sent by the host application and preprocesses the information. The information is sent in JSON format, so it must be decoded. The `NSExtensionContext` parameter context contains the extension item as well as an array of attachments. Since this recipe handles only one URL, you will have to deal with only the first item in the list of attachments.

The code checks to see if the item conforms to the type of `kUTTypePropertyList`. This checks to see if the data contains dictionaries that contain `JSON` information. This is necessary because you are dealing with URL data and will be using JavaScript to communicate between the extension and the browser. If the data is of the proper type, an

NSOperation is queued. This operation will extract the dictionary of information and call itemLoadCompletedWithPreprocessingResults to handle processing the data:

```swift
func beginRequestWithExtensionContext(context: NSExtensionContext) {
    // Do not call super in an Action extension with no user interface
    self.extensionContext = context

    var found = false

    let extensionItem = extensionContext?.inputItems.first as! NSExtensionItem
    let itemProvider = extensionItem.attachments?.first as! NSItemProvider

    let propertyList = String(kUTTypePropertyList)
    if itemProvider.hasItemConformingToTypeIdentifier(propertyList) {
        itemProvider.loadItemForTypeIdentifier(propertyList, options: nil,
            completionHandler: { (item, error) -> Void in
            let dictionary = item as! NSDictionary
            NSOperationQueue.mainQueue().addOperationWithBlock {
                let results = dictionary[NSExtensionJavaScriptPreprocessingResultsKey] as!
                NSDictionary
                let urlString = results["currentUrl"] as? String
                println("URL selected: \(urlString)")
                self.itemLoadCompletedWithPreprocessingResults(results as [NSObject :
                AnyObject])
            }
        })
    } else {
        println("error")
    }
}
```

The itemLoadCompletedWithPreprocessingResults method takes the dictionary of JSON data and attempts to extract the URL to be bookmarked.

In this method, you would deal with the data by transforming it or saving it, depending on your extension's function. If this was a real bookmarking application, you could save it to a local Core Data database. Actions can perform any action and, in addition, return information to the host application. In a Share Extension, you can communicate with the host app via JSON and JavaScript. The doneWithResults method takes a dictionary of name/value pairs and converts it into JSON using the NSItemProvider class. doneWithResults does the opposite of beginRequestWithExtensionContext. The data to be returned is converted to an NSItemProvider and wrapped in an NSExtensionItem. This will be passed to the host application and handled via JavaScript.

Even if the Action extension does not need to return data, you must notify the host application by calling NSExtensionContext.completeRequestReturningItems. Then you can release the extensionContext by setting it to nil:

```swift
func doneWithResults(resultsForJavaScriptFinalizeArg: [NSObject: AnyObject]?) {
    if let resultsForJavaScriptFinalize = resultsForJavaScriptFinalizeArg {
        var resultsDictionary = [NSExtensionJavaScriptFinalizeArgumentKey:
        resultsForJavaScriptFinalize]
```

```
    var resultsProvider = NSItemProvider(item: resultsDictionary,
        typeIdentifier: String(kUTTypePropertyList))

    var resultsItem = NSExtensionItem()
    resultsItem.attachments = [resultsProvider]

    self.extensionContext!.completeRequestReturningItems([resultsItem],
    completionHandler: nil)
    } else {
        self.extensionContext!.completeRequestReturningItems([], completionHandler: nil)
    }

    self.extensionContext = nil
}
```

This JavaScript handles the call to `completeRequestReturningItems`. The method `finalize` receives the dictionary of data that we returned from the extension. The JavaScript can manipulate the DOM of the current page or, as in this recipe, it displays the message the extension returned:

```
finalize: function(arguments) {
        var message = arguments["statusMessage"]

        if (message) {
            alert(message);
        }
    }
```

The Code and Usage

The code of this recipe can be used to add an Action extension to an application. To use the code, start by adding an Action extension target to your application. Then replace the contents of the `ActionRequestHandler.swift` file with the contents of Listing 11-5. Update the contents of `Action.js` with the contents of Listing 11-6. Don't forget to set the types of content your extension will apply to in the extension's `Info.plist` file.

When you run the application, choose to run it within Safari. Then click the Share icon in the toolbar. If the Bookmarker action button is not visible, you may need to swipe to the right in the action buttons and click the "More" button. When you tap the Bookmarker button, you will see the URL printed out to the console, and then a dialog is displayed in the browser confirming the action has taken place.

Listing 11-5. ActionRequestHandler.swift

```
import UIKit
import MobileCoreServices

class ActionRequestHandler: NSObject, NSExtensionRequestHandling {

    var extensionContext: NSExtensionContext?
```

```swift
func beginRequestWithExtensionContext(context: NSExtensionContext) {
    // Do not call super in an Action extension with no user interface
    self.extensionContext = context

    var found = false

    let extensionItem = extensionContext?.inputItems.first as! NSExtensionItem
    let itemProvider = extensionItem.attachments?.first as! NSItemProvider

    let propertyList = String(kUTTypePropertyList)
    if itemProvider.hasItemConformingToTypeIdentifier(propertyList) {
        itemProvider.loadItemForTypeIdentifier(propertyList, options: nil,
            completionHandler: { (item, error) -> Void in
            let dictionary = item as! NSDictionary
            NSOperationQueue.mainQueue().addOperationWithBlock {
                let results = dictionary[NSExtensionJavaScriptPreprocessingResultsKey]
                as! NSDictionary
                let urlString = results["currentUrl"] as? String
                println("URL selected: \(urlString)")
                self.itemLoadCompletedWithPreprocessingResults(results as
                [NSObject : AnyObject])
            }
        })
    } else {
        println("error")
    }
}

func itemLoadCompletedWithPreprocessingResults(javaScriptPreprocessingResults:
[NSObject: AnyObject])
{
    let url: AnyObject? = javaScriptPreprocessingResults["currentUrl"]
    if url == nil || url! as! String == "" {
        self.doneWithResults(["statusMessage": "Recipe Bookmark Failed"])
    } else {
        self.doneWithResults(["statusMessage": "Recipe Bookmarked"])
    }
}

func doneWithResults(resultsForJavaScriptFinalizeArg: [NSObject: AnyObject]?) {
    if let resultsForJavaScriptFinalize = resultsForJavaScriptFinalizeArg {
        var resultsDictionary = [NSExtensionJavaScriptFinalizeArgumentKey:
        resultsForJavaScriptFinalize]

        var resultsProvider = NSItemProvider(item: resultsDictionary,
            typeIdentifier: String(kUTTypePropertyList))

        var resultsItem = NSExtensionItem()
        resultsItem.attachments = [resultsProvider]

        self.extensionContext!.completeRequestReturningItems([resultsItem],
        completionHandler: nil)
```

```
    } else {
        self.extensionContext!.completeRequestReturningItems([], completionHandler: nil)
    }

        self.extensionContext = nil
    }

}
```

Listing 11-6. Action.js

```
var Action = function() {}

Action.prototype = {

    run: function(arguments) {
        arguments.completionFunction({ "currentUrl" : document.URL })
    },

    finalize: function(arguments) {
        var message = arguments["statusMessage"]

        if (message) {
            alert(message);
        }
    }
}

var ExtensionPreprocessingJS = new Action
```

11-5. Creating a WatchKit Application

Problem

You want to display alerts and content on the Apple Watch.

Solution

Create a WatchKit Application.

How It Works

The Apple Watch launched recently, and developers can now create watch applications that allow a user to interact with iOS applications from their watch. A watch application is similar to an extension, except that the "view" of the app lives on the watch. The remainder of the processing and functionality is still handled by the phone.

Create a new iOS Single View Application, and name it Counter. Then add a new target. (Select File ➤ New ➤ Target from the menu.) In the dialog, select "WatchKit App" from the "Apple Watch" section under iOS. On the next dialog deselect "Include Notification Scene" and "Include Glance Scene." Two new targets and groups are added to your project: Counter WatchKit Extension and Counter WatchKit App. The extension runs on the iPhone. It contains the Model and the Controller portion of the code. The WatchKit App contains the User Interface. Apple has done this, so processing happens on the phone rather than on the watch. This will be updated in the future, but as of publication this is the current environment.

Even though the app interface runs on the watch, the code executes on the iPhone, and the two communicate over Bluetooth, developers do not need to worry about any of that. Connecting the user interface to the controller is as simple as it is for an iPhone app. Open the Interface.storyboard file in the "Counter WatchKit App" group. It looks similar to an iPhone storyboard, just smaller. Such a small screen does not have many layout options. When elements are placed on the screen, they are pinned to the top or bottom and the sides.

Drag a label onto the scene, and move it to the top. Select the label, and open the Attributes Inspector. The Attributes Inspector is used in the same way in a watch interface. Change the font to System Bold, and change the size to 40 points.

In the position section (shown in Figure 11-8) are options for pinning. There are three options for each. Horizontal options include Left, Right, and Center. Depending on the side you pin, you can resize the element.

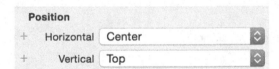

Figure 11-8. WatchKit user interface positioning attributes

If you select "Center," resizing the element will continue to keep it in the center of the watch face. When you add other elements, they will continue to stack one on top of the other. If you want to place two elements side by side, you can use a Group to position them. Vertical positioning options are Top, Middle, and Bottom. Similar to horizontal, the height of an element can be adjusted based on where it is pinned. Add a button and pin it to the bottom. Allow it to take the full width of the screen.

Adding an IBOutlet and IBAction are exactly the same in WatchKit. Click the Assistant Editor. Click+Drag the label, and create an IBOutlet named counter. Then Click+Drag the button and create an action named increment. You do not need to worry about how these outlets are connected; iOS takes care of it for you.

Now open the InterfaceController.swift file in the "Counter WatchKit Extension" group. This view controller runs on the phone and does all of the work for the Watch application. The default template comes with stubs for the most common events in the life cycle. awakeWithContext is the first method to trigger. The method willAppear comes next, like viewWillAppear does in a UIViewController. A third method, didDisappear, is executed after the view is hidden from screen.

When awakeWithContext executes, the interface is loaded and IBOutlets and IBActions are connected. This is where you can initialize your interface elements. The UI elements of WatchKit are different from UIKit and have slightly different APIs. In awakeWithContext, add this line to set the text of the label:

```
counter.setText("\(count)")
```

Then add the following code to the increment method. This will increment the counter and update the label's content:

```
counter.setText("\(++count)")
```

The Code and Usage

Listing 11-7 contains the complete code of InterfaceController.swift for this recipe. To use this code, add a WatchKit App target to a new iOS Single View Application. Update InterfaceController.swift with the contents of Listing 11-7. Create the Storyboard scene as indicated in the recipe and connect the outlets. Before you run the application, launch iOS Simulator. The Watch App needs to run in an external display. In the menu, select Hardware ➤ External Displays ➤ Apple Watch. You can choose 38mm or 42mm based on your preference. A second window will appear. Now return to Xcode, check that the Scheme is set to Counter WatchKit App, and run your application. The WatchApp will appear in the new window. Tap the button and the count will go up on screen.

Listing 11-7. InterfaceController.swift

```
import WatchKit
import Foundation

class InterfaceController: WKInterfaceController {
    var count = 0

    override func awakeWithContext(context: AnyObject?) {
        super.awakeWithContext(context)
        counter.setText("\(count)")
    }

    @IBOutlet weak var counter: WKInterfaceLabel!
    @IBAction func increment() {
        counter.setText("\(++count)")
    }
}
```

Index

Get the eBook for only $5!

Why limit yourself?

Now you can take the weightless companion with you wherever you go and access your content on your PC, phone, tablet, or reader.

Since you've purchased this print book, we're happy to offer you the eBook in all 3 formats for just $5.

Convenient and fully searchable, the PDF version enables you to easily find and copy code—or perform examples by quickly toggling between instructions and applications. The MOBI format is ideal for your Kindle, while the ePUB can be utilized on a variety of mobile devices.

To learn more, go to www.apress.com/companion or contact support@apress.com.

Printed in the United States
By Bookmasters